Voices of Syria

Voices of Syria

War-weary refugees tell their stories

KATRINA HOOVER

© 2016 by TGS International, Berlin, Ohio.

Cover and layout design: Rosetta Byers
Maps: Gavin Miles
ISBN: 978-1-943929-28-3
Printed in the USA

Published by:
TGS International
P.O. Box 355
Berlin, Ohio 44610 USA
Phone: 330-893-4828
Fax: 330-893-2305
www.tgsinternational.com

TGS001279

Publisher's Note

Care has been taken to report conversations and interviews in this book as accurately as possible. However, some liberty has been taken in wording of dialogue in an attempt to clearly convey the key points of the conversation. Also, because of working through an interpreter, there is an increased possibility that not every detail is 100 percent accurate. The chronology of events and interviews has also been altered in places for the sake of coherence.

For purposes of information security, the names of all characters in this book, other than the author and her co-workers, are pseudonyms.

Table of Contents

Voices by the Mediterranean

Voices from Hama

Voices from Aleppo

Voices of Jordan

Voices from Across Syria

Voices from Damascus

Voices from Daraa

Reflecting on the Voices

Epilogue

Endnotes

About the Author

Preface

August 27, 2015. That morning as I sat in the mall, waiting for my car to emerge from the service shop, I thought about my upcoming trip. In two weeks, I was scheduled to board a Royal Jordanian jet in Chicago for an eleven-hour flight to Amman, Jordan.

Online, I checked the weather in the Middle East. It was late afternoon in Beirut, Lebanon. It was 88 degrees there. After a short flight from Amman, I would land in Beirut. I would be spending a week in Lebanon and then about a week in Jordan. After that, I hoped to go visit a friend in Jerusalem for a few days.

In the calm of the morning hours at the mall, I pondered my expectations. I expected to be exhausted when I arrived, and I expected to continue to be exhausted throughout the whole trip. Interviews would be exhausting, especially in an unfamiliar culture where I was working with interpreters. Flying, for me, would be not only tiring but probably nauseating.

I really wanted to see the Mediterranean Sea, and if possible, step in it. I kept picturing the Apostle Paul on the Mediterranean Sea on his trips to visit the churches. And I thought that perhaps a body of water, even after two thousand years, would still be similar to what it was like back then, at least more so than the land.

Beyond that, I hoped to do my job well—and come back safely.

People who had never been there told me what a dangerous place it was. I'd read the news stories, heard about the violence. I'd read up on ISIS and their atrocities, including the beheading of journalists. I found messages like this: "The Department of State urges U.S. citizens to avoid all travel to Lebanon because of ongoing safety and security concerns. U.S. citizens living and working in Lebanon should understand that they accept the risks of remaining in the country and should carefully consider those risks."[1]

I walked through the streets of Elkhart, Indiana, my hometown, on a Sunday evening and thought about how beautiful it was. In just a few days now, I would be leaving Elkhart, the city of extremes! There was breathtaking beauty, and there was heartbreaking poverty. There were happy, secure children as well as lots of needy ones. I had held a massive ice cream party on my porch that week for fifty neighborhood children, with blobs of Neapolitan ice cream melting on the porch boards and three friends scooping flavors until they were sticky.

I passed the purple retaining wall wrapped around the McDonald's parking lot, pockmarked with missing bricks. I touched the wall lightly, fingertips grazing it, as I passed. *What if I never come back?* I wondered.

Yet despite the fears, I felt confident. That morning, my church family in Elkhart had circled around me and prayed. I was sure I would feel the power of that support for days.

I was so blessed. If I died tonight, God could not have given me anything more. His presence with me right now made moments like this one eternal. And His presence is something we can never outrun.

I was following the news more closely now and reading about the Middle East. Three significant news items stood out.

A few weeks before my departure date, a trash crisis developed in Beirut, Lebanon. The problem actually started in the middle of July when the government quit collecting garbage, but by late August, the Lebanese had really become angry about the stinking city. Citizens blamed the government for not picking up the trash. I began to worry that my trip would be canceled as news agencies began to talk of rioting and barricades. I really needed to go to Lebanon, because that was where a lot of my interviews with Syrian refugees were supposed to take place.

On September 2, one week before my departure, the body of a Syrian refugee boy washed onto the shore of the Mediterranean Sea. The *Wall Street Journal* posted an article comparing the photo of the little boy, his Velcro shoes still on his feet, to history-changing photos of the past. Britain, France, Germany, and the United States all agreed to take action and accept more refugees. "Once in a while, an image breaks through the noisy, cluttered global culture and hits people in the heart and not the head," the newspaper said.[2]

And then, on the final day before boarding the plane, I noticed another news item from the Middle East.

A dust storm.

"The storm has been making its way to Israel from Iraq and Syria over the past week," an Israeli newspaper announced.

I again checked the weather forecast for Amman and Beirut, my first two destinations. Dust.

"The storm also hit Lebanon's coastal capital of Beirut on Tuesday, a day after it engulfed the eastern Bekaa Valley," the paper added.[3]

The phrase that caught my attention was "from Iraq and Syria." The refugees were coming from Iraq and Syria, and now a dust storm was coming from the same place. The dust storm, like the refugees, had moved into Lebanon and Jordan. Like the refugees, the storm came without warning.

It just came and settled.

My last day at the hospital where I work as a nurse in heart surgery was long and busy, but God was so faithful. Despite a few tears, fifteen hours of work, and several emergencies, He sustained me and reminded me of His great love. He blessed me through my co-workers: well wishes, hugs, and a prayer.

A gift bag of travel treats came from my friend and veteran traveler Christine.

Three succinct imperatives came from the three men.

"Don't do anything stupid," Chris said.

"Be careful. Don't go to Syria," Dr. Halloran said.

"Be safe. Come back," Dr. Dickson said.

My fellow nurse Sue cheerfully reassured me that she would not mind working for three weeks straight in my absence.

At O'Hare airport now, I'm waiting at the ticket counter. I just finished talking to my dad and my sisters on the way to the airport, treasuring my last moments of cell phone service. I'm still in the USA, but it feels like I'm already in the Middle East. The man ahead of me wears a long white linen robe from wrists to ankles, under a brown suit coat. His closely-cropped beard is an orange color that doesn't match the hair beneath his round, flat-topped cap. He and the people around him speak Arabic loudly and happily as if they are completely unaware of how the language sounds to my naïve Midwestern ears. A woman behind me, wearing a long robe and a headscarf, steps up close beside me every time we move forward in line, as if space were a precious commodity that should be used up completely.

I'm standing at the ticket counter now. "You are going to Beirut?" The man raises his eyebrows.

"Yes," I say. I guess I'm a little surprised too.

"You will get your bag in Beirut," he says, as if he expects me to change my mind halfway there.

You have to go to Beirut if you want your suitcase, he seems to be thinking.

Once through security, I spot a young man with his forehead on the carpet. For a second I think he's in need of medical attention. Then it occurs to me that perhaps he's stretching. Finally, after noticing other men around him with mats spread on the floor and arms raised to the sky, I realize he is praying.

I'm on the plane now and flight attendants are closing overhead bins. I'm about to lose phone service.

Good night, America.

The Middle East

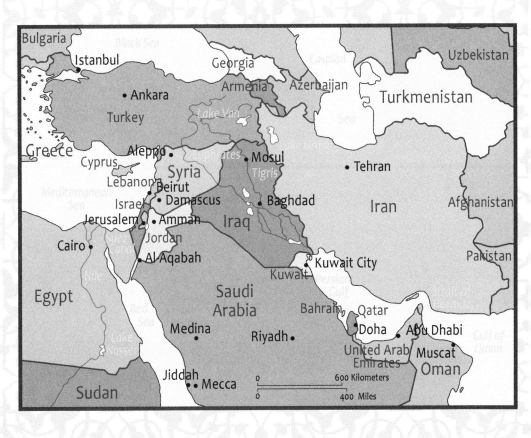

Syria

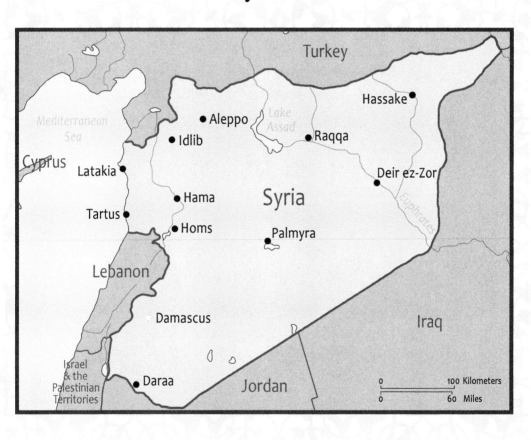

PREPARATION

CHAPTER I

"I love Damascus."

"PEOPLE LEAVE SYRIA BECAUSE THEY want peace," said my seatmate.

I hadn't expected to be talking with a Syrian so soon, certainly not on an airplane. We were waiting on the runway in Amman, Jordan's capital, for our flight to Beirut, Lebanon. Outside the windows of the plane, the Amman airport was a fog of dust from the recent dust storm. My stomach was still churning from the previous eleven-hour flight from Chicago.

Usually I keep to myself on planes because of my trouble with nausea, but I felt that this man was worth talking to. He had a kind, quiet manner and wore a gray, pinstriped dress shirt. Except for his poor English, he reminded me of my father.

"Are you from Amman?" I had asked when I sat down.

He looked at me as if he knew that I had heard all the news stories and seen the body of the boy washed up on the seashore.

"I am from Syria," he said almost defensively, with a hint of pride, as if warning me that he would not apologize for this.

"Oh! I am here to write a book about the Syrian refugees," I said. I spoke slowly, separating each word so he could understand. I also spoke slowly because I didn't know if it was polite to talk about Syrian refugees to a Syrian.

"I don't speak English well," he said. "You talk so fast."

He told me that he was traveling to Damascus, the capital of Syria, and would arrive late at night. He was flying to Beirut first, and then driving to Damascus by car because there was no road from Amman to Damascus.

"There is no road from Amman to Damascus?" I asked, surprised. I had maps of Jordan, Lebanon, and Syria in my backpack under the seat in front of me, but I didn't want to encourage my nausea by trying to read.

"I love Damascus."

The plane began to move.

"There is no *safe* road," he said.

"Oh."

He showed me pictures of his three children on his smartphone. They were teenagers, young adults. One was studying in Jordan, but the other two lived with him in Damascus.

"I've always wanted to go to Syria," I said. "Would it be safe for me to go?"

He looked at me sadly.

The plane accelerated into takeoff, and we left the runway.

"No," he said.

"But you still live there . . ."

"I love Damascus," he said. "Syria is my home. I cannot leave."

I was about to interview dozens of people who had left Syria. Would they speak with bitterness and malice about the country? Would they distance themselves from it? Or would this be their sentiment as well? *Syria is my home. Why did I have to leave?*

The last I saw him, he was at the baggage claim in the Beirut airport.

I hope he made it to Damascus.

CHAPTER 2

Welcome to Lebanon

When we landed in Lebanon, it was late evening. I hadn't slept well since the morning before.

For the first three hours of my flight from Chicago to Amman, Jordan, I had paced back and forth from my seat to the closet-like bathroom to throw up. Finally I had drifted off into a restless sleep, and the nausea was kept at bay until we began our descent into Jordan.

In Amman, I had met Keith and Jana, an American couple who would be traveling with me and introducing me to the people who were working with refugees. Married just a year, they were currently living in Jordan and working with refugees there. They were friendly and welcoming, without being overbearing. They kindly watched my luggage while I tried to revive myself in the bathroom.

I stopped at a little airport shop. When I battled motion sickness, pretzels were the only food that sounded appealing.

"Pretzels?" The man at the counter had squinted up at me, frowning.

"You know, those . . . pretzels . . . kind of like crackers or chips . . ." I trailed off, because his face was completely blank. "That's okay, no problem."

I purchased a Diet Coke at an airport McDonald's. They accepted my U.S. dollars, but I got a Jordanian dinar as change.

When Keith and Jana and I prepared to board the plane for the short flight to Beirut, Lebanon, I warned them about my nausea. I suggested they sit far away from me if they knew what was good for them.

However, after talking to the Syrian man in the gray pin-striped shirt, my physical state had remained stable. As the plane began to dip and circle, I suddenly realized that I felt well—thanks, I believe, to the prayers of my family and friends. When we hit the runway, I was shocked that I felt so good, better than when I had boarded the plane.

We stepped out into the humid night air in Beirut, still hazy from the dust storm. We met our driver who stood waiting among a crowd of cabs. He worked for a Christian organization here in Lebanon that was helping the refugees. He and his co-workers would be driving us around and interpreting for us during our entire time in Lebanon. Keith and Jana knew this driver from their previous visits. He was friendly and talkative. We talked about the dust storm and the trash crisis. Our driver was knowledgeable about the political situation, but in my tired state I absorbed only snatches of his explanations.

". . . they made a problem of it with the contractors, and so the garbage on the street . . . and the pressure is higher . . . assassinated . . . Now when things like these happen, there is give and take under the table, among all the leaders . . . Saudi Arabia . . . Iran . . . Shi'ite . . . Hezbollah . . ."

"What were those? Barriers?" I asked, as we rushed past something that looked like construction materials.

"Yeah, a barrier," our driver said, explaining that a political leader was afraid and wanted extra protection near the place he lived. "Everybody thinks he is important. 'I am important; protect me.' "

Our driver's cell phone began to ring, and he answered it. I found that the ringing cell phone would be a constant presence throughout our entire trip.

"Alo?"[a] he said into the phone. A rapid stream of Arabic followed.

"Khallus,"[b] he said as he hung up the phone. Jana explained that I would hear this word often.

The driver kept talking.

"It's about politics in the big countries. It's like playing a game. That's why when people ask me which political party I support, I say *none*. Everybody is playing a game, like playing Monopoly. You know, give me the yellow, I give you the red. And at the end I will close my eyes and say 'bye-bye' and go to something more beautiful," he added.

---

a *Hello.*
b *A word used to express frustration or finality.*

As we talked about the trash crisis, we looked out the windows expectantly, but so far we had not seen any banks of trash. Photos in the news made the city look terrible.

"They started collecting it," our driver explained, laughing about how the news media was misrepresenting the city to the world. "They don't show you everything."

"They show you the worst," Keith said, nodding.

Our driver agreed and told us about his personal journey with understanding different countries and cultures. "About four years ago, something happened that made me correct my way of thinking about countries I didn't know a lot about. Someone was telling me about Pakistan, how beautiful it is and how nice the people are, and I was surprised. I said, 'Are you sure about that?'

"Then I went to Brazil," he continued. "I visited a church there with the brother who was taking me around. There was a youth meeting, and I was telling them about Lebanon and the believers, and they were amazed and asked me, 'Do you have churches?' "

The driver spoke the question in a hushed, worried tone that made us all laugh.

"I said, 'Yes, we have churches.'

"They said, 'Are they underground? Are the Muslims okay with churches?' "

Our driver told the Brazilian Christians that he lives in a Christian area, and they were again surprised.

" 'You have Christian areas?' they asked. Then I told the brother I didn't want to go to any other churches that day. He thought I was angry, but I said, 'No, I'm not. I want to go home and change my presentation.' It was so funny."

In the back seat, I remembered my own fears about coming to Lebanon and Jordan. Would I be kidnapped or beheaded? The travel warnings on the U.S. Embassy sites were dire. I had spoken with someone who had lived in the Middle East. "You know, it can be dangerous over there," he had told me, "but once you arrive and you see people getting up and going to work, it just feels normal."

Suddenly Keith spotted a pile of garbage. "There's some trash!" he announced triumphantly, and we all laughed. "Now I saw my trash. I guess if you'd situate your camera right, you could make a pretty good story out of that pile of trash."

I looked out the window. In the darkness, I could see that we were at the base of a huge hill, lit up with lights.

"We are going up the hill to the left, where the convent is," our driver told us.

I had heard we would be staying in the guesthouse of a convent.

"Hopefully by tomorrow morning it will be a little clearer, because it's very pretty when it's clear," Keith said. He turned to our driver. "Was the sandstorm here as bad as you've seen it in your life?"

"I've only seen one other in my life," he said. "This one was stronger."

I couldn't stop looking out the window at Beirut. "Oh, everything is covered in dust!" I said. "I didn't notice it until right now. Look at the cars! That would be a big job to clean everything."

We were approaching our destination, spiraling up a series of mystifying streets high above the Mediterranean Sea. We drove up to a guard shack, and a smiling man greeted us and opened the gate to the convent. We drove in. In the darkness, I saw stone walls, grape arbors, and white-walled buildings. The pole lights above us were small pools of light in the dusty air.

"My colleague will be by at 8:00 in the morning to pick you up," our driver said. "You're going to the Bekaa."

It was hard to believe that in just a few hours, we would be visiting the refugees!

Nineteen hours after standing at the ticket counter in Chicago, I arrived at the convent. Nuns in full dresses, veils, and rope belts met us and gave us keys to our rooms, which opened off of a long, dim hallway. Our rooms were air-conditioned and furnished with sensible furniture and light-colored quilts. They were lined with white walls and tile floors.

Would I have the physical strength to travel to the Bekaa Valley, over nauseating mountain roads, in just a few hours?

Syria

The country of Syria is shaped like a rough triangle, with its base resting crookedly on the countries of Jordan and Iraq. The left (or western) edge of Syria borders Lebanon and the Mediterranean Sea, and the third edge of the triangle borders Turkey in the north. The Euphrates River, mentioned in the book of Genesis, runs through the country of Syria from the mountains of Turkey to Iraq and the Persian Gulf. The Orontes River, with its mouth in the Mediterranean Sea, starts high in the mountains of Lebanon, but runs mostly through western Syria. On its banks, cities have been built and major atrocities been carried out.

Unlike most places on the globe, Syria has been inhabited by people nearly since the beginning of time. The historian Josephus records that Syria's capital, Damascus, was founded by Noah's great-grandson, Uz. It was already a thriving city in the time of Abraham.

Like much of this region, Syria was conquered, in fairly quick succession, by Babylon, then Persia, then Greece, and then Rome. When Constantine legalized Christianity, the region became Christian, but a few centuries later, Muslims invaded. A huge battle was fought at Yarmouk in A.D. 636, close to the modern-day border between Syria and Jordan.

Syria became a predominantly Muslim state, and in 1097 the "Christian" Crusaders came to free the land from Muslim rule. They mostly failed, but not before they left a legacy of terror. Close to Aleppo, Syria, a Crusader recalled that "our troops boiled pagan adults in cooking pots; they impaled children on spits and devoured them grilled."[4]

In the following years Syria was invaded several times by Mongol invaders. During these wars, the blood of thousands of Syrians was shed.

The Ottoman Turks controlled Syria for the four hundred years from 1516–1918. Then World War I changed everything. As the Ottoman Empire disintegrated, European powers lay claim to some of the former Ottoman territory. France claimed Syria, and the European powers drew lines to create the boundaries of modern-day Syria. World War II saw more changes in government, but Syria finally declared independence in 1946.

In 1963, the Ba'ath Party took control of Syria, and in 1970, one of their top leaders, Hafez al-Assad, was sworn in as Syria's president. President al-Assad was an Alawite, a member of a minority group living primarily in the mountains near the coast. Even though they were small in numbers, the Alawites were powerful and had no real rivals among the more numerous Sunni Muslims. The Alawites were Muslims too, but they had different beliefs than the Sunnis, and they even had a few ideas that were almost Christian. Some Sunnis, especially deeply religious ones, felt the Alawites were heretics. It made them angry that a small group of less-than-genuine Muslims was in charge of the country.

President Hafez al-Assad began to develop the modern state of Syria with roads, schools, and hospitals, but he also ruled with an iron fist for thirty years. Perhaps his brutality was best demonstrated by a massacre in Hama in 1982. Hama was home to a group of religious Muslims called the Muslim Brotherhood. They felt the Alawite government of President al-Assad must be overthrown. They set off bombs in Damascus and shot at members of the government. They even opened fire at President al-Assad himself one day as he was waiting to welcome an African dignitary, but he escaped with only an injured foot after kicking a grenade out of the way.

President al-Assad responded to these attacks by executing a number of prisoners who belonged to the Muslim Brotherhood and burying them in a mass grave. He arrested, killed, or tortured members of the Muslim Brotherhood whenever he discovered them.

Finally, when a car bomb went off in Damascus and a plot to topple the government was uncovered, President al-Assad had had enough. He sent thousands of soldiers to the beautiful, unspoiled city of Hama to destroy it. He gave the responsibility of this project to his ruthless younger brother Rifaat, who was said to have compared himself to Stalin of Russia. In just a few weeks, an estimated 20,000 people, many of them civilians, had been killed (although exact numbers were hard to obtain). The "Old City" of Hama was flattened, and the picturesque Orontes River ran red.[5]

President Hafez al-Assad had two sons, Basil and Bashar. Basil was the oldest. He had an outgoing personality and was in line to inherit the presidency from his father. He loved to drive fast cars. His brother Bashar was quiet and studious and wanted to be an eye doctor. Bashar al-Assad studied at the school of medicine in Damascus and then moved to London to specialize in ophthalmology.

In 1994, Basil al-Assad was killed in a car accident, and Bashar was called home to a military school. In 2000, when the senior President al-Assad died, Bashar al-Assad entered a role he never expected to fill, president of Syria. The constitution had to be amended because it said that a president had to be forty years old, and Bashar was only thirty-four. The next year he quietly married a Syrian Sunni from London.

Most Syrians were hoping President Bashar al-Assad would be different from his father. As time passed, people became disappointed that he didn't make more changes. He was accused of being too passive by some and too dictatorial by others. In 2008, a travel writer mused, "The most common question asked of this enigma is, 'Is he really in control?' Until he can make a clean break with the past and put more of his own stamp on the country . . . the shadow cast by his father will not fade."[6]

The Uprising

On March 6, 2011, a group of boys spray-painted words on a wall in Daraa, Syria. The boys, about a dozen, were younger than fifteen years old. Their graffiti said, "The people want to topple the regime." It was a common Arabic slogan that had been used in the revolutions of other Arab countries. Although the boys were only children, their action was, for Syria, a "rare and dangerous show of defiance."[7]

The boys were arrested and tortured.

A few days later, a Facebook page sprang up called "Syrian Revolution 2011." It called for a Day of Rage. Protests sprang up in several Syrian towns. In just a few more days, the protests spread to include thousands of people. People who supported President al-Assad's regime also gathered, waving pictures of their beloved president and promising him their support.

President al-Assad, seeing that the protests were growing, began to offer concessions. He appointed a prime minister to bring change. He closed down the country's one casino to please the Sunni Muslims. He promised to grant the wishes of some of the people groups who felt they were being overlooked.

In spite of this, protests continued. Fridays, the days when Muslims worship, became regular protest days. Friday, April 22, 2011, became known as "Great Friday" with tens of thousands of people demonstrating. One hundred people were killed. One month later the death toll had reached 1,100. On June 3, another Friday was named for its 50,000-strong protest, called "Friday of the Children." This came shortly after the body of a thirteen-year-old Syrian boy who had been arrested by the regime was returned to his family, mutilated. Later in June, President al-Assad gave a public speech, passing blame for the conflict.

In the fall of 2011 a video was posted online of Syrian soldiers forcing a prisoner to say, "There is no god but Bashar al-Assad." It was later removed from the Internet site.

By this time, Arab nations were recalling their ambassadors from Syria, and nations around the world were condemning the acts of the Syrian government. The Arab League removed Syria from their ranks in late fall, and Jordan's King Abdullah called on President Bashar al-Assad to step down. Just before Christmas 2011, the United Nations announced that 5,000 people had been killed in Syria's war.

Early in 2012, a general in the Syrian army defected to join the opposition, which was now known as the Free Syrian Army. He reported that 20,000 fellow soldiers had also left the Syrian army, most of them Sunni Muslims.

On March 15, 2012, demonstrations marked the one-year anniversary of the conflict. Again, both anti-government and pro-government crowds formed. Toward the end of May, 108 people were killed by the regime in a massacre in Homs; 48 of them were children.

By July, Aleppo, Syria's largest city, was the scene of constant fighting. The important city was divided, weakening the economy of the entire country. Later in the fall, government forces bombed civilians in Aleppo who were standing in line waiting to get bread. By New Year's Day 2013, Aleppo's airport was shut down.

By June 25, 2013, the death toll in Syria had reached 100,000. By this time, any hope of dialogue seemed to be permanently gone. President Bashar al-Assad promised to strike down the opposition with an iron fist.

On August 21, 2013, the regime released deadly chemicals in the suburbs of Damascus while people were sleeping. Hundreds woke up choking and gasping for breath, later dying in makeshift hospitals as their friends attempted to splash water on them. Family members took photos and videos of the victims, to ensure that their deaths would not be ignored.

And as these events were occurring, Syrians by the thousands were fleeing their homeland.

The Opposition

Humans have a tendency to want to choose sides. It is easy to assume that if one side in a conflict is wrong, the opposing side must be right. When both sides act in deplorable ways, those watching are often left feeling depressed, confused, and hopeless. When a conflict splinters into more than two sides and multiple parties are all exhibiting hatred, revenge, and a lust for power, the feelings of confusion and hopelessness only deepen. Such is the case with the Syrian civil war.

While much has been made of the peaceful protests that began the war and elicited a heavy-handed response from the government, perhaps less media attention has focused on the movements that developed in response. Peaceful protestors and defectors from the Syrian military soon organized themselves into a force that was intent on overthrowing the government. This group was known as the Free Syrian Army.[8] But from the beginning, there was a lack of unity among various factions of this army, and other than the removal of Bashar al-Assad, their goals often varied widely. While some envisioned a more democratic Syria, others longed for a more Islamic state.

As time passed, these rifts became wider. In addition, many foreign players began to enter the war in Syria, each one siding with a Syrian faction that they thought would advance their goals in the region. Because of this, the war in Syria has often been called a proxy war. Radical Islamic jihadists found Syria to be fertile territory for recruiting angry, oppressed Sunni Muslims who were enraged by the atrocities of the al-Assad government. Yet even these groups could not always function together as a cohesive unit. The best-known split occurred between an Al Qaeda affiliate known as Jabhat al Nusra and a group that became known as the Islamic State in Iraq and Syria, or most commonly by its acronym, ISIS.[c] ISIS leaders were originally active in Iraq, but sensing an opportunity in the chaos of Syria, they took over large swaths of territory there, claiming to form a caliphate, or Islamic state, with the Syrian city of Raqqa as its capital. Their cruel and barbaric practices soon became infamous around the world, and world governments that had once seen al-Assad's government as the enemy began to redirect their rage toward ISIS.

---

c   *This group is known by several other names, including the Islamic State of Iraq and the Levant (ISIL), the Islamic State (IS), and colloquially in Arabic as Da'esh, an acronym for its Arabic name.*

VOICES

OF THE BEKAA

CHAPTER 3

"God has watched over us."

We met promptly at 7:30 a.m. on the morning of September 11, in the dining room of the convent. It was a large, silent room full of tables. Places were set for us and a few other visitors, but most of the white tables were empty. Tall windows let in the morning light, and I got my first hazy but real glimpse of the Mediterranean Sea.

We knifed off portions of soft and hard cheese and helped ourselves to Lebanon's thin bread along with Turkish coffee, olives, and candied apricots. They offered cucumbers and tomatoes also, but that was too much of a stretch for me for breakfast food.

Our driver for the day came into the breakfast room early. He was a quiet man with closely-cropped curly dark hair. I had heard that schedules were sometimes behind in the Middle East, but not with the team we were working with. In the days to come I was to learn more about them. Throughout our entire time in Lebanon, workers from this organization would drive us around, take us to visit in the homes of refugees, and interpret for us. The staff members who were our drivers and guides in the refugee camps usually did the interpreting as well. We had various drivers and interpreters, but they were all Arabic-speaking Christian believers. I was blessed by their desire to reach out and serve the refugees, who were mostly Muslim, and I found the team to be hospitable, prompt, and organized.

We were ready to set off across the Lebanon Mountains to the Bekaa Valley now. The drive would take an hour or two. Our driver had washed the coat of dust from his vehicle, so it was spotless.

"God has watched over us."

We drove out through the sliding gate of the convent, the endlessly cheerful watchman waving and smiling from his small guard house. We took a few turns, went down a hill, and then started going up the other side of the mountain. Far below us and behind us, the pale blue of the Mediterranean Sea, still wrapped in dusty haze, was visible if we looked back. We took a few more turns and climbed a few more hills, winding through small towns packed with honking cars and motorcycles.

Then we took another turn and found ourselves on top of the mountain, with another mountain ahead of us. We twisted and turned, dropped and rose a few more times, passed terraced gardens and a chateau set high on a hillside, to climb the second range, and suddenly, there was the Bekaa Valley, spread out below us, as flat as Indiana.

There were two military checkpoints along the mountain road. I asked our driver what they asked him, as the camouflaged, armed men spoke a few words and waved us through.

"Nothing," he said. I suppose he was tired of visitors expressing alarm over a commonplace event. He told us that they only asked questions if they were looking for someone in particular.

Our interpreter explained to us that some of the refugee camps in the Bekaa Valley were built in farmers' fields. As we descended, vineyards and vegetable fields flashed past our windows. We turned a few corners, and our driver eased the vehicle into a lane covered with crushed white rock.

We had arrived at our destination. My purpose for coming was now to be realized. I was very near the refugees now. I felt a bit of happy apprehension. Throughout the next few days, over and over again, I would hear the voices of Syria.

An interpreter from our host organization was with me now, and together our small team walked into the tent camp. Beside the gravel lane stood an elderly man in a traditional red-and-white-checked scarf.

"I miss my home, my land," the man said. He was wearing a loose, gray, long-sleeved robe. "Before the war, we were happy and comfortable. I worked in the field, growing wheat and barley, and I had some livestock, some lambs

17

and goats. There were mountains and flatlands.

"But suddenly we were bombed by barrels, and we had to leave immediately."

"Barrel bombs[d] are very common in Syria," the interpreter said to me on the side. "Planes come and drop barrel bombs over everything. If people in a certain area are not on the side of the government, the military randomly picks part of that area and bombs it."

"As soon as they started bombing, we ran away," the elderly man continued. "Some people left with cars. Some people had to walk. But my wife is disabled, so we had to get a car. The last thing I saw when I was leaving were barrel bombs falling. One hit a neighbor of mine. He passed away.

"At least my children are all safe. I have six boys and four girls, and they're all married and in a safe place. Two are in Jordan and the rest in Lebanon."

The organization that was hosting us was distributing food in the camp today, and the distribution was beginning now. We were surrounded by shouts of men, the revving of a motorcycle, and the chatter of children. Close to us, gallon bottles filled with cooking oil had been unloaded onto the gray, dusty ground.

"God has watched over us," the old man in the red scarf said above the clatter, and we parted ways.

---

d   *Barrel bombs are unguided bombs that are typically made from a barrel-shaped metal container filled with explosives, shrapnel, and chemicals.*

CHAPTER 4

"This crisis brought us to despair."

OUR INTERPRETER, WHO WAS ALSO our guide, led us to a tent housing a family with nine young children. The tent had a real wooden door hung in a doorframe. The wood skeleton of the tent was covered with white plastic stamped with the symbol for UNHCR, the refugee arm of the United Nations. The floor was bare cement. The children, although their clothes were well-worn, were dressed cheerily in bright rainbow colors: red, green, orange, yellow, and blue.

Only eight children were present when we arrived, because the oldest boy had gone to get water. The eight sat in a line on the cement floor, the sun streaming through the sides of the tent and lightening the dark heads of hair. They were all barefoot. One of the oldest girls, perhaps about ten, held a baby brother in a red suit.

"A, B, C, D, E, F, G . . ." one of the children chanted, showing off her knowledge of English. We laughed and applauded her.

"We were living in proper houses in Syria," the man of the house told us, chuckling ruefully as he looked around at the plastic and cement.

He was a tall man with a black mustache and beard, and he was dressed, like the camp itself, in dusty white clothes. His white T-shirt frayed at the collar, and over it he wore a long-sleeved shirt, rumpled, stained, and partially buttoned. "We were settled and everything was good. I used to sell vegetables and fruit. I used to rent a small shop and sell from there. The children were too small to help me at the time."

He began to speak about the war. The row of children listened silently.

"The war was the worst thing I've lived through. I was afraid of being arrested. I was afraid for the children, for their safety. One day when the rockets were falling, we just took the children and left. First we moved from village to village. Finally we came to Lebanon.

"Since we left, many awful things have happened in Syria. A rocket hit our house. I lost my mom. My oldest brother disappeared and has been missing for three years. My younger brother was injured, and they had to fix his leg."

The man's wife arrived with a two-liter bottle of a dark fruit cola, and an oval silver tray of glasses. She passed the drinks around the room.

"Thank you, that's wonderful," I said, relieved to find something cold to drink in the intense heat.

"*Shukran, shukran,*ᵉ" our guide said.

As the woman settled on the cement floor beside us, she began to talk about Syria. She talked about how she longed to see her parents, her family, and her friends. Even by phone, they were almost unreachable. Her parents had never met her two youngest children, the new babies of the family that had been born since they arrived in Lebanon.

She was dressed in a black hijab, the traditional head and neck covering worn by Muslim women, and a royal blue dress embroidered with silver designs. Her eyes were bright and intelligent.

"This crisis brought us to despair," she said, speaking loudly and energetically. "Growing up, in our safe homes in Syria, we used to hear about Palestine. That was the place of war and conflict. And now we have experienced it too. The Syrian families are separated all throughout the world now. We are refugees in many countries. Our dream is to be settled in Syria again. We want to go back to our homes and see our families, friends, and neighbors."

As we talked, the Muslim call to prayer rang out over the camp.

"We want our children to have an education, to become doctors and lawyers," the man said. "I feel that I am not giving them the best, and I feel guilty because of that."

Listening to their father, the row of eight small children grew silent, their huge, dark eyes sober with understanding.

"We had six children in school in Syria," their mother added. "We feel sorry

---

e   *Thank you.*

for them because here they're not getting their chance for proper education."

I smiled at one of the little girls, and she smiled back, pleased to be recognized. The line of children began to rock and jostle as the conversation went on. A few rubber bands appeared, and the children pushed and shoved and began a miniature rubber band war. A motorbike roared up to the entrance of the tent. The oldest son entered, lugging a large bottle of water from the spring.

Our guide, clearly skilled at turning the conversation to the spiritual, addressed the mother of nine.

"Have you ever forgotten to feed or dress your child?"

"No," the mother said, shaking her head.

"Maybe one day you might," our guide went on. "But there is a verse in the Bible where God says that even if a mother forgets her child, He will not forget us. Remember that God never forgets you. You are very precious in God's eyes. As God protected you in the past when you were in the middle of Syria, He can still protect you and help you to the very end."

The man of the house changed the subject. He talked about the countries that were helping the refugees. "We thank them a lot, and we respect them for taking refugees, and for their support. We hope that everyone will follow their lead. And we thank your organization," he said directly to our guide.

"We are trying our best to help you," our guide said. "We're doing this because of God's calling, not out of our own strength. We are nothing without God. We couldn't do this if He hadn't put this love inside of us."

As he talked, everyone watched him, their eyes quiet and thoughtful.

"Keep close to God and tell Him that you want to know Him," our guide concluded. "The most important thing is not to know *about* God, but to know God Himself. Maybe some night I will call my dad, and he won't answer the phone. But my heavenly Father answers any time I call Him."

The family thanked us for visiting. We thanked them for the soda and, slipping on our shoes, stepped back into the intense heat.

The System

The idea of having modern nations is a new concept in the Middle East. Most of the national boundary lines, and even some of the names of the countries, were created by European powers after the world wars. As Thomas Friedman said, "The borders of these states consisted of neat polygons—with right angles that were always in sharp contrast to the chaotic reality on the ground."[9] The tribes and political and religious groups living inside these straight lines didn't really get to choose whether they suddenly wanted to be part of the same country as the other tribes and groups.

However, as presidents and kings took leadership of these countries, order began to develop. With central governments and armies, the countries were able to build modern highways, run electricity to rural areas, and create public school systems. Even in Hama, Syria, after huge sections of the historic city were flattened in the government's 1982 massacre, President al-Assad built a new hospital, schools, public housing, and mosques.

In Syria, despite the brutality of the leaders that was evidenced whenever someone tried to cross them, many Syrians still appreciated the systems their leaders had carved out of the ancient desert lands. Perhaps they forgot how much of a role the government had in making Syria a relatively stable place to live, but even when complaining about the government, they often referred to it as the "system."[10]

CHAPTER 5

"We were walking with death."

EVEN IN THE MORNING, IT was sweltering inside the tents. As the day progressed, the tents grew even hotter.

The woman we visited now was dressed in black. A solid black scarf wrapped around her head, and she wore a black dress accented with yellow flowers. Her children screamed and slapped each other. The bare room had a cement floor, with walls of white plastic. A fan hummed from the corner.

The woman began to talk. She told us how she didn't have enough money to pay the rent for the tent they were living in.

"I remember how I was living in Syria with my husband," she said wistfully. "We were living really happy lives. Everything was cheap. My husband provided everything back then. He used to take very good care of me. I didn't need to work or do anything.

"My husband and I were relatives, but I didn't know him growing up. But once he saw me, he liked me."

"Did you like him too?" I asked.

"Oh, yes," she smiled. She giggled and looked at the floor. "We were married for five years. My husband was a metal worker, a little bit like a blacksmith."

She talked on, her memories circling back to her husband. She told us about their wedding. It had been a triple wedding. Two of her husband's brothers had gotten married the same time she and her husband had. The wedding celebration had gone on for three days, in a tent outside their house. They had had a special kind of rice and bulgur. There had been singers as well as special lights, because the party had gone into the night.

"It was really nice," she said, relaxing at the memory.

Then one morning at 5:00, everything changed. The five happy years ended.

"Around fifty soldiers entered the house. We were awakened from sleep by the commotion. They killed my husband and his two brothers. The three of them were married on the same day, and they died on the same day. I begged the soldiers not to kill me and the children; that's why they let us go. The children saw it happen. My eldest son has psychological problems now and always hits his brothers."

Her daughter was sitting on the floor listening. "My daddy is in heaven," she echoed. "He was killed by the army."

By the time her husband had been killed, many of the woman's neighbors had already fled from Syria. The young widow felt she had no choice but to leave Syria too.

"I was one of the last to leave, but I left everything immediately. Shortly after we left, we heard that they took a bulldozer and knocked the house down. It took us from 7 a.m. to midnight to get to Lebanon. We had to stop many times along the way.

" 'Why are you leaving?' the soldiers asked me at the checkpoints. 'Where is your husband?'

"I told them, 'My husband is traveling,' so they would allow me to leave. Then they told me that I had to go and bring a letter of approval from my brother-in-law, so that I could take the children with me. I did not find my brother-in-law, but I paid the mayor some money, and he prepared a written statement for me. We had no food, so the children were hungry.

"When we came here, it was difficult. But we praise God that we have something to sit under, that we have a roof over us.

"Since my husband died, I always have this fear, especially when night comes, and I'm alone with the children. I miss him, and I don't want to go back. My husband died and my house is struck down, so I want to stay here. But if I have a chance to move to another country with my children, I will go."

However, as we talked on, the lady told us, "If everyone else went back to Syria, I would go. I would like for my sons to have the same job that my husband had. My father wants me to remarry, but I told him, 'No, I just want to raise my children.' "

"God in heaven," Keith said, "He sees, He knows, and He is like a father to your children."

Our guide directed us a few tents down to the mother-in-law of the lady we had just visited. She was the mother of the three men who had been married on the same day and killed on the same day.

"I had five girls and five boys," the older woman told us. "I raised them twenty-one years without their father, and now I have lost three boys." The woman began to cry. "And now I am raising my grandchildren without their father."

"She is raising the children of one of her dead sons," our guide whispered to us. "Their mother abandoned them and ran away to marry someone else. This is very unusual in the Muslim culture."

One of the woman's five daughters lived in the tent as well, helping to care for her abandoned nieces and nephews. This daughter had her own story to tell of the morning the soldiers had entered the home and killed her brothers. She had also been shot and her leg badly injured.

In the middle of the mayhem, the soldiers had ordered her to leave, so she and her mother escaped to the hospital. Her mother sat in the hospital while her daughter was in surgery for two hours, getting pins in her leg.

As the mother waited outside the room where they were doing the surgery, her sons were brought to the hospital, dead. Someone took her to see them. She could not even cry; the shock was so great.

"I was in surgery when all this was happening," the daughter explained to us. "They put screws in my leg. The next day they discharged me. I was on a wheelchair when they rolled me out. They released people from the hospital as soon as possible, because sometimes the soldiers would come to the hospital to arrest people who had been injured. As soon as I was discharged, we began our journey to Lebanon. We left on foot."

"Didn't your leg still hurt?" I asked.

It was a stupid question, but I was in shock as my mind tried to absorb what she was telling me. How could this be? She had been shot and had received emergency surgery. She was discharged in a rush from the hospital the next morning so that she would not be tracked and arrested. Then she had fled to Lebanon—on foot, with a freshly pinned leg?

"Yes, it still hurts," she said. "The journey to Lebanon took us twelve days. The road was so dangerous, and we were some of the first people to try it," she said.

They hadn't risked going the legal way, where they would be questioned. They had come by illegal routes, walking. Where they could, they paid people money to get through or to take them a distance by car. But often they walked.

"It was really hard," the daughter said. "We moved from place to place. It was difficult finding food. In one place we went for two days without food. Once, they started shooting at us, so we left everything, even our phones, and started running. Both my brother and I had been injured previously, so we were slow. I kept falling, stumbling, and falling again. The worst thing was that my brother needed medical attention. He was bleeding. There are hardly any words to describe what happened on that journey. We were walking with death all the way."

With some pride, the young woman showed me the wound on her leg, now a white scar like a claw mark. She seemed to have mentally rebounded from the horrible experiences. She talked with us in an even, clear voice, but her mother's sadness was impenetrable.

The mother and daughter had parted ways that dreadful morning. While the daughter fled on foot to Lebanon, the mother fled to her brother's house in the country, still in Syria. Her brother had a farm, and she had stayed there. For twenty days, she knew nothing about the rest of her children. Once she found out that they had safely arrived in Lebanon, she followed them.

Here in Lebanon, in the refugee tent, far from danger, the tears came. She mopped the corners of her eye with a crumpled Kleenex, and dropped her head, swathed in a black scarf, into her hand. I asked her about the three-day wedding of her three sons, but she could not speak.

"I miss home," she said, crying. "I miss visiting the tombs of my children. This is my last wish, to be buried next to them."

"We care for you, and we will pray for you that God will give you peace and strength," Jana said.

As we gathered to pray for the mother, daughter, and grandchildren, the Muslim call to prayer sounded again.

CHAPTER 6

"We want to go back."

WE WERE SITTING NOW IN another tent on thin floral cushions. The walls of the tent were draped in a bright red satin cloth. Outside, separated from us only by a black mesh screen, children walked past in the dust.

An older woman dressed in black began to speak. She had ten children, three boys and seven girls. She had gray tattoos[f] under her eyes and on her jaw and chin. They looked like perpetual tears.

"We were happy before the war," she said, "even though we were poor. Before the war, we came to Lebanon a lot and went back to Syria. My children worked here in Lebanon before the war. But my husband was working in Syria. He was a truck driver in Syria. He loved the truck. He delivered things near our home.

"Then the army came to our house at 4:00 one afternoon and asked us to leave. Our home was confiscated, so we took all our children and left the same day.

"I lost one of the three boys," she said. "He worked in Lebanon as a construction worker, and he helped us financially before the war. He lived here in Lebanon for four years, and then he went back to Syria to get married. When he went back to Syria, he disappeared. I sold all my jewelry to pay for the people to search for him, but no one knows anything about him," she said. "I don't have the energy to do anything. My husband died here in the camp two months ago because he was so filled with grief about the loss of his son. My children can't find any work here in Lebanon now. We have passports to go to other places, to Germany, but we don't want to leave because we want to know about my son. What if we would leave, and then

---

f *Facial tattoos are not uncommon among elderly Arab women.*

27

find out that he was still alive and needed us?"

The daughters in the family occasionally interrupted as their mother talked. One of them got up, left the room, and returned with a silver tray for us. It carried a glass of water, a pot of coffee, a footed white sugar bowl with a mismatching lid, and tiny china cups.

"We want to go back to Syria," the mother continued. "Life here is expensive, and we can't continue like this. I want to go back to our home, but there is no safety or security there now. Also, my sons are wanted in the Syrian army, and I am afraid to lose another son."

The sister-in-law of the first lady began to speak. She was dressed in blue and tan and had listened as her sister-in-law spoke. She agreed to tell us her story as well, but she wanted us to come to her tent.

"Before the war, we were happy and comfortable," she said, when we were all settled on her floor in her tent. "Sometimes we got carry-out food from a restaurant close by. The restaurant made chicken and kebab, and other Arabic food. Sometimes we cooked. I cooked different kinds of kebab and *kibbeh*."[g]

Our interpreter turned to us, at a loss.

"This is hard . . . Lebanese food and Syrian food are somewhat similar but there are also differences. I don't know if there is a word in English for *kibbeh!* But perhaps you have seen *kibbeh* here in Lebanon."

"Is it deep-fried . . . like rolls?" Jana asked, motioning with her hands.

"Ay, ay, ay!" the woman said energetically.

"Exactly," our interpreter said.

"They fill it?" Jana asked. "Kind of like falafel, but it's bigger?"

"Exactly," said our interpreter again. "Some make it bigger."

"Our house was well-furnished," the Syrian woman continued. "We had books for our daughters.

"But then the Syrian army came and surrounded our area. They stayed for three days around our home, and they didn't let us go out. After these three days, they told us we had to leave. We left at 8 a.m. We brought nothing with us when we came to Lebanon. I miss my home, my security and safety, and my neighbors. We haven't heard anything about them. I want to go back to our home in Syria. I hope I can go back to that same street again.

---

g   *A Middle Eastern food made with bulgur and stuffed with meat.*

"We want to go back."

"Here, my daughters work one day and are off five or six days. There's no work. No one helps us—only you," she pointed to our interpreter. "We hope to go back to Syria, but the second choice is to go to another country. When we go back to Syria, you can visit us there."

VOICES

OF LEBANON

CHAPTER 7

"Refugees are the most resilient people."

LEAVING THE BEKAA VALLEY, WE passed a shepherd urging a herd of brown and black sheep past a garage. Around us lay carefully cultivated fields. There were rows and rows of cabbages, and vast vineyards surrounded by fences. There were fields of squash planted on rows of black plastic. They reminded me of my father's straight rows of vegetables back in Wisconsin, except for the layer of white dust. The dust had settled everywhere. Car washes were running a good business. The apple orchards and grape vineyards shone white with dust under the hot Lebanese sun. According to my guidebook, these Lebanese fields receive about 240 days of sunshine each year.[11]

Into this peaceful valley, the refugees had poured, uninvited. Many of them were living in the fields of the Lebanese farmers.

We arrived back at the convent, weary after a long day of interviews. After taking some time to recover and rest, we met in the convent's white cafeteria. We had helped ourselves to zucchini pizza, grilled fish, and pasta, when a young man walked in. He introduced himself as George Wheeler and joined us at the table. He was an American working as an intern with the local organization that was helping the refugees. Having degrees in economics and sociology, he had also previously worked with refugees in Minneapolis.

We invited him to join us at our table, and he agreed. From the minute he sat down, we talked about refugees. We talked about the body of the Syrian boy which had just washed ashore and how, as a result, some countries were promising to accept more refugees. President Obama had just agreed to accept 10,000 Syrian refugees to the United States. This sounded like a big number unless you considered that Lebanon, a country the size of Maryland, was hosting 1,000,000 refugees. It was also a small number when compared with the 60 million people living as refugees world-wide.

The United States accepted a total of about 70,000 refugees per year, George told us. But, with his economics degree, George understood why no country wanted to take in a big crowd of poor people in a short time.

"The main question with refugees is, 'Whose problem is it?' " he said. "Most people want to say, 'Not mine.' Anyone can say, 'Well, glad that's not my problem; I hope someone else does something about it.' But what does that do?

"There are three things you can do with a refugee. You can wait for the crisis to end and let them move back home. You can help them assimilate into the country they're in currently, where they're probably living in a camp or substandard housing. Or you can resettle them to a new country.

"The average wait time for a refugee in a camp is sixteen years," George informed us. "Many refugee camps in Africa or Asia have the third generation of refugees there. Many of them are unskilled laborers, and other countries don't accept them.

"For example, there are Congolese refugees throughout Africa, but people are not very interested in resettling them. The Congo has been at war since the Congo's been around. It has the highest number of mineable resources for computers . . . gold, zinc, copper, all of that. Whoever controls all of the Congo will basically be able to provide every cell phone we need for 300 years. There are about 250 ethnic languages in that area. So that means there are more than 250 groups of people saying, 'This is our territory.' "

Jana left to find hot water for tea.

"Do the refugees know that they might have to live for years in a refugee camp?" I asked. "It seems like maybe if they knew what they were getting into, that they might not have a life in the camps, they would try something different."

Perhaps there was nothing different to try.

"That," said George, "is why refugees are willing to take the risk of dying in the Mediterranean Sea. As long as staying in a country means death or something worse than death, no amount of infrastructure or technology will stop people from leaving, because they have nothing to lose."

George kept talking as we stirred sugar into the tea Jana had found. He explained how the Geneva Accords of 1952 had defined what a refugee was in the post-World War II era. A refugee was someone who was oppressed by his own country, or someone who could not use legal means to escape hardship. "For example," George said, "some people leave a country because they are the 'wrong race' and will be killed. Others leave their country because they think the situation there is hopeless, and there is no chance of making a living."

George pointed out that the United States was a country that mostly got to choose its refugees. Most refugees to the United States have been acknowledged and assisted by the United Nations and have been accepted by the U.S. Through the UN, these refugees get protection, the right to work, and a new start to life. After a year they get to apply for green cards, and after five years they can apply to become citizens.

By contrast, the Syrian refugees just "showed up" in Lebanon and Jordan and said, "I'd like to be a refugee, please."

As we talked, the convent's kitchen workers picked up our now-empty plates, loading them with a clatter onto a rolling cart.

"Even though refugees seem like an economic burden," George said, "there are a number of positive things about accepting them into a country. Refugees are the most resilient people I've ever met. And immigration has been really good for the American legal system, which makes money on all of the paperwork. Applying for a green card costs money, applying for citizenship costs money. Also the number of really good ethnic restaurants shoots up," he added with a smile.

"The Syrian refugees seem to be a bit different than the refugees from the Congo or Somalia. Some of the people in the United States seem to feel some responsibility for them. Also, Syrians have more resources, so they can try to flee their country more than some people can."

"Yes, a lot of Syrians were prosperous before this all started," Keith said. "You know a lot of people in the West are pointing fingers at the other Middle Eastern countries. 'Look! These are your brothers! Why don't you take care of them?'"

"Right," George agreed. "When the current concept of refugees was defined in 1952, the West loved to help people who were fleeing communists. They were scientists, chess masters, people like that. So they were really skilled people who could assimilate into the country easily. And now we have people who are not as technically developed and who look different from typical Westerners. The West isn't sure if they want them, but many of the Middle Eastern countries don't want them either."

"Sometimes," I said, "I just get overwhelmed by the problems of the world, but then I realize that it comes down to me doing what I can do in my neighborhood. What else? You can't always see the end results, but that's what I've been called to do."

"Nobody can fix every problem," Keith agreed, "but we can all play a little part."

"We need to be willing to open our homes and open our hearts," Jana said, "instead of just looking at the news and saying, 'Oh, there are 60 million refugees.' "

"One thing that I find very interesting in all of this," George said, "is that most of the major characters in the Bible were refugees of sorts at one time. Jesus himself was smuggled to Egypt. Moses, Abraham, and David were all hunted or driven away by famine at one time or another. Paul, Daniel, and the apostles . . . they can all relate to being strangers in a strange land."

After the energizing meal and conversation, we stepped out into the courtyard. From the hillside where we stood, we could see the lighted boats on the Mediterranean Sea and the lighted buildings of Lebanon spread out both on the slope below us and on the mountains above us.

The beauty engulfed my heart. I felt with a rush that Beirut, Lebanon, was the most beautiful place I had ever been.

Yet, like a refugee, I thought of my own home. What would it be like to wonder, *Will I ever return?*

Syrian Troops
in Lebanon

When Syrian refugees began to pour into Lebanon, it was natural for the Lebanese to remember the many years Syrian troops had been stationed in their country and the ways they had mistreated the people of Lebanon. Syrian forces first came to Lebanon in 1976, as Lebanon's civil war was beginning. They were intended to act as a peacekeeping force. But as time went on, they seemed to function more as an occupying army, pursuing Syrian interests at the expense of the Lebanese. Power plays and assassinations continued for almost thirty years. The Syrian forces stayed in the country until 2005 when the sentiment against them was so great that they permanently left Lebanon.

CHAPTER 8

"He sees the whole picture."

OVER THE WEEKEND THAT I spent in Lebanon, we rested. One day I wandered down a path at the convent to a low stone wall where I could sit with a view of the hillside. It was packed with brown, white, and red-roofed square buildings looking as if they could slide down the hill at the slightest touch. I looked down on the tops of grape arbors, and far, far down to the Mediterranean Sea.

The convent library was a dizzying spread of books. The spine titles were written in Arabic, French, and English, almost evenly divided. It reminded me of Lebanon's splintered past and divided present. Lebanon had been split into many different cultural groups long before the Syrian refugees arrived.

In the convent's round chapel, with Arabic books in the benches, I was struck by the mosaics at the front of the room. One showed a woman handing a water pot to a man at the well—Jesus and the Samaritan woman from John 4. In the context of war, people groups, and refugees, the woman at the well was a refreshing symbol of Christ's power to change lives.

In the evening we found an open-air restaurant on the shore of the Mediterranean Sea with waves literally crashing in beneath us. I ordered a grilled fish, which came whole on a bed of fresh lettuce, eyes, scales and tail still intact, its mouth resting on a cut lime. I removed the skin, ate the top half, and dissected the spinal column and ribs, picking off meat as I went. It was delicious.

We then circled around the restaurant and picked our way down a sandy bank to the beach. We stood in the sand with the waves sliding in over our feet as the sun dropped toward the edge of the sea. Silhouetted teenage boys leaped off each other's shoulders into the water just as others had done, I supposed, two thousand years ago.

As I watched the boys leaping and playing in the sea, I thought again of the refugees. How strange that everyone here was happy and carefree, and only a few miles across the mountain were people whose lives were at a standstill!

We ended the night with coffee, also outside among palm trees, with the hills of Lebanon lit up around us in the darkness and the sound of the waves surrounding us.

As we waited for a taxi to take us back to the convent, we chatted with the Lebanese coffee shop workers. They had an interesting perspective on the Syrian refugees.

One of the workers talked about how harshly the Syrians had treated the Lebanese in years past. Yet he didn't seem to be bitter.

"Now they are being treated harshly," he said. "But God knows. He's up there. He dealt with them His way. I'm not making fun of them. I don't know why this happened to them. God is great; He knows how to act. That's God's way. He sees the whole picture."

"I think it's nice that the Lebanese are helping them," I said.

"In my village," the young man said, "there were some Syrians who hid in the schools. They lived in the schools because there were no other places available to stay. So I opened my home to two families. I had an apartment beside the house, so I gave it to two families. I told them, 'I don't want rent; just stay for three months until they make refugee camps for you.' They stayed there three months."

But as I was coming to realize, not all the Lebanese were so welcoming or positive about the Syrian refugees in their country. Across the table, Jana was talking with a girl who spoke wonderful English. She had heard about our project, and now she turned to me.

"This is a very sensitive issue, writing a book about the Syrian refugees," she told me. "And right now, there are too many books about Syrian refugees."

CHAPTER 9

At the Warehouse

ON MONDAY MORNING AS WE lurched over the mountain roads heading back to the Bekaa Valley, we discussed the Sunnis and the Shi'ites. George, whom we'd met in the convent earlier, was traveling with us today, so the conversation was brisk.

Our driver's opinion was that the Western media wanted people to think that the Sunnis (represented by Saudi Arabia) were the peaceful Muslims, and the Shi'ites (represented by Iran) were the violent Muslims. However, he said that all extremist Muslims were Sunnis, including ISIS and Al-Qaeda. The particular brand of Islam that spawned ISIS had started in Saudi Arabia.

"In those sects of Islam," our driver said, "if you don't follow their law and pay the tax, they have to kill you. It's not that they just leave you alone, they have to kill you. To be very honest with you, this is the true Islam. It's not what people are trying to show, that Islam is a religion of forgiveness. No, not at all."

"We have Pakistani neighbors in Amman," Jana said. "And they are respectful of Christians, of us, and of our Holy Book. But they also say that Islam is a religion of peace."

"I've worked with a lot of Sunnis," George said, "especially with Somali refugees in Minneapolis, and they're good, nice people. Probably 95 percent of any population is more concerned about feeding their family and that kind of thing. It's just the 5 percent you've got to look out for."

As we made our way down the other side of the mountain, we talked about the way the Middle East was evolving. Our driver thought it was likely that Syria would be split into four pieces to match the ethnic divisions that the war in Syria had exposed.

39

George remarked that he was surprised Lebanon had managed to stay together as long as it had. It was more diverse than Syria, yet it still managed to stay unified as one country.

"During World War II the West made a bunch of countries over here and didn't ask anyone how they felt about the boundary lines," George said. He felt that a lot of the political issues were still scars from these decisions.

"Some people say you just have to solve it . . . figure it out, find a solution," Keith said. "It's not that easy."

George agreed. "Just solve it? The fastest way to do that is make new countries, and that's violent."

"Ten more minutes," our driver announced, as we made our final descent into the valley where the refugees lived. "Did you hear about Saudi Arabia's offer?" he went on. "Saudi Arabia offered to build 200 mosques in Germany for the refugees, and someone suggested, instead of putting this money to build 200 mosques, just host a few refugees. And Saudi Arabia refused."

"There's a growing question of, why is Europe taking all these Muslims, when there are very, very rich Muslim countries not taking refugees?" George said.

With a lurch, we pulled into an alley with shop signs in Arabic, green plants in pots, and a tangle of electric lines swooping overhead. Down the street, a shop announced "Scanner Auto Diagnostics" beside American logos: Ford, Jeep, Dodge. A brown cat padded across the dirt alleyway, followed by a gray cat. A man two doors down sat on several tile steps in khakis and a dress shirt, smoking.

We had arrived at our host organization's warehouse in the Bekaa Valley. They used this warehouse to store the items that were distributed to refugees. It was cool and clean and smelled like burlap sacks. Young men loaded a waiting truck, everyone talking Arabic, their voices echoing in the warehouse. Pallets were loaded with parcels for the refugees. Some pallets held unpackaged items: boxes and boxes of white meat tuna, labeled in Arabic and English, shrink-wrapped packages of black tea, clusters of olive oil bottles, boxes of "High Foam Washing Powder," and tin cans of beef.

I found George by the parcels.

"What all is in here?" I asked George. "Do you know?"

George had helped pack parcels for a number of days in Beirut. He laid a hand on the lumpy parcel.

"There is toilet paper at the bottom," he said, checking off the items with a slap on the burlap parcel, "eight rolls. There are peas, and then tomatoes, fish, tea obviously, two kinds of pasta, larger cans of some vegetables. Then some things they get in big bags and put into smaller bags, like chickpeas, rice, lentils, and other basic items. This whole parcel is for a family of five for about twenty-one days. The idea is that it's not a full thirty days, so that people don't become entirely dependent, so once a month they get three weeks' worth of food."

The truck had disappeared; apparently, we had missed an announcement in Arabic. Upon asking, we were told that the truck had been pulled around the corner to a second building for loading. "Just down there," we were told, so the four of us walked over to the second building.

I wandered among the pallets in this warehouse, spotting cooked fava beans in a tin can, a box of processed cheese, and a loft full of tissue.

"Take it, please," one of the relief workers said to me, pressing a black package of chocolate-filled wafers into my hand as though I had been working and deserved a break.

Here I learned a little more about the work that the organization was doing. In addition to food, they provided heaters and blankets as donations allowed. They also brought medical and dental teams from other countries to provide physical and spiritual support for the refugees.

The more I heard, the more I began to appreciate our hosts' efforts to maintain relationships with everyone they served. The needs were vast.

"Every day, we have six or seven families calling, 'Can we get a food portion? Can you come and visit us?' " our driver said. "There are six hundred people on the waiting list. We can't deal with that. They call and we say, 'We don't have any places. But we can take your name, just in case.'

"We don't only distribute food. We maintain a good relationship with every family! We do follow-up visits. We do Bible studies. Expanding would require more staff. We are trying to make a good system and have a good process in place before we expand."

The truck was almost loaded now. A worker hurried by with a scales, and a light plastic table was tossed onto the truck. The tailgate was already closed, and above it was a higher gate, swung shut and chained on one side.

We drove the remaining few minutes to the refugee camp. As we pulled in, children ran up the path to the truck. A little boy in a blue shirt and tiny plastic sandals stood close to his mother, clutching a half-eaten green apple. Mustached men in red-checkered scarves and ankle-length robes greeted us.

I looked around both ways. On one side of us loomed the mountains over which we had come from Beirut. On the other side were the mountains over which the refugees had come from Syria.

A blistering sun was already burning down onto the plain, baking the white rocks of the refugee camp and tanning the children dressed in colorful clothes. Not far from us, a blue blanket was spread on the ground, covered with red peppers drying in the sun. Smells of mud or sewer lurked nearby, but thankfully there was also a gentle breeze today.

George jumped up into the truck full of food parcels; Keith began filling black bags with hygiene items. Jana and I mingled with the children and young women. We were ready to hear more of the stories of Syria.

VOICES

FROM HOMS

Homs

Homs is the third largest city in Syria with a pre-war population of at least 823,000.[12] It was known as a friendly town with corn-on-the-cob stands, coffee shops, parks, and gardens.

In the Roman era and beyond, Homs was an important center of Christianity. Although Muslims later took over the city, Homs is still home to many Christians. There is a Christian quarter in Homs, and the city has an array of both churches and mosques.

Because cities in the Middle East have been around for so long, many of them have a historic section known as the "old city." Most of the old city of Homs was destroyed during the Ottoman Empire, but there are still sections of fortified wall.

In pre-war Syria, the souk (marketplace) in Homs was a beautiful place for tourists to visit. Its lampposts, vaulted ceilings, and stonework gave it a reputation as one of the most beautiful souks in Syria. Here visitors could wander, watching carpenters, metal-workers, knife-sharpeners, and cobblers plying their trade. Spices, gold, and apparel were top purchases for tourists.

Tribal Politics

Perhaps because he was planning to be an eye doctor rather than a president, President Bashar al-Assad failed to deal with the tribal politics in Syria like his father had.[13] His father, Hafez al-Assad, had taken Syria's tribal groups seriously, inviting them to be part of his government. He knew his group, the Alawites, were a minority, so he wanted more people on his side. He made sure the other groups had schools and hospitals. He gave them positions in Parliament and made sure they got revenue from their local oil fields.

Tribal connections, or connections between relatives, mattered a lot, especially in rural Syria. As one expert on the Middle East explained, there are tribal affiliations all over Syria that are so strong that the people can often operate as isolated, independent groups during times of war or unrest. Or, if one member of a tribe is in danger, any other member will take him in, just because they belong to the same tribe.

Another Middle Eastern writer further explains that these tribal traditions reflect the geography and history of the desert.[14] Not too long ago, Bedouin tribes lived in the lonely desert where there was not enough grass or water to share with other tribes. The grass or water belonged to the tribe who could fight hardest. There was no central authority to call on. There was no police station, no 911 center, no courts of justice. All of that was managed by people who stuck up for each other within their own tribe. Thomas Friedman, a journalist who has lived in the Middle East and written extensively about it, said, "In such a lonely world, the only way to survive was by letting others know that if they violated you in any way, you would make them pay, and pay dearly." The tribes would retaliate in a way that would make everyone take them seriously.

When Bashar al-Assad became president, the government policy toward the rural tribes changed. The younger al-Assad either did not know or did not care about the previous relationship the government had with the tribes. He often filled their positions with Alawites, people from his own group. Then a drought hit the rural areas, and Bashar al-Assad's government did little to help the tribal people living in the desert. Finally 800,000 of them migrated to the cities to survive. They took their families with them, and they also took their animosity toward President Bashar al-Assad, who had ignored their plight. One such movement landed in Homs, in an area called Bab al-Amr.

Some say that it was these tribes from the desert, who had once been included but now were overlooked, who first came out in the anti-government protests at the beginning of the war. They encouraged their relatives to join the protests.

"Blood ties are powerful," one expert on the Syrian war says. "During many of my interviews in the countryside, people said that in the early days of the uprising, they could go anywhere in the community and hide with relatives. Anyone trying to escape from security services would find open doors with tribal relatives willing to protect them. But in big cities like Damascus, no one would be willing to do that. The tribal ties aren't there." [15] Yet even in big cities like Damascus, family ties and family pride are so strong that beggars are rarely seen.[16]

Even relatives working outside of Syria were invited to join the anti-government effort. Money and support poured in from Saudi Arabia and Kuwait, where relatives had gone for jobs. Similar tribes from other Arab countries sometimes offered their support as well.

CHAPTER 10

"The most precious thing we left was peace."

MANY COLORFUL CHILDREN STOOD AGAINST a backdrop of dusty white as we walked through the camp. They seemed to be everywhere, slinking along the sides of automobiles or motorbikes, trying to catch a glimpse of us. They clustered in groups, looking at us, talking Arabic. They wore sports T-shirts, bill caps, and shirts with American cartoon characters. The older girls wore hijabs and full-length skirts. There were many pairs of deep brown eyes and many heads of dark, dark hair, standing out against the cheery yellows and reds in their clothes.

Thankfully, the morning was still cool. Our driver led us down the main street, then veered off into an alley. Wooden frames held walls of tarp, plastic, burlap, and corrugated tin. The roofs were strewn with dusty tires, holding the plastic in place. Lines of laundry hung on rope beside the houses. Empty plastic water bottles lay along the sides of the tents. Occasionally, a refugee tent was wrapped in the colorful plastic of a billboard, but even the advertisements for potatoes or McDonald's were covered with dust.

We walked up to a square tent. Cement blocks anchored one side of the plastic to the ground, and a tire was visible on the roof.

A tall man in a plum-colored robe stood in the doorway. He greeted our guide warmly and invited us to come inside. It was clear that everyone in the camp recognized and trusted our guide.

Just inside the door of the tent, we all took off our shoes. We entered a room with floral curtains on the walls and a huge, floral mat with a waxy finish on the floor. Low cushions lined the walls. A square black plastic clock hung on the wall, bumping up against the wooden slats of the ceiling. A single spiral light bulb hung from the center of the room.

We took seats on the low cushions around the perimeter of the room.

The man of the house was balding, with a whitening beard and a black mustache. Other family members joined us: a woman in a black hijab, several children, and a brother in khaki pants and a polo shirt.

This family had lived in Homs, Syria, before the war began. In Syria, the man was a construction worker.

"People raised cattle in our area," the man told us. "And it was also industrial. The agriculture was slow because of the government. They took our agricultural places and tourist attractions and built castles on them for their own use."

The woman in the black hijab was the tall man's wife. She spoke now.

"We used to make sweets and gather for coffee! We used to laugh and talk while the children would play." Then, as if reminded of her duties by her own words, she slipped away to the tent kitchen.

Her husband talked on about oppression and war. Whenever the conversation strayed to other subjects, he always brought the topic back to the oppression they had faced.

"Because of the pressure, I had to move out," he said. "We were bombed, persecuted, and arrested."

His eyes were small, but serious and bright. He didn't make eye contact with me long. If I happened to glance his way, he looked at the mat on the floor. I remembered that I had been warned not to make eye contact with Muslim men and had been told that many of them do not shake hands with women.

"I am from Bab al-Amr. The people in our area were oppressed by the government, so they rose against the government," the man said. "Because of that they were attacked and bombed. Bab al-Amr was one of the regions that was brutally hit. If I would go back to Syria and say I am from Bab al-Amr, they would kill me or imprison me for life. This is what happened to a man I knew who went to see his family. When they found out he was from our street, they arrested him. He has been in prison now for four years.

"I was once arrested in front of my house and was held for two days. They struck me and forced me to say things I didn't believe. There was no reason for them to arrest me. We were sitting in front of our house peacefully.

"My brother was helping people; he was going to get medicine for children. He and our cousin were passing by a car that was out of gas, and they were both murdered, hit by rockets."

As he spoke about his brother's death, he became animated, waving his long arms and chopping the air with the palms of his hands.

Other people on their street had suffered tragic fates too. Elderly people had their homes broken into. The intruders would douse the old people with gasoline and then set them on fire because they refused to leave their houses.

"Eight people, they set them all on fire on this street," he told us.

His wife returned from the tent kitchen carrying a tray with a pot of Turkish coffee and a little cluster of tiny cups. We passed the tray, each pouring the thick coffee into our individual cups. Despite the heat, which was beginning to pour through the sides of the tent, the coffee hit the spot.

The man's young son spoke up, "We used to go out to get bread, and they used to come and shoot us, using the big tanks."

"In Syria we once tried to buy vegetables," the woman added, as a baby wailed in the background. "We were near a checkpoint, and the soldiers opened fire on the people that were buying vegetables. I left everything and fled."

When the war became unbearable, the family had left their home and fled the country. They hired a driver to take them across the border into Lebanon.

"The driver knew the people and how to get himself through," the man said. "We had to pay him to take us through."

As we talked, flies began to circle. It got hotter as the sun pushed through the plastic and screening. I took another sip of the Turkish coffee, which ironically was getting too cool.

"If you go to our street now," the man said, "they say it feels like a deserted street, but people are living inside. Once, the government went to that area and said, 'Come, we brought you bottles of gas and bread for free.' People came out and they started filming that to show the public that people are still there, and being treated well. But they did that only as long as the cameras were running. It was a political statement."

"We miss our house and our possessions," the man said, "but the most precious thing that we left was peace, and the gathering of the parents of the families and the neighbors. We used to see our neighbors all the time. Our parents would come and check on us. Now it's been four years since I've seen my parents. This is the thing we miss most."

Like the man on the plane, these Syrian refugees wanted to be at home. They wanted to return to normal, to their coffee breaks and their family gatherings, to a place where women talked and laughed while the children played.

"We will pray that you would be able to go back and have these family gatherings again," our guide said. "We want to support you as much as we can so you will be able to go home."

Then, undaunted by the heat and flies, our guide told our Muslim hosts the story of Jesus. The guide was just a young man, but he spoke fearlessly, with a face full of joy and peace.

"I believe that Jesus came for all people," he said. "He didn't come to certain people. He came for the Christians, the Muslims, the Druze, Jews, for everyone. The Jews didn't accept Him. They crucified Him. But whoever accepts Jesus will be saved, because Jesus died to save everyone. Just like God prepared a lamb to die on behalf of Abraham's son, Jesus was the Lamb who died for all of us.

"If we confess our sins, and believe with all our heart that Jesus died because of these sins, He will put our sins away. This is what happened in my life. It's not enough to do good deeds. Good deeds will not take me to heaven.

"When my sins were forgiven, it was as if a mountain was removed from my shoulders. I started a new life. The first thing that God changed was my dirty tongue and the thoughts that I had. There was no more lying or cursing. My heart that used to envy could now easily forgive, because I allowed Jesus to enter my heart. I won't hide the change from others, because this decision determines where I will go in eternity. Now it's everyone's chance to do this. I'm not saying just words, I am sharing my own experience. And I repeat that Jesus didn't come just for certain people."

All five Muslim family members listened very quietly. The face of the woman in the black scarf was one of curiosity, with a hint of desire that these words might be true.

We ended with a prayer.

Keith prayed in phrases, as our guide interpreted.

"Our Father God in heaven, thank you for your goodness and your love to us. Thank you that you love this family, even though they have been through many problems. Thank you for Jesus, who came to take us away from our own problems of the heart. I pray that this family would be able to go back to Syria in the future. But most of all I pray for their hearts and souls that they could experience peace and love. Thank you for their graciousness and their hospitality to us. Please be with them and keep them in your hand."

When the prayer was done, the woman of the family wiped her eyes on her black hijab.

"We thank you for your visit," said the man. "We are really privileged that you have come. At least we feel we are being heard and listened to."

Bab al-Amr

Whether or not it was because the desert tribes felt ignored by President al-Assad, the neighborhood of Bab al-Amr in the city of Homs was a hotspot of the Syrian war. A young singer from Bab al-Amr wrote songs about the need to overthrow the government, inciting the tribes to action.[17] The war had been going for barely a month when twelve people were killed in Homs. Their funeral was a huge public event; the coffins were carried by hand from the mosque to special graves that were usually reserved for leaders. The funeral procession was like a rally, encouraging everyone to continue the fight against the regime.

Then in October 2011, ninety Syrian soldiers from the Bab al-Amr area defected from the government army. Also that fall, the rebel army took control of this section of Homs. Tanks and soldiers descended on Bab al-Amr and supplies were cut off. Food, water, and electricity all became difficult to find as these areas of Homs were collectively punished. People were malnourished, fresh water was scarce, and rodents abounded. As a result, disease spread. Besides sickness, many people suffered disabling injuries from the constant rockets and shells.[18]

On February 3, 2012, nearly a year after the demonstrations began, the Free Syrian Army held a demonstration in Bab al-Amr. It was the thirtieth anniversary of the massacre of 20,000 people in Hama. They wanted everyone to be reminded of the awful things President Bashar al-Assad's father had done. The rebel army took photos with tanks they had captured from President al-Assad's Syrian Army.[19] But less than a month later, after endless bombardment from the government forces, the rebel army withdrew, and the government claimed Bab al-Amr.

Funerals now became commonplace and hasty, if they happened at all. When shells were raining all around, it was not always possible for corpses to be retrieved by family members. Empty lots were turned into cemeteries, but even so, space became limited. One thousand people were buried in the first year of the war alone. People began to bury their loved ones next to their houses.

In an article entitled "When the Grave Becomes a Luxury," an author from Homs wrote, "They now say: lucky are those who died before. At least they had someone to give them a proper burial and mark their graves."[20]

CHAPTER 11

"I don't know how I got the bullets."

No floral wall curtains adorned the next tent we visited—only white plastic, pieces of it frayed and tearing. The man of the house, wearing a bright orange polo shirt, reached above his head and turned on an overhead fan. The fan had no power plug, only two bare wires sticking out of the cord, but he slid the wires into the two slots of the outlet, and the fan began to spin.

We took off our shoes and sandals, piling them on the white rocks at the entrance.

The man's wife, her head wrapped in a leopard-print hijab, settled in a corner on the mat floor and promptly began to breastfeed her baby. The Muslim women were very modest, so I was surprised to learn that breastfeeding in public was perfectly acceptable.

Leaning against a torn screen, the man told us about their lives in Syria. "We used to live in peace," he said. "Our daughters would go out at night."

His wife, juggling the baby, began to talk. She told us about how she had met her husband and about their wedding. She told about celebrations and family gatherings that she remembered from Syria. Even though the family had not been wealthy, they loved to get together for birthdays and family gatherings and play music and cook good food. They would serve rice, bulgur, yogurt, and salads. A sheep would be slaughtered for the celebration.

"Did you have cake for the children's birthday parties?" I asked doubtfully.

"Yes," she said. "And candles. One candle for each year of the child's age."

Their oldest daughter, a shy girl of about eight, was still dealing with the emotional trauma of the war. She was in the kitchen, avoiding our conversation.

The man held out his right wrist to show us a bullet scar. He also had a bullet in his leg. I thought I heard him say, "I don't know how I got the bullets," but that didn't make sense to me, so I decided to clarify this. *How could a person get shot and not know it?* Turning to the man, I said, "I would like to know how you got the bullets in your arm and leg."

"I don't know," he replied. "I just fell on the ground."

He had gone to a hospital in Syria after he was shot, but it was not a real hospital. It was a field hospital that had been set up to help the injured people. The bullet in his leg was still there and hurt him to the point of interfering with his ability to work. But it would require surgery to remove it. A nerve in his arm had been cut.

Our tent conversations were prone to interruption. Our guide was well known in the camp; everyone loved and trusted him.

An older woman in dark blue with a black hijab entered. A little girl appeared in the doorway in a clean red dress, her hair braided in a thick, black braid. She nibbled on a rippled potato chip and appeared to be a visitor in the house, probably here to see us. A large gray-haired lady entered through the front door to ask our guide about school registration for someone.

"Not today," he told the woman, explaining to her that we were focusing on hearing the stories of the refugees today.

The man with the bullets hadn't wanted to leave Syria, so he had tried moving his family temporarily to different places. But the trouble grew worse and worse.

"My niece was killed," he told us. "She was my sister's child. She was going to get married and she was shot in the head by a sniper. Things got worse and worse. Finally, so many rockets came down on our street that it destroyed almost all of the houses. So many other people had left, and I finally decided we needed to leave. I was the last to leave."

The shy daughter from the kitchen appeared with a tray of drinks for us. The cups clattered as we passed and shared them. She stayed as far away from us as possible.

The man's wife had come to Lebanon first, with their three children. The journey took them from 8 a.m. until 9 p.m., not because it was so far, but because they were continually stopped at checkpoints. At every checkpoint, they had to get out of the car and answer lots of questions. Mainly they were asked, "Why are you going to Lebanon?" Many times the people at the checkpoints asked for money, which their hired driver paid out of the fee he had previously charged.

"This is the first time we've lived in a tent," the man said. "In Syria, they put an insulating material in the houses so it wasn't so hot. But, no matter how hard it gets here," our hosts said, "it is not as bad as it was when we left Syria."

With the sandstorm and the heat, it had been hard to sleep. But even blowing sand and no air conditioning were better than living with the constant threat of danger.

Several people talked at once as they began to discuss the government. A cell phone rang, adding to the clamor in the sitting room, growing hotter each moment as mid-morning turned to midday. The baby began to jabber, as if joining the discussion. The woman re-adjusted the little girl on her lap and gave her a yellow ball, which she began to chew. Jana reached for the baby and held her, playing with her.

"We were afraid of the government because things were getting worse and worse, but we couldn't say anything," the man said. "Prices were getting higher. They used to come and collect taxes from us and oblige us to pay."

Still, they wished to go back.

"We left behind things from the house," the woman said, "but there's nothing more precious than the country. I don't want to go anywhere else. I want to go back to Syria. I'm afraid to travel to Europe. I'm afraid of the sea."

"Our house was destroyed," the man added. "But we just wish to go back, even if we have to go back and sit on the ground."

CHAPTER 12

"We just need a little bit of news."

WE MOVED TO A SECOND camp to continue distributing food. Jana and I played clapping hand games with the children while the men prepared the truck for a second distribution of food. The little girls called out a chant and taught us to slap our hands against theirs in a rhythm that matched their words. Jana's Arabic allowed her to converse with them somewhat, but I could only rely on smiles and gestures.

One of our guides came to check on us. If anything didn't go as planned, he suggested that I make noise. "In this culture, you shout!" he said with a smile.

As the distribution progressed, the white bundles disappeared to their respective tents. Women hoisted the bundles onto their heads. Sometimes the recipient had a motorbike, and the parcel bounced away across the rocks, balancing on the bike. Little children helped to carry black sacks of liquid soap and oil.

Across the driveway of white rock, a pile of striped green watermelons was piled on the bed of a truck. Another collection of watermelons lay on the ground at the end of the truck. A plastic lawn chair near the tailgate made me think that someone had been peddling them. An empty watermelon rind lay nearby.

Two little girls tussled with each other while talking to Jana, everyone laughing.

"One says they're sisters; one says they're not," she explained.

As soon as we had an interpreter, we began chatting with a lady in a zebra-striped dress, right out in the sunshine in the middle of the busy food distribution. She wore a black hijab, with one end wrapped around the lower part of her face, allowing only her nose and eyes to be seen.

"Before the war, Syria was safe and secure," she told us, "especially for the women. We were free to go to the market without someone asking what we were doing. The marketplace was a combination of shops on your right and your left. We would spend a thousand Syrian pounds to buy everything on our shopping list. We could have bought clothes for four or five children. Now, the thousand pounds is worth nothing. It takes almost 100,000 Syrian pounds to get the same items. Once a week we would go to the marketplace to get vegetables and clothes. If a child had a birthday, we would prepare sweets and buy the child new clothes.

"Syrians have a lot of children," the woman added. "We don't have one or two. I have seven.

"We were living in the middle of Homs, and it was being bombed repeatedly. And we had small children. That's why we chose to leave Syria," she said. "If we would have been alone as grownups, we could have settled down in Syria, but because we have a family, we fled away. People were predicting that the war would be big, so we decided to leave. We came in the night. We took a taxi and then moved to another taxi. It was dangerous. The soldiers asked us lots of questions.

"After we came here, we heard that our house in Syria was destroyed by the shelling. Our neighbors were still there, and they called us up on their cell phone and told us about it. Everything I owned was still in my house. I didn't bring anything from there besides a few needed things."

"So what do you miss most?" I asked.

"I miss everything about Syria!" the woman exclaimed. "My nation, my people, my house, my things—I remember everything every day. My sisters and families are still living there, and I'm missing them a lot. Please pray for us always and remember that we need this support," she begged as we parted ways.

We walked across the driveway to a woman in purple who was standing in the shade of the food parcel truck. She wore a purple dress with large black butterflies on it. Gold shone among her teeth. When she smiled, she kept her mouth closed.

"We were so happy in Syria before the war," she told me. "I have one boy and one girl. My husband worked in construction, and we lived in Bab al-Amr."

"Ooooh!" my interpreter said.

"We are from there. Because of the children we had to flee. We left in the middle of the fighting. We saw the bombings, and the army came into our house. Then we fled in the night. We went at night because there was less chance of being shot by snipers.

"We didn't come to Lebanon immediately. It took us one month to come here. We stayed inside mosques along the way."

Behind us a motorbike arrived, idled loudly in our ears, and then accelerated even louder as we strained to hear each other's words.

"We miss our places, our nation. I am ready any time to go back to Syria. Does anyone not like his own country? Now we are suffering in this place, moving from one camp to the other. In winter the water comes into our tents.

"Come into my tent now," she said.

We followed the lady in purple the few yards to her house. She had made her surroundings attractive, despite the conditions. She cultivated greenery in the little courtyard at the front of her house, although I couldn't recognize all the plants. A rooster balanced near a woven basket, and another rooster walked beneath him close to a black hen.

Nestled in a corner against the plastic, a tiny brown goat eyed us suspiciously. It had a perfect tiny mouth, long brown ears, and a sharply pointed hoof on the one visible brown foot. A small brown horn was forming in the curls on its little head.

"My daughter bought her," the woman explained. "She didn't give her a name."

The woman led us into her house.

"No, you don't have to; it's okay," she protested as we started to slip off our shoes.

"My house was different in Syria," she said as we looked at her sitting room with the cement floor. "It was not like this; it was made of wood. It had a large room with a big closet with four sections and a mirror and two beds. Everyone had his own room. Here we are sleeping on these mattresses on the floor."

She took us to her kitchen. Apparently, her favorite color was purple, judging from her dress and several purple plates loaded in a rack at the side of the kitchen. Jars and bottles were lined on a top shelf against the plastic. A few pots and pans and a skillet were sitting on a lower shelf. Like the other rooms, the floor was bare cement.

We asked the woman what her kitchen had been like in her house in Homs.

"Don't let me remember!" she sighed. "It had rinsing basins and porcelain on the floor. Now we are learning to use new tools to make our food. We can't make the same kinds of food as we did in Syria. It's very hard to get good meat here. It was so cheap in Syria, but here it is not cheap at all. We don't have an oven, so we can't make the sweet desserts here. We would need a small electric oven to make sweets. At home, we fried them in oil and dipped them in sugar syrup. We made cakes with an electric oven. Besides not having an oven here, it's not easy to get ingredients," the woman lamented. "I don't have access to them."

As we prepared to leave, another woman arrived. Keith also walked up to join us.

"This is my mother-in-law," the woman in purple said. "Her son has been kidnapped in Syria, for three years so far. His wife is still in Syria, waiting for him."

"I don't have any idea what's going on with him," the mother-in-law said, her sadness present in every Arabic syllable, her sniffs an attempt to corral her tears. "He was here, and he went back to Syria to get his family, and they arrested him. I tried to find out where he went, in which jail, which prison. I appointed a lawyer to defend his case, or to find him at first, but they couldn't. For the last three years I have tried everything I can think of to find him! I gave out his name, his mother's name, all the details, just to locate where he might be!"

She showed us her ID card. In Arab countries, our interpreter informed us, the mother's name is a reference to help identify people.

"But no one is answering," the woman went on. "I paid the lawyer, and they asked me to give them 18 to 20 days, and they would give us an answer. But the lawyer took the money and disappeared."

We exhaled in a collective group sigh.

"Those lawyers change their phones so you can't find them. You can't call them back. They change the SIM card. It's easy for them to take advantage of people," the woman explained. "We just need a little bit of news—any, any news about him!"

CHAPTER 13

"He went back to Syria."

WE VISITED YET ANOTHER REFUGEE camp, this one next to a high hill of dirt that looked like it had been man-made. Dusty children had turned the hill into a sliding range, bouncing down it in their clothes, creating human tracks on the hillside. A dumpster was overflowing near the entrance to the camp, and chickens and children played among the piled trash bags. Nearby, a bright patch of marigolds bloomed.

We were quickly invited inside another tent.

"Shukran," our interpreter said as our new hosts passed us drinks.

They had brewed a pot of Turkish coffee and passed it on a tray with tiny china cups and a glass jar of sugar with a spoon and a lid.

"Thank you," I said.

"We came here at the beginning of the war," said an older woman with a white hijab. "My husband and my son are still in Syria. I haven't heard from them in a long time."

Although the floor was bare cement, I was surprised to see a heavy piece of furniture in the corner. Their tent also had a good view, through its screened sides, of the valley's green fields. On one curtained wall, a picture was hanging askew.

"Everything in Syria was very cheap. My husband was a teacher in the school. He was an Arabic teacher for children ages seven to ten. My son was a truck driver. I would stay at home and cook. My house in Syria was so different from our tent here. It had four rooms and one bathroom. My children's homes all had three rooms in every home. But now all the houses have been destroyed."

"We were in our house when planes began to bomb in our area. The army came to our home in the morning. 'Leave your home and don't come back again,' they said. 'You don't have much time or we will kill you.' So we ran, and then we came here by car.

"My husband was with us the first time we came to Lebanon, but after some time he went back to Syria. His mother was sick and had problems, so my husband left to go back to Syria and take care of his mother. Now we don't know anything about him. My son, he never left Syria. I saw him last before the war."

Outside the screen wall, several children began bullying another child. Our interpreter turned toward them.

"Hey, hey, hey!" he yelled through the screen. The bullies backed off at the sound of his voice, and the conflict ended. If only all wars could be settled so easily!

"We can't do anything," the woman lamented. "We can't go back to Syria and we can't travel to another place. And we don't have any money or any work. The rent of this tent every year is about three hundred U.S. dollars[h] with electricity and water. And we don't have any money to pay this. The store here doesn't want to give us any food because we have many bills. And I have high blood pressure and diabetes, and I had a heart attack."

She ended her dismal tale by taking a plastic bag and turning it upside down. Medications spilled onto the cement floor.

Before leaving for the drive back to Beirut, our driver and guide took us up the dusty hill to get a better view of the camp. The leader knew the best way to climb the hill to avoid the most dust, but the weeds still pricked us through our shoes and clothes.

From the hill, the tops of the tents spread out below us like squares on a carpet, interspersed with the tires holding down the roofs. Wide fields of brilliant green edged the camp. Beyond the camp, in the opposite direction from which we had come, were the mountains that separated Lebanon from Syria. Somehow, Syria seemed so close from this altitude.

"Do you think any of the refugees actually come across these mountains?" I asked one of our guides.

---

h   *U.S. currency is used frequently in Lebanon.*

"No, I don't think so," he said, "because there are soldiers in the mountains. And the Lebanese army is everywhere around the mountain, watching everything that's happening. So no one crosses here. They all go north and cross near a Lebanese Sunni village that is close to Syria both geographically and emotionally. The Sunni Lebanese people support the Sunnis in Syria, so they opened their village for them, and that's where the refugees have been crossing over.

"However, the fighting has also come across at that place. In that same village, terrorists kidnapped 30 Lebanese soldiers last year in July or August. Some people in that village are with ISIS, and they tried to help ISIS get across into Lebanon from Syria. But the village was surrounded by the Lebanese army, so ISIS never managed to capture it."

I looked again toward Syria. What was happening just now across those mountains? What had happened to the husband of the lady we had just visited? What about her son? What about all the other people who had somehow mysteriously disappeared?

VOICES

BY THE MEDITERRANEAN

CHAPTER 14

"We are going to teach about Jesus."

DURING OUR TIME IN LEBANON we traveled south to an area along the Mediterranean coast. It was an area that Jesus had visited, and likely the Apostle Paul. It was now home to a big group of refugees. The refugees we visited there lived in houses rather than in a refugee camp.

The day we traveled there, Keith was running a fever and needed to stay at the convent. Our driver assured Jana that he would make sure someone checked on him.

We drove out of Beirut and headed south, right along the Mediterranean Sea. As we arrived at our destination, our driver pointed out a castle, built on an arm of land reaching into the sea. It was built by Crusaders, he thought, in the 800s. We continued, flanked on the right by the sea, and on the left by Lebanon's picturesque mountains, stacked full of houses. The view of the mountains was like the view from an airplane, where you can see all the houses at once.

"The valleys and mountains are so abrupt," Jana observed.

"Just like the political situation," our driver agreed. "Everything is fine and then suddenly–!"

As we drove along the Mediterranean Sea, I couldn't help but think of Jesus and Paul. It seemed almost as if I might see them today.

We turned off the main road in the opposite direction of the Mediterranean Sea, and immediately up to a warehouse with an overhead door open to reveal a tile floor and a table set up for food distribution. Muslim women, men, and children had already arrived from their homes and were waiting, some sitting on the tile floor which actually extended several feet outside the boundaries of the warehouse as a kind of porch. Motorbikes were parked, with their kickstands in the white dust at the side of the parking lot, but many of the people had traveled the few miles from their homes by bus.

Most of the women were dressed in black, but there were snippets of color in the sea of black. I saw a black hijab with red flowers, and a blue hijab, but they were the exception. Many of the men wore jeans, polo shirts, and bill caps, but there was also an elderly man in a light gray robe and the classic checkered red-and-white head scarf.

The crowd had gathered, waiting to receive their food portions.

A tall, rugged man with graying hair and beard stubble greeted us, and I sensed that he was the leader I had heard about, described by Jana as a "modern-day Paul." His name was Ramzi.

"Welcome, welcome," he said. "I will make some announcements, and then we will talk to the people."

Ramzi shouted a few Arabic words, and the crowd, which had been sitting, leaning against walls and lounging on motorcycles, moved into a semicircle around him. He began to talk loudly now, waving his arms for emphasis. Beyond him and beyond the crowd, the blue waters of the Mediterranean Sea formed a New Testament backdrop for him, and I could just picture the Apostle Paul shouting orders or pleading with a crowd. Perhaps Paul had been here, on this very spot! If he was, I imagined he was very much like this man.

"This year, you are going to get food portions every month, and we are going to increase the number of visits to your houses. Concerning schools, if you want your children to be in our school, you have to notify us. When you get your food portion, please tell us that you want them to be in our school. Those who want their children to be in the public schools here in Lebanon should go to one of those schools in the area here and tell them.

"I hear that lots of people are visiting you and using our names, but these are not people I am sending. I insist that the faces you see here are the faces you will see in your homes."

"There are other organizations in the area," my interpreter explained to me, "who are going to people's houses and saying they are with our organization, and they are not."

Many of the Muslims in the tightly packed semi-circle surrounding Ramzi were new to the program, my interpreter said, which is why he was explaining things so thoroughly.

"You know that I personally visit you," he said, "so don't listen to other people who come and use our name.

"Another thing I need to tell you again is that our school is a Christian school. Our aim at school is to show the love of Christ. So I don't want anyone to come here and tell me, 'Why are my children learning Christian songs?' or 'Why are my children learning about Jesus?' This is how our school operates. We are going to teach about Jesus. If you don't want your children to learn about Jesus, you can put them in the public schools. I do not force anyone to sign up their children for our school. You are all free. I will help your children to adjust to other schools if you want. But if you want to put them in our school, they are going to learn about Jesus, and no one can change our minds. I will not compromise about this!

"The help you get is not conditional. We give you the food, and there are no conditions, but when it comes to the rules of our school, we're not changing those rules. The children will be learning about Jesus. I have nothing to do with the public schools. I will only try to ensure that no one there will mistreat your children, and I will take care of helping you understand the system. But in my school I am responsible for the teachers, for the staff, for the children, for their safety, and for their food."

"Ramzi is the principal of the school," our driver interjected. "That's why he says, 'My school.' "

"Those of you who know us, know that we do not treat people differently. I don't want you to come complaining about what we are giving other people. Everyone is equal. If you want to be part of our big family, you have to respect all of this. All of you have my phone number. If anyone has a problem, you can call me. I don't mind even if you call in the middle of the night. I'm being sincere about this. What's most important to us is the safety and education of the children and your food and well-being.

"There was an incident in one town. A Syrian lady was married to a Lebanese man. But she told us that her husband is in Syria, and he's missing. We later found out that her husband is Lebanese, and she's been hiding the truth; she's been lying about it. I look at this as a wrong representation of Syrian men, because she said her husband is Syrian, and he left her. And this reflects badly on the Syrians. This is not acceptable. We're not judging, but please tell us the truth. Do not lie; do not hide such information.

"I behave according to the Bible, so when you give me one piece of information, I take it seriously. I believe you; I do not assume you are lying to me. So I don't want things like that to happen again. Let this be a new year, a good year."

CHAPTER 15

"You have to show them love."

THE SCHOOL WAS LOCATED ABOVE the warehouse where food was distributed. We climbed the steps to visit it. It was a small school with five rooms. Each room was decorated with bright colors. Oversized, laminated pencils were labeled with the names of classes: English, Bible, Math, and Music. Welcome posters for Grade One and Grade Two were written in both Arabic and English. Paper kites flew high on a bulletin board, with the words, "Soar to new heights with Jesus." Even the refrigerator was decorated with a colorful sign proclaiming, "God is love."

Our interpreter was also a teacher in the school, and she told us about the variety of needs there. Some students had been out of school for several years because of the war, so they were way behind in their classes.

There were non-academic needs as well. One refugee student had told her, "Miss, I don't understand when you tell me this. You have to hit me."

She had told him, "No! I won't hit you! No matter what you do, I'm not going to hit you. I'm only going to speak to you quietly and ask you to behave."

"It's because of his father," she confided to us. "He always comes here with bruises on his hands. So after we talked about the solar system, he came back to school and said, 'Miss, I can't believe it! My dad said that I'm really, really smart because I told him what you taught us about the solar system.' He was so proud that his father actually complimented him!

"So there's a lot more than teaching these children to read and write," she went on. "Working on their personalities, and fixing the damage . . .

it's very challenging. I'm very sensitive. At the beginning, I had nightmares about this every day, and it was really hard, but I know that we are making a difference in their lives. I hope we are!"

"I'm sure you are," Jana and I both agreed.

As we talked, we heard some commotion in the next room. We walked over and found one of the teachers exclaiming over a brown-eyed boy whom she was seeing for the first time since summer break.

There were other teachers in the room, so we sat down for an informal interview with a few of them. The teachers were all from the Lebanese Christian community. "What do you enjoy about teaching?" I asked them.

"I like when I see the children enjoying the songs and prayers," one said.

The other teachers agreed that seeing the children grow spiritually was their favorite part of teaching.

"One time I came into the classroom and the children were being noisy," one teacher told us. "And I said, 'Please keep it quiet. I'm sick today, and I need the calm and quiet.' And then one of the children, one that you could tell always enjoyed the prayers and songs, said to me, 'Miss, I want to pray for you.' And then they all closed their eyes, and the boy started praying for me."

The teachers talked about their joy in seeing this change and the progress from day to day.

"One of the children accidentally hurt his friend's finger, and he immediately told him, 'Sorry,' and the other boy said, 'Don't worry.' Then the boy told the teacher, 'Before we came to the school, we did not know how to be polite and use these words, but you have taught us to say *sorry, please,* and *thank you* and words like this, and now they just come out of our mouths. We're used to using these words now.' You can see a lot of change in them . . . they live in violent environments and this is strange to them that people are polite to them and use these words."

Another teacher recalled a child who felt conspicuous because his head was shaved.

"He was very shy about it, and he came to school wearing a cap on his head, and he wouldn't take it off. If anyone would try to move it, he was very tense about it. He had his head on the table all the time. During recess he didn't want to talk to anyone. But all of his friends banded together . . ."

The interpreter had been telling us the story, but here the teacher herself began to talk to us, using slow but sufficient English, with occasional help from our interpreter.

"First, I came to him, and I said, 'Jesus loves you if you are beautiful or if you are normal. He loves you however you are. He just loves you. If you are short or thin or fat, Jesus loves you.' And I reminded him of the song 'I am very special in the eyes of Jesus.' We began to sing it, and all the class joined us. And all of his friends encouraged him and sang the song with him. Finally, he lifted his head up, and all his friends started shouting his name. I said, 'If you are strong enough, remove it,' and he removed his cap. It was a huge step for him."

"I had a boy who knew nothing, nothing at all," another teacher said, "but he looked at me with those blue eyes and said, 'Please teach me! Please!' "

"It shows how passionate they are to learn," our interpreter agreed. "They really want to learn. But some of them are active and aggressive in a negative way."

"It's difficult because of all the violence they've been through," one of the teachers said. "You always have to show them love. You always have to show them the love of God, and that's difficult when you want to discipline a child, and at the same time be very loving to that child. This is a challenge."

"The age range is also difficult," one teacher said. "Some of these children have been out of school for a while, so there are a range of ages who are in the same classroom. Even if they are the same age, one child might know more than the other, and it can be a challenge to keep the whole class together. The schools in Syria are weaker than the schools in Lebanon. The children enter schools at an older age. And everything is taught in Arabic in Syria. In Lebanon we teach in either English or French, depending on the school."

"Sometimes too we find it difficult because Arabic has different dialects. In Syria they all speak Arabic, but sometimes they use different dialects, so sometimes it's hard for us to understand them. Sometimes I ask a student, 'What did your friend say?' If we can't understand, we ask other students to help us."

They explained that in one dialect, a certain word meant *boy*, but in the other dialect it meant *baby cow*. The possibility for confusion was clear.

"You have to show them love."

Jana and I were lost in a clatter of Arabic as the teachers shared experiences and word differences.

"We have to make our own dictionary!" one of the teachers suggested, as they all laughed.

"I'm impressed with all of you and the job you are doing," I said.

"By the grace of God," one of the teachers said. "If it's up to us, we can do nothing. Every day we pray together. It's His work, not ours."

CHAPTER 16

"We bribed the person at the checkpoint."

WHILE WE WERE AT THE school, we talked to a young Syrian lady in a floral hijab. She was working as a cleaning lady at the school, and a staff member told us about some positive things that were happening in her life.

"Our cleaning lady had been receiving food portions from us," he told us privately. "She came twice for the food distribution, and we visited her and prayed with her and her children. And then when she came to the school to clean, I encouraged the ladies to sit with her and talk to her about the love of Christ. In the first session they told me that she was interested in knowing about God. I assigned one lady to disciple her two days a week, using Scripture to talk to her about God."

He was excited about the faith they were seeing in this lady. She would be able to reach other Syrian women in a way they could not.

The cleaning lady told us about her life in Syria and the journey to Lebanon. "I've been in Lebanon three years. We had to come here suddenly because the fighting started and all of that. But I went back to Syria once a year ago. After that I came to Lebanon again."

"I'm married, and I have two daughters. We used to live in very good conditions; we were safe and stable. But when the war started we were always stressed and fearful, and we had hard times.

"I had a job where I used to work with beads. We would put the beads on wedding dresses, different colors. We used a piece of thin metal." She used her hands to trace imaginary tools in the air as she spoke. "It's not a needle. It's a bit thicker, and it has a kind of hook on its end. We'd flip the clothes, and we'd put the beads from behind, and sew the thread through it. There was a person who used to give me the dresses, and then I would do them and give them back to her.

"I was happy because I had a job. I would think, *I have a job, I have to finish my work.* I would work for three hours a day, and after that I would go visit my relatives, and then we would go out to the gardens and sit and enjoy nature.

"My parents owned land. They had fig trees and olive trees. So we used to take our food there and sit under the trees. It was a good way to have fun and rest and enjoy each other's company. My parents had better living conditions than other people. We had a happy life."

"Tell me about your wedding," I said.

"My husband knew about me through his cousin," she said, laughing at the memories. "He came to my house, and he saw me and he liked me. That first time he came, he talked to me a little bit. He asked me what I do, if I had an education. And then he started coming for three consecutive weeks, and we got to know each other more. I liked him too, and we were engaged for nine months and then got married. Of course we had a celebration and food, and we did it in a big hall. But in Syria the women are alone and the men are alone. We are separated. I wore a white dress.

"Also at our engagement we had a party, but it wasn't in a hall. It was in one of the relatives' houses, but the women are separate from the men there as well. I had a new dress for that occasion too, and I fixed my hair.

"Before I got married, I used to work at home and also in a factory. And after I got married, I continued with my job until after I had my oldest daughter, and then when I was pregnant with the other daughter, I had to stop. I couldn't continue working there."

But then, as we had heard from so many others, the pleasant life in Syria had ended—without warning.

"My husband was working in Lebanon, and I was in Syria. We did not have any intention to actually move to Lebanon. But all of a sudden the army came into our town and tanks appeared everywhere, and they started bombing the houses. So I was scared, especially for my daughters. In one night everything changed. I did not know what happened. I took my daughters and left. It took me nine hours to get here. They asked me a lot of questions along the way at checkpoints. I got a cab here, and we had to stop regularly at checkpoints. Every time we'd stop they would search the whole car and ask for identity cards and check through everything before they let us move on. Still, my journey was easier than for some people, because my husband was already in Lebanon.

"I did have some trouble at the border, though. I don't know if there's an English word for this, but we have an official certificate that has not only the name of the person but also the names of my husband and the children. And there was some mistake in the spelling of my daughter's name. They wanted my uncle's approval in order to travel, and they gave me a hard time about it. But eventually we bribed the person at the checkpoint and they let us go."

Christians in the Middle East

Christianity began in the Middle East with the birth, life, death, and resurrection of Jesus Christ. Since that time, Christians have always inhabited the Middle East, and from the fourth to the seventh centuries, Christianity was the dominant religion there. In the centuries to follow, the predominance of Christianity waned somewhat, but it continued to play a significant role in the region.

Yet in recent decades, factors such as war, persecution, emigration, and low birth rates among Christians have caused the population of Christians in the Middle East to drop considerably, even to the point where some have predicted its extinction there.

As is the case throughout the world, the Christian community in the Middle East is divided into many different sects and denominations. Many of these groups began centuries ago and are sometimes referred to as the "traditional" churches. They include groups such as Copts, Greek Orthodox, Maronites, Syrian Orthodox, Greek Catholics, and Armenians.[21]

In the Middle East, a person's religious identity is a significant factor in their personal identity. A person's religion is recorded by the government and printed on their identification paperwork. In some locations it is difficult, if not impossible, to have this changed.

Understandably, then, the term "Christian" in the Middle East is often used as more of an ethnic label that signifies a person's ancestry than a statement about one's spiritual status. Middle Eastern Christians who value their religion as more than a historic identity are often referred to as "believers" or "born again." A variety of evangelical churches have also sprung up in the Middle East in the last few centuries.

For radical Islam, though, personal beliefs about Christian teachings are not the issue. Any association with Christianity is reason enough to be a target.

At a church in Jordan, we saw small mosaics made with tiny stones, bordered and backed by wood. They were designed to be coasters for coffee mugs. The background stones were white, but red stones had been placed among them to form an Arabic symbol.

"This symbol is the sign the Islamic group ISIS paints on the front of Christian homes," the pastor of the church explained to us. "It's the Arabic character *nuun*, like the English letter *n*,"he said. "The word they use for Christians starts with the letter *n*, so that's why they use this letter.

"ISIS marks this letter on the houses of Christians before they kick them out or before they kill them or steal things from them. It's a symbol that anyone is free to steal from the house because it is a Christian house, and they can do to Christians whatever they want.

"They use it as a sign of shame, but we want to turn it around and say we are proud of being called Christians regardless of how they use it. We are showing it to the world instead of hiding it or being afraid of it.

"We have trained people to make these mosaics, and then we will sell them to support the refugees and raise awareness. When they make this sign, the Christians feel this work belongs to them, and they know it will create awareness all over the world for people to pray for them."

He held one of the coasters in his hand.

"I think it resembles the cross in a way. The cross was supposed to be a sign of shame too."

Refugee Perspectives

The perspectives of refugees fleeing the war in Syria vary widely. While the majority of refugees are Sunni Muslims who fled from the atrocities of the Syrian government, many Christian refugees and members of other minority groups who fled faced greater threats from rebel groups like ISIS or Jabhat al-Nusra. Many Christians prefer to see the current government of Bashar al-Assad remain in power, not so much because they agree with his policies, but because they see his more secular government as more tolerant and protective of their minority status than any form of Islamist government would be. And, as interviews in this book show, many of the refugees are not loyal to any of the groups. They just want peace!

CHAPTER 17

"Our hearts are swollen."

BACK DOWNSTAIRS IN THE WAREHOUSE where the food distribution had taken place, I got the chance to visit with several Christian refugees. Behind the pallets of white sacks, we seated ourselves on plastic chairs.

The first two ladies I spoke with were from a Syrian town called Hassake, near the border of Turkey. Here, I got another perspective of the war and heard a narrative I hadn't heard to date. I also heard the term ISIS used by refugees for the first time. I even began to pick out the Arabic term they used, *Da'esh*. They had expressions of terror and fear as they used it.

"ISIS is in our town right now," one of the ladies began. "There are lots of bombings and explosions. The houses are falling on people's heads. I'm talking about my relatives. In one family, four people died. In another family, five people died. Lots of children are dying. The last two years have been very difficult, and ISIS was right next to our houses. The children were scared all the time. They were afraid of the bombs, so they covered their ears so they wouldn't hear the loud noises."

One of the women had been in Lebanon for a year, but the other had been there only a month.

The lady who had come most recently was speaking. "A year ago ISIS came and took our town, but the army fought them off. Around two months ago they came again, and the army also fought them off again. But they had so many ways of spreading terror. ISIS would send explosive cars into the town. The car would come in and explode inside the town. And they were hitting us with bombs from outside the town. That's why I finally escaped. The bombings were hitting right next to our house, so I took my daughter and left."

"So your friend left almost a year before you," I said to her. "Why did you stay?"

"We had hope that things would calm down. We witnessed lots of things. The bullets were passing above our houses. We used to hide inside. Then things would be quiet for about a month, so we would think finally everything is going to be fine, and then there would be fighting again."

"Since we're here, we heard that our relatives were killed," the other woman offered. "We read the news online. We even saw their pictures, and yesterday was their funeral.

"We have lots of family and relatives that are still there, and our hearts are with them. My brother is still there. Our hearts are swollen. I am exhausted physically and emotionally. We've been living in war for five years. For the past two or three years it was just getting worse and worse.

"Some days were quieter and calmer than others. I would be able to go out and buy groceries. But also sometimes while we were buying groceries, all of a sudden there would be fighting again and explosions, and we just would run to our houses."

"What bothers me the most," one of the mothers said, "is that my children, a ten-year-old and a seven-year-old, are always drawing bullets, and guns, and blood on the paper. That's all they draw; that's all they talk about. They talk about the different kinds of weapons they know. These are children! They have been seeing so much violence. I wish I would have brought his drawing book with me."

Our interpreter's voice began to shake.

"My youngest child here in Lebanon heard fireworks the other day, but he thought they were bullets, so he covered his ears. And I was telling him, 'Don't be afraid, those are just fireworks.' I am shivering on the inside as I remember these things."

"Was it harder for you in Syria because you are Christians?" we asked the women.

"Yes, definitely. ISIS thinks of us as infidels, so they behead the Christians. I want this to be known. I want people to know that this is what is happening to the Christians in Syria. We are being very honest."

The women talked about their future plans.

"Our hearts are swollen."

"I am filling out some legal documents to go to Canada, but they aren't processing the documents for me in Lebanon. Why are they waiting? I wish they would start working with the legal issues. I have two brothers and two sisters in Canada. My brother wants to come to Lebanon from Syria, but he's waiting for legal documents to be processed."

One of the women found a photo on her phone and showed it to me. It was a scene of destruction. A water truck filled with explosives had pulled into the town and exploded.

"We lived far away from this, but even in our house all the glass shattered and fell because of the explosion."

The women took turns then, showing us pictures on their phones.

"My memory card was destroyed with pictures before the war," one of them said. "But I can show you some things. These are the people who died recently. Four from the same household. This girl is eighteen years old, and these are thirty, thirty-seven, and forty-five. These two are sisters, and this is a mother and her daughter.

"Do you know what this paper is? In our culture when someone dies, they put those fliers in towns next to the churches and the houses, on the walls. They say that this person died and they state who his relatives are, and they state where the funeral is going to be, and where you can go to give your condolences."

One of the women showed me a picture of her church.

"We have a festival in this area; we call it the Festival of the Cross. Those are boys playing their instruments, and those are the people in the church. This is a Syriac church, and those are our traditions. Here is another picture of the church. It has a courtyard outside," she said.

My interpreter and I squinted at the phone screen in the dim light of the warehouse.

"This picture was taken just a few days ago in Syria. The next day bombings and explosions started because they saw that the Christians were having festivals and celebrations, so ISIS bombed the town the next day. They don't know for sure that the bombings were related, but that's what the people say. And ISIS also hits the Kurdish people, not only the Christians."

"Before the war, five years ago," I asked, "was it a peaceful town?"

"Ay, ay, ay!" the women chorused.

"I think their facial expressions give you an answer!" my interpreter said.

"It was like the difference between earth and heaven," they said. "We used to celebrate; we used to dress nicely; we used to decorate our houses at Christmas and Easter. Here is a picture of my husband and children at church. This is the boy that's always afraid now. This is at Easter.

"Also at Easter, we have special sweets that we make, called *maamoul.* They are stuffed with either dates or nuts, and then they sprinkle them outside with white sugar. Then there's this other kind of food that's made only in the town where we lived in Syria, so not even in the rest of Syria. It's called *legia,* and it's made of dough, and it has lots of spices in it, lots of cinnamon and other things."

The ladies put their phones away and returned to the gloomier subject of their escape from their city of Hasakah.

"When we decided to flee, we couldn't leave by road. We had to fly because ISIS is on all the roads. Even to reach the airport there were lots of government checkpoints, and they asked lots of questions. It wasn't easy to get to the airport. But the government won't keep anyone from going. As long as they have the proper documents, they can go.

"We did not personally see people from ISIS. We knew they were surrounding the town, but we saw them only on TV, not in person. But two months ago when there were conflicts between the Syrian army and ISIS, the army killed some of the people from ISIS, and then they dragged them into the town and dragged their bodies on the streets to show the people that they killed them. Even some Muslims from our town were cooperating with ISIS, so the army killed them and showed the bodies."

"We are all emotionally tired. My daughter is always afraid," one of the women said. "She wakes up at night and cries. She probably remembers the *voices.*"

It took me a little while to understand that the lady meant her daughter was afraid of the loud sounds of war she had heard. In Arabic, the same word is used for *sound* and *voice,* which caused the translation to come through in this way. But the explosions really did have a voice, even if it wasn't a human one. The voices of the planes and rockets had spoken to many of the refugees, telling them it was time to flee.

"What we hope is for the war to end, so we can go back to our countries and back to our homes," the lady continued. "Our country is precious for us, and our families and relatives. It's like a mother who lost her children. Even if we go to Canada, we hope to go back to Syria. No matter where we go, it's our country; it's our home, and it's in our hearts."

CHAPTER 18

"Everyone is wearing black."

THE NEXT CHRISTIANS I VISITED with in the warehouse were a group of three—a mother and two daughters, all of them dressed in black.

"We are from the city of Aleppo, and the war there brought us here," they said. "If it weren't for the war, our lives would have been very different. Even the wind in our country is different."

"I used to speak some English, but I forgot," one daughter said clearly in English.

I soon learned that both of the daughters were married, although their husbands were not present at the interview. One had married an Armenian man in Syria, and the other had married an Iraqi man in Lebanon. Although they were dressed in black, these ladies were wearing stylish clothes and wore make-up. They had a distinctly different appearance from the Muslim refugees.

The mother of the two sisters was dressed in practical black clothes that made no attempt at beauty or style. Around her neck was a photo hanging on a black chain. The metal link holding the photo was silver, as if she had painted the necklace black.

The mother lifted the photo in its plastic casing, proudly, for us to see. It was a head shot of a young man with a pleasant face, facial hair, and a half-smile.

"My son," she said. "He's a martyr. He died in the war almost a year ago. In Syria there's a law that when a boy is eighteen years old he has to serve in the army for three years. He finished his three years of service, but because there was a war, he had to stay."

"ISIS came from behind and killed him. The bullet hit his head, and it was just seconds before he died," one of his sisters told us.

"I have his voice in my phone, talking to me," the mother said. "I even have pictures from his funeral. When he died he was twenty-one years old." She pressed a button on her phone and a singing voice came through the electronic speaker. "That's him singing for me."

The voice stopped singing and started speaking. The recording was from four days before he was killed.

"Hi, Mom. How are you? I miss you so much. Take care of yourself. I hope you're happy. My mom, you're my life." He then said something funny, teasing her, something unclear even with the English translation. "I miss you. I love you. I want to drink coffee with you. It would be the best thing in the world if I could sit and have coffee with you. Mom, I want to kiss your hands. Tell God that you're pleased with me."

His sister lowered her head as the recording played and wiped her eyes. Then she started speaking. "My younger brother is almost eighteen now, so we're trying to do something so that he can evade the army. We don't want him to join. He is here in Lebanon, and we're trying to make his papers legal so he can stay, or go to another country."

"There has been so much fighting in our neighborhood in Aleppo," the mother said. "The building we lived in is on the ground. It all fell down. Even the places that did not have conflict do have conflict at the moment. So they didn't have my son's funeral in Aleppo. They had it in Homs."

The ladies began to play a recording from the funeral. Gun shots exploded from the phone. Even though the shots were salutes for the dead soldier and not actual violence, they were chilling to hear, even through a phone. After the shots, was a strange, flute-like *woo-loo-loo-loo*. The banging of the salutes and the shrieking of the *woo-loo-loo-loo* left an unearthly and eerie atmosphere in our safe little plastic office at the back of the warehouse.

"That *woo-loo-loo-loo* is something done in weddings," my interpreter explained. "But for deaths at a young age, people do the things they would normally do in weddings for the person's funeral."

"My son was very kind," the mother said. "He used to always tell his sisters, 'Take care of mom and don't upset her.' The recording I have from him is from four days before he died. The night before he died, he did not have enough megabytes to send me a recording of his voice, so he just sent me a text. He told me, 'Light up a candle for me because we are going to fight ISIS tomorrow. Don't worry about me; just light a candle for me.' That was the last message I had from him.

"Four days later the priest came and told me that my son was a martyr, and he died. When he told me my boy died, I couldn't even think straight. I said, 'Which one?' even though my younger son is here in Lebanon. I couldn't even think.

"They spent fifteen days looking for his body, and then they found it. I went to Syria to attend the funeral, and then I came back to Lebanon. My daughters did not go due to paperwork issues at the time. But even though I went they would not let me see his body. They wrapped him in the Syrian flag.

"I hope that my younger son can emigrate to a different country. His documents are not legal in Lebanon, and I'm afraid they'll send him back to Syria, and he'll have to join the army. I already lost one child. I don't want to lose the other. Emigration is very expensive. I hear that some people are going to Turkey and the sea, but that's dangerous too and he might also die. Lots of people are dying."

Another engine started behind us. The food distribution was wrapping up. Soon we would take a lunch break, I hoped. I didn't think I could bear any more of these stories right now.

"Two months ago we went back to Syria to make a sort of anniversary for our brother who passed away," one of the daughters confided to us in conclusion. "It was his birthday. We went to make a birthday for him even though he passed away.

"While we were there, we noticed that everyone is wearing black, not only us. Everyone has tasted this cup. Almost everyone has lost a loved one."

My conversations with the Christian refugees intrigued me. In some ways they were very similar to the ones I had with Muslim refugees, in other ways very different. I was still trying to understand the fact that in this context "Christian" was an ethnic label, not necessarily a statement about one's beliefs. However, many of the Christians did have firm beliefs in the truth of God's Word, and some of them were growing in those beliefs. I recalled a conversation we had had with our driver several days before.

"The mother head of the convent where you are staying is the sister of the head of the party that started the war in Lebanon," he had told us. "But she's a nice person, a very nice person," he added. "I doubt you will see her at the convent. She comes only occasionally. She's the head of all the convents. And actually they are active, these nuns," he went on. "I know about them. They buy New Testaments to distribute to people.

"The Catholics in general have copied the evangelical church. My family comes from the Catholic background, and my cousins and uncles are still Catholic. They were not totally engaged in their churches, but now they are. They didn't have any Bible study groups, but now they have them. So they are copying the evangelical church. I believe sometime they will be ahead of us! They have a hierarchy in their church, a structure and order which we are losing in our evangelical communities. We have a head of the council of churches, but he has no authority. Each church can do whatever it wants with services, activities, and small groups. They are good things, but this diversity is weakening the power and the structure. Sometimes other groups, Catholics or even Muslims criticize the evangelical churches because of this. 'Everyone believes in different things. You have no point of reference!' "

We had listened in silence for a while until Keith spoke. "I've thought about something already," he said. "If we could collect all the good out of every different church group and put it into one church . . ."

"Ha, ha!" our driver had laughed cheerfully. "That's a dream!"

CHAPTER 19

"I want to be invested for Jesus."

WE WALKED UP SEVERAL FLIGHTS of steps to Ramzi's office. He had a room facing the Mediterranean Sea. Windows opened onto a balcony, and a breeze blew in from the water. The highway we had traveled ran beneath the building. Beyond it was sand and dirt and a margin of weedy grasses, and beyond that was the flat blue green of that storied body of water. Perhaps Paul or Jesus had looked out from just this spot!

Besides a desk and office chair, there were several couches. Even though we were exhausted and ready for lunch, Ramzi was still going strong. He was always moving, always talking, always being distracted. We took seats for a moment until he was ready to go.

As we drove toward a café, the refugee workers began to talk about some of the difficulties of working with the refugees.

"I went home and went to bed at 7:00," our driver said of his early days of learning to work with the organization. "My mom thought I was sick or something. I was so tired."

He also recalled one rough food distribution at a refugee camp. It got crowded. "We were surrounded by men, and I thought, *This is it. I'm going to be slaughtered.*"

At the café, Ramzi walked in, greeted everyone cheerily, and grabbed a basket of packaged towelettes for our table. Everyone seemed to know him.

In between phone calls, he ordered food for all of us and made sure we had something to drink. It seemed his phone was always ringing.

Finally he sat down at the table. He had agreed to share his personal story with us over lunch.

"I'm not going to share all of my testimony," he said. "It's too long. I'm just going to give you highlights. God called me to be part of His family, and it wasn't by accident. God was preparing me to be a leader for my people, especially the Muslims and poor people."

Ramzi talked so fast, sometimes I had to stop him and ask him to repeat.

"I was a child the first time I heard about Jesus. As a child I said, 'I want to follow this God.' I started in an evangelical school, but unfortunately they didn't teach the Gospel. We heard about Jesus only through the movies or through the TV. Are you familiar with the cartoons that are stories about Jesus? I heard about Jesus through these when I was eight years old, and from a pastor who had a talk show program. He was always talking about Jesus and he would say, 'Put your hand on the TV and pray with me.'

"My father is the head of his family. People obey and respect him. I am the youngest child, but I am more social than my two siblings. I was the one who was expected by my father to have a bright, successful future. He wanted me to go somewhere, to be somebody important and successful. He had high expectations for me.

"I was only sixteen years old when I was an interpreter for soccer players. They brought players from Africa to play with our local teams. Most of them spoke English. I was sixteen years old, and I was interpreting for this tall, black soccer player." He chuckled at the memory. "I interpreted from English to Arabic, and sometimes from Arabic to English.

"I went to Beirut University. I have three majors: political science, a master's degree in international law, and English literature."

Ramzi went on, telling us more about his youth. He had been a devout Shi'ite Muslim. He told us about Ashura, a Muslim holiday that commemorates the death of a Muslim leader. To express their sadness, some Shi'ite Muslims would cut or beat themselves to share in the suffering of the Muslim leader who was killed on this day.

"I did it," he said. "I used knives to cut my head until the blood would come. I was very committed. I did it four or five times. But it began to trouble me. I asked myself, *Is this my destiny? Is this the kind of God I want to serve? One who wants me to beat myself and bleed for him?*

"I was a fighter. From 1989 to 1991 I was part of the Lebanese war in the south. In 1993 I fought in the war against Israel for seven days. In 1996 I also was part of the war between Hezbollah and Israel. From 1991 to 1996, every summer, I attended military training to be equipped to be ready for the war.

"But I kept having these questions. *Why am I here? What is my work? What is my destiny, to keep fighting, to be a soldier? If I die, where am I going? To heaven as a martyr, or not?* I lost a lot of friends, most of my friends, during the war. One of them passed away in my arms.

"Then I was in my parents' home in 1993. A military airplane was destroying the neighborhood. The bombing was so close to me that the front part of my parents' home was partially damaged by a bomb.

"But despite this close danger, nothing happened to me. And then I had this dream. In my dream, I heard God say, 'Son, I will take care of you.' In the religion I grew up with, you are not God's children. I wondered, *Who is this God that spoke to me as if I were His son?*

"Years passed. Around 2004, I found a small tract saying 'God loves you.' To me it was something new. In my religion and background, you are like slaves. You are not God's children. I liked it, and I found the cell phone number of the person who wrote the tract. I called him and he came. He was an American, and we sat together and we talked.

"We talked a lot. I was talking about politics most of the time, and he was talking about God. Then he gave me the New Testament. I spent a day and a half, and I read all of it. Well, it was amazing, but I told the American, 'I didn't understand it. I have a master's degree in international law; why don't I understand this book?'

"He said, 'You have to read it with open eyes and an open heart.' And he helped me a lot.

"And I said, 'I want to follow this Lord. He's amazing. He's different than others.' "

"Was it mostly because you found him to be a God of love?" I asked. "Is that the main difference?"

"Exactly, exactly," he said. "Because I used to be this person who had to work hard to gain things."

The waiter arrived with the food. The chicken shawarma^i sandwiches came

---

i *Sliced, seasoned meat, usually roasted on a revolving pole in front of a heat source.*

on white plates. They were cut in seven pieces and lay in a ring with fresh lettuce in the center and french fries piled on the side. Three shallow bowls sat on each platter holding pickled vegetables and several dips. The sandwiches were black with the heat of the grill and peppered with seasonings.

"Some people are not bold enough to share their faith," Ramzi continued. "They become believers, and they keep these things to themselves. And I don't want this attitude. If you eat at a good restaurant, you invite everyone. You tell people, 'This restaurant is good!' So it is the same when you become a believer and you become a new person; your life is totally changed, and you have to invite others to this. To me it's the same concept."

His phone began to ring. "*Alo*," he said into the phone.

Between phone calls, Ramzi finished his story.

"For six months after I became a believer, I didn't do anything besides read the Bible and share my faith with others. Finally, the people kicked me out of the city I was living in. For my dad it was a disaster. He was preparing me to be a diplomat for the Lebanese government in one of the cities around the world.

"I told him, 'I want to be invested for Jesus,' but he thought I was crazy. In his way of thinking, you should keep your religion to yourself; you don't share it with others! You can believe in it, but at the same time you should have a good job and make a lot of money. To my mom too, a successful man is one who has a good job that makes lots of money. A successful man has a good career and people respect him. A person who makes a career of sharing his faith did not meet her expectations. So it was something new to my family, talking about sharing the love of Christ with others, and being invested for someone who is God. How can you be invested for God? For them, God was a master and we are His slaves.

"Besides, my dad had put a lot of money out for my education. He expected me to be something. He expected me to have a good reputation, to honor the family name. I had been popular and well-liked. I used to play soccer. I had a social life. I didn't do anything wrong according to the Muslim principles. Suddenly, everyone was complaining about me, how I was sharing the Christian faith with their children. So when I became a believer, my parents felt like they lost a son. It was difficult."

"I was dating during the time I became a believer, and I talked to the girl I was dating and she became a believer too after three months. We married as Christians and had a Christian wedding.

"Our daughter is also a part of our testimony. My wife was taking medications when she became pregnant, and the doctor encouraged her to have an abortion because the medications could have caused birth defects. Having an abortion was against our principles as believers, and we refused. The doctors looked at me and said, 'You are crazy! Or maybe your God is strong enough.' I told him that my God is strong enough, and that I trust God, and this baby will be fine. And my daughter is a healthy child.

"I am also in a good relationship with my parents now. They tried to get me to compromise many times, and I refused. So finally my dad said, 'This is what he believes, so we have to respect it.' He collected all my family about a year after I became a believer and said, 'He's doing good work, and I don't want any of you to hurt him.' And then my mom became a believer herself! But she's afraid of telling people about it. It's not easy for a person like my mom to say, 'I'm a believer and a follower of Jesus Christ.' "

"Do you think that fear is what keeps a lot of Muslims from accepting the love of Christ?" I asked.

"When Mohammed shared his philosophy about Islam, he included two instructions that stopped the Gospel from spreading among the Muslims. First, he said, 'You don't have a right to doubt the Quran. You have to take it as it is.' Second, he said, 'You don't have the right to ask questions about Islam.' These two instructions discourage people from finding out about Christ. Also, in Islam, they kill you if you change your religion."

We asked Ramzi about his safety. Would he be in danger if his story was told?

He admitted that a respected Muslim leader in Iran had at one time written to request his death. This leader asked other Muslim leaders from the same background to sign the document as well to give it more force, but they had refused.

"They got scared because blood was involved," he said calmly, as if he were not talking about his own potential murder. "When you share my testimony, just don't use my real name."

CHAPTER 20

"We kept on paying ransoms for a whole year."

Next we drove to a place beside the sea. We looked at each other. Perhaps we were going to get in the water for a bit? We were all dripping with sweat.

"No, we are coming to visit a family who lives here," Ramzi said.

I could not get enough of the Mediterranean Sea. As we climbed out of the vehicle, my eyes sought the blue-green horizon. A light breeze blew off the water.

There was an apartment building beside the beach, several stories tall. Some of it was painted brick red, but part of it remained a tan cement-like color. Arabic writing framed a metal garage door on the first story, and symbols from BMW and Lexus were painted on either side of the door.

"When you finish your visit, call me. I will need a towel," our driver said as he looked longingly at the blue-green water.

We entered through a side door around the corner from the Lexus symbol and climbed the stairs to the upper apartment. Open windows looked out over the sea, and laundry flapped from a clothesline strung within reach of the window.

The people in the house had been wealthy in Syria. In fact, they had furniture in the apartment now. There were a number of young children there, one girl with striking blue eyes and a stunning full smile. Her mother and grandmother, who both looked young enough to be her mother, were dressed in floral hijabs.

We were offered seats on the couches. As we settled in, a young man, the son of the older woman, got up and left the room.

Our driver gave us some background. "The girls in this family go to our school," he told us. With the help of our interpreter, the two girls began to sing a Christian song they had learned at school.

Halfway through the song, Ramzi threw his head back and yelled, "Good job!" He was clearly a favorite of the children from times past.

The children sang the song again, this time in English.

"Jesus, Prince of Peace, glory, hallelujah."

Everyone clapped at the end of the song.

The ladies brought us little cups of juice. My interpreter and Jana and I all thanked them and took the juice. Ramzi and our driver, the two men in our group, both declined. They didn't need the sugar, they said.

"We had a good life and a perfect location in Syria," the older woman said. "My husband was a butcher in Syria, and he did a lot of beef for stores, so we used to be wealthy. We had visits among our family and relatives. We had lunches and dinners together.

"My daughter's family came here to Lebanon to stay, after the danger became so great that they had to keep moving from place to place. But my husband and I and our younger son were still in Syria. Because of the war, my husband, who had been wealthy, had spent all his savings. And it was cheaper to live in Syria.

"But my husband would come to Lebanon to visit my daughter's family here. And it was on one of these trips from Syria to Lebanon that disaster struck. My husband and son were at the border, trying to cross into Lebanon. They were stopped and questioned. The soldiers arrested my husband, and he disappeared.

"My son has never fully recovered from that night and the horrible experience when they captured his father at the border. It was dark, and after the soldiers took his father, he told them that he didn't know how to find his way back by himself. He told them he would not leave until they released his father. But they didn't listen to him, and they made him leave alone. My son went back to Damascus on his own. He has been in psychological distress ever since they took his father. Also during the war, a stray bullet hit his eye, and he can't see out of that eye any more.

"We kept on paying ransoms for a whole year."

"I did my best to find my husband. We kept on paying ransoms for a whole year to bring him back, but he was already dead, and we didn't know that. People would tell me, 'Pay this person,' and 'Pay this person. Give bribes to these people, and they will let him out.' But my husband was already dead. He died in prison, one month after they arrested him, but no one told us that.

"After I found out that my husband was dead, I came here to Lebanon, and I brought my son with me. We had no one left there. We were able to come here without any problem. I left all of my possessions in Syria. These things you see are all second-hand items or things people gave us. Sometimes I stay with my daughter, and sometimes I stay with my son. I cook for both of them, and I am a babysitter for the children!"

"My mom is the best cook. Even now, I still can't cook that well. My mom comes here to help me! She can make all the dishes," the daughter said.

"I don't want to go back to Syria anymore," she continued. "I want to stay here. My father is not there. I don't want to go back."

We could hear the waves of the Mediterranean Sea hitting the beach in the short pauses in our conversation. A gentle breeze blew in, cooling us off just a bit.

"We are thinking about emigration," the younger woman said. "Some people called my mother from the United Nations, asking her if she's ready to emigrate."

"I didn't want to before," the older woman said. "But now because of my son, and needing treatment for his eye, I'm willing to think about it."

CHAPTER 21

"The people were dying in front of us."

At another building close to the sea, we walked up an outdoor flight of steps. In the tiled patio leading to the apartment, a homemade wooden ladder leaned against the side of the building, giving access to the roof. Vines climbed up the wall with the ladder, and an orange plastic lawn chair added color. It was a beautiful spot, in striking contrast to the sadness of the refugee stories.

The woman's sitting room floor was covered with a pink and yellow mat woven in a pattern of diamonds and squares. Brown cushions bordered the room, and we took seats on these.

This apartment housed one of the new families being assisted by the refugee organization. The lady in the house had two young daughters. Her husband was working.

"Honestly, it was a very good life in Syria before the war," the woman told us wistfully. "It was much, much better than here. Our children were in schools. If you would come to this house at the beginning of the winter, you would see water dripping from the walls and the ceilings. We did not have that in Syria; our house was well-built. Before I got married, I used to work in a medicine company in distribution. Here we are having problems with our daughter's education. They won't let us register because they give priority to Syrian families who have been here before and to Lebanese children."

"I will work on that to help you," Ramzi said.

"I already paid $120, and they still want around $450 and a bit more. And they told me I can pay a little at a time."

"The people were dying in front of us."

"Can I see the United Nations registration paper?" Ramzi asked. "So I can work with the school."

When she produced the paper, he got to his feet and came across the room, the paper blowing in the air from the fan. Ramzi looked at it, promising to get her daughter in a public school and return the money to her if he possibly could.

Traffic roared by, drowning our words.

A small daughter leaned on her mother's lap. The mother stroked her head with a gentle, slow movement as she began to recall her last memories of Syria, after the war began and life was no longer good.

"During my last days in Syria the conditions were terrible. Our area was in a hot location where there were lots of fights. The people were dying in front of us. There were bombs. We had no food, no water. To avoid the fighting, we moved from village to village.

"We had to make our own bread inside the towns. There was no bread in the stores, no fuel, no water. There were checkpoints everywhere. We were afraid to move around. Even now, just a few days ago, my husband's cousin went to Syria, and they stopped him at the border and captured him.

"When we finally decided to come here, we left in the evening and went to another area. Then we were on the road two days in a car. We brought nothing at all with us. We went back and forth to get more legal papers that we needed in order to cross. Then there were army movements going on close to the border, and they wouldn't let us cross because of that. So we stayed two days at the border before we could get in. The whole trip was scary.

"Imagine if you had spent your whole life's earnings to buy a house, and then your house is destroyed. We did that. We had purchased our own house. But we never got to live in it because of the war. I have not heard what happened to my house in Aleppo, or the furnishings inside of it."

"In our culture," Ramzi explained, "when we say 'I didn't live in it,' it doesn't mean that you didn't live in it at all. You may have lived there for six months or one year, but you didn't get to live your life there."

"I'm worried because my husband doesn't have any registration papers," the woman went on. "He is avoiding passing by any officials."

"We will pray for the safety of your husband, but don't worry, they will not send him back," Ramzi said. "They will not send the Syrians away."

Ramzi had told us before we arrived that this woman had struggled with mental problems.

"At this point I'm not taking any medications because they told me that because I'm pregnant I can't. But I used to take them before I was pregnant. I haven't seen my doctor since before I got pregnant. He has not been checking in with me. I went to the hospital yesterday, and they made me pay $200 even though the receipt said $66."

"I will talk to the hospital," Ramzi said. "I will take your receipt and bring you back your money. I will take care of this."

"I don't want to bother you with this," the woman said.

"Not at all," Ramzi said.

"I'm worried to bother people."

"I insist," Ramzi said, as a cell phone began to ring. "Come tomorrow, and we'll go over the issue about your daughter's education."

"When we first came to Lebanon we were living in another house that was half furnished, but we could not afford the rent, so we moved here. But this house leaks. We need the house to be fixed so it does not leak. We put plastic on the door because the winter is coming. Thank you so much for your help, but I'm really desperate about the house because of my children."

"We have friends in other organizations that might be able to help even if we don't do this," he replied. "Is there anything you don't like about the food portions we are giving you?"

"You are giving me something," the woman said. "I'm not in a position to complain about anything. Thank you for all you are doing for me. I hope that my children have a life better than the one I am living."

She rearranged her hijab. Her voice was quiet and sad, yet proud.

"Lots of Syrian people live in this area, and the Lebanese are having trouble with them," the woman added. "The Lebanese assume that all the Syrians are bad people. There are lots of people that are destroying the reputation of Syrian people. I never had to ask for help for someone to get my child in school. That was a right. Now I feel humiliated that I have to ask for someone to put my children in school. I won't ask from anyone except your organization."

"The people were dying in front of us."

"Regardless of all of this," Ramzi said, "I am sure that there is hope for you and the Syrian people. They have a good reputation, and we love you. And don't hesitate to contact us and ask for help. We will solve the money issue and the children's school thing, and we will talk to another organization about your house. God bless you, and I hope you can go back to your country."

It was time for us to leave, so we had a time of prayer. I prayed for the woman and her family, praying for peace and the return of the money and the presence of God and someone to fix the house.

"I am going to write in my book about all the wonderful people I met from Syria," I told her in parting.

VOICES

FROM HAMA

Hama

Hama, a beautiful town on the winding Orontes River, was known for its tall wooden water wheels, gardens, and riverside trees. The water wheels, which groan and squeak as they turn, are up to 20 meters high. Known as *norias,* they were originally built because the river was much lower than the surrounding fields. The *norias* dipped the water out of the river and transported it to aqueducts which took water to the land. Seventeen *norias* still exist of the thirty built in the thirteenth century.

Much of the town's beauty was destroyed in 1982 when President Hafez al-Assad, father of the current leader, crushed the Muslim Brotherhood uprising there. "Only those who knew this city before this calamity can fully measure the damage," a Syrian guidebook says. A travel writer from 1955 described Hama as "extraordinarily unspoilt with houses that overhung the water and an extensive old town in which modern buildings rarely intrude."[22]

Bashar al-Assad's ruthless younger brother had silently planted soldiers in the city prior to their planned attack in order to silence the rebellion of the Muslim Brotherhood. Then on February 2, 1982, a day that was said to be cold and drizzly, the Syrian army attacked.[23]

At first the Muslim Brotherhood fought back. They were fighting for their beliefs and probably hoped to start a revolt that would echo across Syria. With cries of *"Allahu Akbar,"* they confidently fought off the government intruders. Snipers hid in the minarets, the towers of the mosques, and shot from above. Piles of garbage and large rocks became barricades behind which fighters hid with guns. Speakers from the mosques continually repeated, "Rise up and drive the unbelievers from Hama." But when President al-Assad's younger brother saw that the Muslim Brotherhood would not give up, he called in reinforcements. Twenty tanks rolled into Hama, no longer firing at certain targets, but now bent on utter destruction. For three weeks, the battle raged on as the Muslim Brotherhood hung tightly to certain areas of the city. Finally much of the city, including historical architecture, was rubble.

Although journalists were strictly forbidden in the city over this time, reports emerged that many survivors were shot and thrown into common pits, or gassed in their houses by cyanide channeled from canisters through rubber hoses. Finally, when the river was running red, President al-Assad's younger brother brought in bulldozers to completely destroy the already broken neighborhoods. He followed this with steam rollers that turned three areas of Hama into flat lots of broken cement, each the size of four football fields. He then found students to clean up the area, wash away the blood, and restrain the dogs.

When journalists were finally allowed in, Thomas Friedman found the city of Hama silent. The water wheels were not squeaking. Walking over the empty broken lots, he ran into an old man and asked him where the houses were, and the people. The old man told him that he was probably walking on both.

In 2011, as the Syrian revolution started, a video clip began to circulate on social media. From a high bridge in Hama over the Orontes River, near the picturesque wooden wheels, men were tossing a pickup load of bodies over the railing. The river again turned red, as the chanting mobs shouted *"Allahu Akbar!"* When someone far below walked toward the river bank, the men doing the deed warned that no one was to pull the bodies out.

The old President al-Assad was gone, but the red river was back.

Authoritarianism

Many people have puzzled over the brutal actions of the leaders of Middle Eastern countries. It seems surprising that Syrian President Hafez al-Assad was in power for thirty years despite the 1982 massacre of 20,000 of his own people.

Like the nomads of the desert, President al-Assad believed that if he was crossed, he needed to send a clear message to the people so that he would never be questioned again. He knew that Syria was full of little family cliques and tribes and religious affiliations who would love to see him ousted. He believed that the only way to win was to smash rebellions. "Restraint and magnanimity are luxuries of the self-confident, and the rulers of these countries are anything but secure on their thrones," Thomas Friedman said in 1989 of President al-Assad and Iraq's leader, Saddam Hussein.[24]

President al-Assad was not only brutal, but also smart. "Men like Assad and Saddam are dangerous and long-lasting because they are extremists who know when to stop. These men know how to insert the knife right through the heart of one opponent, and then invite all the others to dinner,"[25] Friedman said. He went on to say that many predecessors of these men were just as brutal, but their reigns were fleeting because they were *only* brutal. President al-Assad balanced massacres with new hospitals and roads. He balanced putting the Alawite sect in control of the government, with granting parliament positions to the tribal groups in the desert. He was brutal, and his people remembered the 1982 massacre with hate, but they were also happy to live in a country with affordable healthcare and schools.

By 2000, when President al-Assad died and his son Bashar became president at thirty-four years of age, not only was 1982 a distant memory, but people were hopeful that the junior al-Assad would part ways with his father.

However, people in Syria were still cautious about discussing politics, especially with strangers. As one guidebook to Syria says, "The Syrians can be a little reserved on some topics, such as their own government's actions. This is tied to the fact that most people still believe someone's always listening, and during Hafez al-Assad's reign they were probably right."[26]

CHAPTER 22

"They started dying and dying."

ONE OF THE FAMILIES RAMZI took us to visit was a family who had lived close to Hama. We pulled up at a block house with a propane stove by the front door.

Inside the house, the walls were simply the other side of the block wall. The floor was cement, but a patterned rug covered part of it. At the edge of the room, a cement ledge had been poured, which served as built-in seating. A window in the wall opposite the door was open, and the light from it made the room less dusky. On the right side of the window, a family photo in a thin purple frame was posted on the block wall.

We took seats on the rug, the cement bench, and several low cushions. Our driver began to play quietly with a little boy and a stack of playing cards.

Ramzi exchanged pleasantries with the woman of the house, a young, slender woman wearing long black sleeves, a white skirt, and a zebra-print hijab. He spoke with her about school transportation for her son, the little boy who was present.

She then began to talk about her son's medical condition. While he was in the hospital for other reasons, medical personnel had drawn blood samples and found there was something wrong with her son's blood. He had leukemia.

"This was the most difficult thing ever. I stayed inside for two months after I found out," she said. "I couldn't even open the door for people and tell them what happened. I was very sad. He was one year and four months old when they discovered it. He has been receiving treatment for the past four years."

"We always share the story of the boy with others, and we always pray for him," Ramzi told her. "At school I tell the teachers to watch if he is weak or fragile, and to make sure that he is eating."

In response to our questioning, the woman began to speak about her former home. "It was beautiful in Syria, especially where we lived near Hama, before the war," she said. "We lived on the ground floor. We used to plant cotton, tobacco, and vegetables. Our area was very nice. Our house was not like this one."

"Was it worse?" our driver asked, teasing her.

"No!" she said. "It was lovely. We lived in the mountains, and we could view the whole village from our house. I had four rooms, a kitchen, and a bathroom. In Syria they take good care of houses. Houses are important there. They have lots of green, lots of trees, and many plants. But now . . . there is nothing. I want to show you a video someone sent me."

She picked up her phone. Mournful music began to play.

"Everything was destroyed," she said as pictures of broken block houses and desolate brown mountains began to flash on the screen of her phone. "This is the village where I used to live, but I did not recognize it.

"In 2012, my husband came to Lebanon and found a place for me to live," the woman told us. "And then four months later he asked me to come to stay. We came here legally on the bus. I did not bring anything with me from Syria—just a few clothes for the boy. I put the picture in my purse." She glanced at the picture high on the wall in the thin purple frame, a family photo of six or seven people and a bouquet of flowers. "It was difficult to come here, and we had to stay two days on the road. We had to take a long road to get here."

"How are your parents and family doing who still live in Syria?" Ramzi asked.

The woman again raised her eyes to the family photo. Then her head fell.

"I don't have anyone left in Syria," she said. "Everyone died."

There was a rare moment of utter silence that was broken only when Ramzi said several stunned words in Arabic that no one interpreted.

Finally he said in English to Jana, "Can you go over and sit with her? She lost all her family."

The woman began to talk again.

"Month after month, they started dying and dying from the plane bombings."

Again there was complete silence. Ramzi put his head in his hands in distress.

Finally he whispered to us in English, "I did not know. We did not talk about that because most of the time I was focusing on this boy. I didn't know that!"

Although he had told us that he visited four hundred families monthly, Ramzi was crushed to have missed this detail.

He turned to the woman and asked her a brief question.

"I have no one left," she said, wiping her eyes. "My husband's family is okay," she said.

"Can you pray?" he asked Jana.

"Dear heavenly Father, thank you for this sweet woman," Jana prayed, her arm around the young lady. "I pray that you would bring her peace in her heart. Would you comfort her in the loss of all her family? Let her feel your love and your arms around her. Father, just give her your strength and help her to know that you care about her."

"I always focused on your son's story because I know that he is going through a hard time. I did not know that you lost your family," Ramzi apologized in Arabic. "What about your husband?"

"Thank God he is able to find work as a laborer. And I am happy that I receive food portions from your organization. No one else helps.

"Ever since I came here from Syria I heard about you. I heard that you register only specific families, not all the families. And then they told me to go and visit. They said if they can help you they will, and if they can't, they can't. I went to your office, and you were nice to me and treated me with respect, and you registered my family."

Ramzi turned his attention to the little boy, trying to lighten the mood a bit. "Is he behaving?"

"A little bit," his mother said, laughing. "He's bored. He wants someone to play with. And sometimes I don't have the time to play with him.

"I have neighbors from our area in Syria," she went on. "We're not related to them, but they're good people. I don't have anyone related to me here besides my husband and son. They're everything in my world, because I have no one else besides them. I hope my son has a good future, and I ask God to heal him. He is studying at school, and he's learning English. I can't speak English.

"I would like to return to Syria. But the thing I miss the most is my family. It is even more difficult for me because I could not even see them when they died."

"Even though we do feel with you, we can't actually feel the way you do," Ramzi said, sitting cross-legged on the Arabic carpet. "But the Bible speaks of a Spirit that gives us comfort."

The woman listened silently, fingering a tissue.

"I asked Jesus to be here and comfort you, give you condolences, and be with you," Ramzi went on. "I'm sure that there's life after the one we have here, and that after that there will be no pain or suffering for those who go to heaven. I am very sorry that you lost your family. Some things are very difficult in life. But God can give us His peace. We should ask the real God to come and bring His peace into our hearts. May He give us comfort. And we pray that He stops the war in Syria. The Syrian people are always asking us, 'Why is this happening to us in Syria?' But I'm very sure that the devil is helping with this because he loves evil and blood and killing.

"May you have a long life, you and your son. You are responsible for his future and his life. I'm very happy because you're worried for him and you take care of him and his future. May God bless you and give you comfort.

"Can we pray for your son? There's a Bible verse that tells us that everything we ask in the name of God, we are given. In the letter of James, it tells us that we can pray if someone is sick. And that's what we're going to do, we're going to pray, and we believe in the power of prayer for healing."

The boy sat in the middle of the group as Ramzi prayed passionately, begging God to heal him. I could hear the poetry and power in the prayer without understanding one word.

After the visits of the day, we headed back to the warehouse. Suddenly, Ramzi, who had declined juice earlier on the basis of too much sugar, whipped the vehicle into a parking spot in front of a glass-fronted shop with gold Arabic lettering on the front window. It was a shop that sold sweets.

Inside, Ramzi asked the shopkeeper to assemble a tray of sweets for us. Most of the sweets were unfamiliar to American eyes.

Sitting in the shop with his mouth full of sweets, Ramzi explained that he would balance out his sweet intake by doing sit-ups the next day. The conversation was in Arabic, but I got pieces of it interpreted to me.

"Thank you!" Jana said to Ramzi when we were all in the vehicle. "Everyone takes such good care of us here. How do we teach the people in the West to be so hospitable?"

"You cannot," our driver answered. "You have to be born here."

"But today you worked hard," Ramzi said.

It had been an exhausting day; there was no question about that. But the blessing was ours.

"I feel so grateful just to hear these stories, and I know that because the refugees know you, they are more willing to talk to us," I added.

"I hope this book gets to many people, and they will read it and understand refugees better," our driver said. "Especially here in the Middle East there is a lack of rules and regulations. People have to suffer legal trauma on top of the trauma that comes from war. And they suffer because of the lack of really credible organizations that know how to help. Here in Lebanon all we had was civil war and corruption for the past forty years, and now we are taking care of refugees too! For every two Lebanese, we now have one refugee, whether from Syria, Iraq, or Palestine."

We pulled into the parking lot by the warehouse.

"Thank you for telling me your story," I said to Ramzi. Meeting him and watching him work with the refugees had been an unforgettable experience.

"It's just *a part* of my story," Ramzi laughed. "God bless you!"

CHAPTER 23

"Don't come!"

AT A FOOD DISTRIBUTION CENTER in Beirut, I met a Syrian Christian from Hama who was working for the organization that was hosting us. He had lived in Saudi Arabia for a time. He could speak English, and it felt freeing to hear a refugee story without going through an interpreter.

"I left Syria and went to Saudi Arabia to make money," he explained. "Many Arab people, and I think Europeans and Americans, go to the Gulf countries for jobs. I had a business major, so I worked with communication between the departments of a construction company. I worked there for six or seven months."

I pulled my map of the Middle East out of my backpack. He showed me the town on the Gulf of Oman, where he had worked, right by the water.

"You can swim there in the winter," he said. "But I hated it there. It is desert, and the people were not friendly. Have you been there? The Muslim culture is very strict. It's a problem to do anything. I almost went crazy. One time I went to Riyadh, five hours by car. The driver didn't have enough fuel. He stopped at a gas station, but they would not sell him gas because it was prayer time. 'But I need gas!' the driver said.

" 'No, it's prayer time,' the owner said. I asked the owner if he goes to prayer. He told me, 'No, but the religious security might catch me and close the gas station.'

"Eventually, I decided to go back to Syria. I had grown up in Hama and lived there until I was eighteen. Then I went to Aleppo to study in the university. The food in Aleppo is delicious. It has better food than any other city in Syria. At that time I never worried even once about war or thought that I would ever come here to Lebanon. I never wanted to come to Lebanon, because it is so much like Syria. The sea is the same. The mountains are the same.

"Anyway, when I was in Saudi Arabia, I was finally so tired of it, I said to myself, *I will go back to Syria!* I came back to Syria in 2011, and fifteen days later the war started. I came back the first of March and the war began the fifteenth of March. I was so glad to be back in Syria, and I had no idea a war was coming. Then the war began. I worked one month, two months, then seven months. I said, 'Oh, Syria will be okay!' But nothing got better, and finally I came here to Lebanon.

"I came here, thinking I could get a job like I did in Saudi Arabia. I called people and sent my resume to different companies: an insurance company, a clothing store. No one hired me, so I moved to smaller companies. Still no one hired me. Finally I tried to get a job as a laborer. I can work! I didn't care! I didn't care if I was working in something different than I have a degree in. I needed to live. I went to one place and he told me, 'Sorry, you don't have good experience.'

"In the end I found one place to work in sales, but it was sad there. It wasn't run by good people. One year and a half I worked every day, under a lot of stress. I was supposed to be getting paid commission, and I was doing a good job in sales. Sometimes I made a sale of $10,000 and the owner gave me two or three dollars.

"I tried the U.S. Embassy, but they wouldn't give me a visa to go to the States. In 2014, after my birthday, it seemed like God brought me here to work with other refugees. Now I'm helping refugees every day. Here, they don't care whether you have experience or not. It's enough if you share the Lord with the people. I don't care if I'm packing the food or going to visits. I feel something different inside too, now that I'm helping people. I'm happy!"

His face reflected his words.

"All of us working with the refugees put our eyes on the same goal. It doesn't matter if I'm an employee, or manager, or president, all the work has the same goal. I don't care about the position, only about the focus and the goal. I never saw this kind of management before. There's no need for personal advancement, because they move the bar for everyone.

"I don't think I'll go back to Syria right now. I could go visit, but that's dangerous. I have two brothers studying in Damascus University. One is getting a master's degree in banking and finance, and the other is studying to be a doctor. My father and mother are both teachers, and they also live in Damascus now. My dad teaches math, and my mom teaches music.

"One day a friend called me and said, 'Don't worry about your father; he's okay.' I didn't know what he was talking about. 'You don't know?' he asked me.

"He told me that a bomb had hit my father's school, and a lot of children died. My father was on his way to the school with his friend when a rocket hit their car. My father's friend had died, and an ambulance had taken my father to the hospital.

"When I heard this I called my family and said, 'I will come back to Syria!'

"My father told me 'No. Don't come. This time the bomb came to me. Tomorrow it could come to you.' He stayed in the hospital for three months and had a lot of surgeries. He is still having surgeries done. A lot of times when I speak with my family I hear *VROOOOM!* from the planes, and then an explosion."

VOICES

FROM ALEPPO

Aleppo

Aleppo competes with Syria's capital, Damascus, for the title of "oldest city in the world." It was a stop on the Silk Road that linked Europe to China, the pathway for goods and ideas to travel back and forth.

Before the war in Syria, Aleppo was famous for its delicious food, its souk, and its ancient citadel, rising high in the center of the city. Because of the traffic in Aleppo over the years, the cuisine was distinct from the rest of Syria, with spicier influences than most Middle Eastern food. The souk still relied on donkeys as the best means of transport in the narrow streets and stalls, and desert Bedouins could be seen in the alleys of the souk, doing their monthly shopping. Like most Syrian marketplaces, the Aleppo souk is divided into different sections for different items. One area is devoted to fabric, another to gold and silver, another to leather, another to perfume, another to rope, cord, and braid. Photos from before the war show a spice booth with huge burlap sacks full of colorful spices, the mouths of the sacks turned down for easy viewing.

"The streets speak a rhythm of sounds," the guidebook says, "from horse-drawn carts over cobblestones to the more frenetic pace of donkey-riding couriers, still the fastest way through the atmospheric, labyrinthine souk that's fragrant with olive soap, exotic spices, roasting coffee, and succulent grilled shwarma [sic]."[27]

A photo of Aleppo at dusk before the war shows a beautiful mosaic of tan-colored domes and walls with the lights of the town blinking on. The minarets beside each mosque glow green.

Aleppo is the largest city in Syria, positioned in the north close to Turkey. Driving south from Aleppo, travelers would first drive through Hama, then Homs, then Damascus, and then finally through Daraa near the border of Jordan.

Far north of the first trouble in Daraa, Aleppo remained immune from the conflict until students at Aleppo University began to demonstrate in early 2012, almost a year after the graffiti in Daraa. In the summer of 2012, Aleppo became an intense battleground. The opposition captured pieces of the city, dividing the city into government-held sections and opposition-held sections. A fire tore through the souk. Citizens fled by the thousands.

CHAPTER 24

"I put my children in the well."

THE LAST DAY WE WENT to the Bekaa Valley, our driver told us we would stop on the top of the Lebanese Mountains for *kanafeh*. He explained that it was made with syrup, soft cheese, and grains, and it was tucked into a kind of bread.

We parked at the roadside, with a *kanafeh* shop on one side of the road, and a drop-off on the other. Blue mountains could be seen across the ravine. It felt like we were stopping on the top of the world.

The workers prepared the cheese, syrup, and bread skillfully and handed the *kanafeh* to us in parchment paper. Nothing American seemed at all similar to the combination of sesame seed-studded bread, chewy soft cheese, and syrup.

Kanafeh in hand, we drove on, and rolled into the refugee camp for our last visit.

"Our story is no different from anyone else's," the father said when we introduced ourselves to a handsome family. The man wore a loose, dark red shirt and pants and sat cross-legged on the sitting room floor. His wife was a quiet woman who inserted comments from the background, where she sat on the floor, dressed in a gown of black and lavender.

Their tent was sparsely furnished, with a bare cement floor and white plastic walls. In the entryway to the house, a wash line had been hung, and clothes were pinned up to dry.

"In Syria, my husband would make hand printing on clothes," the lady said.

"I put my children in the well."

Her husband was a slight man, and we began to discuss his vocation in Aleppo. He reached to his oldest son's black shirt with an Armani stamp as an example of what he used to do. He rested his hand briefly on his son's shoulder.

"Right before the war, we had opened a store, my brother and my family. We were working for ourselves. Right when we started that, the war started and there was no business anymore, and we had to shut it down. And even before the war started, when there was fighting in Egypt and in Libya, they stopped importing things. And so our business had started to go down way before the actual war in Syria."

"I heard that Aleppo has lots of good food," I said.

"Of course, of course," the whole family said, a collective smile breaking out.

"No restaurants, we cook at home. We only eat at home."

"Who's the cook?" I asked.

"Me," the woman said. "But he can also cook really well. But I do most of the cooking. He has very good taste in food, so whenever I cook something, he gives me suggestions and ways to improve it. He tells me, 'My sister's cooking was better.'"

Everyone laughed.

"When the war started, we lost everything," the man said. "Equipment we had and everything else. We would close our store and leave, and when we came back there were things missing. There were no authorities or police to call. We were getting robbed, and we had no control over it.

"There were many people who lost their businesses and were robbed like this. It wasn't only small businesses. There were factories that cost millions of Syrian pounds, that employed a thousand people, that were also destroyed and robbed. Poor people lost fortunes, everything they had, and also rich people with factories also lost it all.

"We would leave, if bombings happened, and go stay with friends in another city. When we would come back, our houses were robbed. Even mattresses, TVs, everything we had—all the houses would be robbed. It would only be a matter of twenty days to two months, and we would come back and it would be robbed."

As their father talked, two young boys, who appeared to be about eight or nine years old, listened silently with matching expressions and dark eyes.

"Are these twins?" I had to ask.

The mother answered.

"There's one year difference between these boys, but the boy and girl over there are twins," she said.

"My favorite food is grilled chicken," one of the younger boys said. "My mom's a good cook, and my dad too."

The older boy, with the twin sister, told us he enjoyed games. He remembered riding his motorbike in Syria. "I don't have one here. I dream about it. I had a motorcycle. And I would ride in front of the house, and I would go to villages nearby."

"I love motorcycles," the father joined in, "and when I see one, I think, *Just give it to me! I want to ride it.*"

I could tell that the parents were concerned about their children's social skills. They insisted that the children interact with us, even if they were shy, drawing them forward into the circle of people sitting on the cement floor of the tent.

The twin sister was standing shyly behind the men in the doorway leading to the kitchen.

I asked her if she liked motorcycles.

"No, I don't like them," she said. "But I can cook some things."

"We depend on her a lot," her father said.

"I don't let the children go up that big dirt hill," their mother said, "because it's dangerous, and they get dirty. In this camp there are a lot of rodents. So we're very careful about that, and we never leave any food on the floor. Cleanliness is the most important thing. Even if we're living in a camp, we still can be clean."

"We have these piles of wood here," the father said. "Rodents and snakes hide in them. I've been asking the neighbors to move them. A little girl was bitten on her toes by one of them. It's very hard for me to sleep at night when I hear the rodents trying to come inside." The man made scratching sounds on the cement floor with his fingers. "I try to sleep, but I hear them, and they keep me awake."

We returned to the discussion of the war. The father had been in Lebanon before the war but didn't enjoy the country. "I didn't have luck in Lebanon.

"I put my children in the well."

'I don't ever want to come back to this country again,' I told myself."

But as the war in Syria had progressed, everybody around them had left, all the young people and the families. There had been only a few old people left in the village, including this man's parents.

"In our area we had bombings all around us for a long time before we actually left. They were destroying the village line by line. The last barrel bomb fell about one hundred meters away from us. We had a well that we had dug, and I had cleaned the well. We were getting bombed, and we could see how the bombs were getting closer and closer and closer. When the bombing became very close, I put my children in the well and said, 'If it hits the well, it's a problem, but otherwise, you're safe.' And so that's how I hid my children about an hour when the bombing became very close."

As the father talked, the children in the room sat quietly, sad and calm.

"The well was a little ways from our house. So we were in there, and the bombs were still coming. Every time my wife and I would say to each other, 'This is the one that's going to destroy everything.' We suspected that at any minute everything around us was going to be destroyed. Our children were screaming. Their screaming reached the sky. We would tell them . . . the only thing we could tell them was, 'Don't worry, this one's far away; that one passed us, we're safe now.' But we didn't believe it ourselves.

"The bombing passed us, but we saw that they were just trying to destroy that whole village in order, every house. Most people had left by that point. Most of the people around us had already gone before we actually left.

"Several times we had gone back and forth between our village and Aleppo, back and forth, back and forth, depending on which place seemed safer. And so though we had a little bit of money, that was all gone from the moving back and forth. We heard that a bus was coming the next day. So if we would be at a certain point at the right time, we could get the bus that was going to Lebanon. And so we were able to get just two pairs of clothing for the children and one blanket and very few of our belongings, and we came on the bus.

"When we left we didn't bring anything sentimental with us, because we had to pay for everything we brought by weight. So we couldn't just bring everything we wanted. It was the bare minimum, because we didn't even have money to pay to be able to come from Aleppo to here. We had to borrow money, and we still haven't repaid that."

"Then when we got to the border, they wouldn't let me in," the woman in black and lavender said, "because my ID was expired. So we had to sleep at the border for three days, and it was cold and rainy. It was just a place where people would pass through; it was not a place to stay. They had tents like this on the border, and so we slept in those. There weren't beds or anything, so we were sitting there falling asleep. And I had a jacket, so I would cover one child and then cover the other one. We didn't have anything protective, and they were shaking. It was very cold."

"Did you have food and water?" I asked.

"We did not have food. We even had to go look to find water. But we wanted to try to be inconspicuous because any soldier or someone could come and say, 'What are you doing here?' So we were hiding and didn't want to cause any kind of commotion or anything, or be needy in any way, so people would leave us alone.

"The three days we were at the border trying to allow her to enter, it didn't work," the man said. "So I brought the children here to Lebanon, left my wife at the border, and went back to try to get some papers. They still wouldn't let her in. So she actually went back to Syria and got a passport. And all of this is debt. With the passport she was able to get in."

"It was costly for me to get the passport," the wife explained. "I had to go to Idlib. In Aleppo, everything had closed, government-wise, and you couldn't get anything done. So I had to go three times to try to get the actual passport, and I would have to borrow money every time. It cost me 50,000 liras to be able to get that done. And that's money that I didn't have."

"We are living in debt; everything is in debt," the husband said.

"Every time I would go to Idlib to get the passport, they would tell me, 'You're from Aleppo, go to Aleppo and do it.' To do any kind of legal document, you have to go to where you were born. And I would say, 'Everything is closed in Aleppo,' and they would just turn me away. Finally, the third time, I was able to do it."

I thought of Mary and Joseph registering at Bethlehem.

"When I was living there alone, I was very, very cautious," the woman said. "I wouldn't even open the house door to guests. It was so different from the way we were living life previously."

"What's the last thing you remember when you finally left Syria?" I asked her.

"When I left, I had not seen my children in three months, so that's all I was thinking about. But the hardest part was leaving my parents." She began to weep quietly. "I don't know where my parents are. And my husband doesn't know where his parents are. Either in Turkey, or maybe still in Syria; we just don't know. And that's the hardest part."

"We can't even use a phone because we have to use these cards to charge it. It's not just a land line, and so we don't even have that connection," her husband added. "If we at least had a connection by phone, our hearts would feel okay, but we don't know anything about them. And they don't know anything about us. We just don't know."

"Our dream is to be able to go back and for Syria to be okay. And we want to be able to educate our children. The older boy and girl were very good in school. The boy is excellent at math. The younger children didn't even get a chance to start school when the bombings had started. So they never got to go to school."

"In school in Syria we were studying addition, multiplication, division, and subtraction," the older boy told me.

"Is it possible for us to be able to read and write and our children can't?" the mother said sadly. "How tragic would that be, that we know how to read and write but our children don't."

"We thank God that here there's peace, but it's hard to make a living," the man said. "I tried to get some work in construction. I went and worked a whole day. And at the end of the day the man who was in charge, he started beating the employees, and he didn't pay us anything. He complained about our work and said, 'I'm not going to pay you anything.' He's an evil man. I don't have a lot of luck when it comes to work.

"Some of the men are getting kidnapped for ransom. They kidnap the man, ask for some money, and then they release them. But I don't have any relatives around here to pay any kind of money. If I get kidnapped there's no hope for me to come back, because no one is going to pay any ransom. I have nobody here. I am not willing to take a chance to go far away for work. I want to stay with my family."

Islam

Islam began in A.D. 613 in Mecca, a city in what is now Saudi Arabia. Mohammed, considered by Muslims to be a prophet, preached to the people of Mecca about the revelations he claimed to have received from the angel Gabriel. He criticized the idol worship of the people of Mecca, and eventually he was run out of town with a small group of followers. He and his followers moved to Medina, where they became much more popular. Eventually, they returned to Mecca and took their revenge on the people who had once rejected them.

After Mohammed died, his followers had a disagreement about who his successor should be, since Mohammed had no living sons. Some of them thought it should be Abu Bakr, a close friend of Mohammed and the father of his second wife. Others favored Ali, who was both Mohammed's cousin and son-in-law. Finally, Abu Bakr was declared to be the successor. His supporters became known as Sunni Muslims.

However, the supporters of Ali continued to support him as well and became known as Shia Muslims or Shi'ites. The Alawites, the religious group that Syrian President Bashar al-Assad is a part of, are an off-shoot from the Shi'ites. Another somewhat mysterious off-shoot group are the Druze, who mostly live in the mountains of Lebanon.

In Syria, the Alawites were historically oppressed and persecuted by the majority Sunni Muslims. For centuries they suffered at the hands of Sunni governments, including during the 400 years of the Ottoman Empire. At times they were massacred or forced to convert to Sunni Islam. The Alawites were poor, usually consigned to the lowest occupations.

However, in the 1900s when the French arrived, they sided with the Alawites. They gave the coastal mountain area to the Alawites and allowed them to rule themselves. Suddenly the Alawites rose both in importance and power, and by 1970, their own Hafez al-Assad became president of all of Syria.

True Muslims believe in professing their faith in God and Mohammed, praying five times a day, giving to the poor, fasting, and making a pilgrimage to Mecca.

Five times a day, mosques announce a call to prayer, and it is at these times the people are expected to pray with their faces pointed in the direction of Mecca. In cities where many mosques are close together, the calls to prayer, now announced over loudspeakers, form a haunting chorus. The first call is between dawn and sunrise. The second call is just after the height of the midday sun. The third call is in the afternoon. The fourth is right after sunset, and the last call is later in the evening.[28]

CHAPTER 25

"I love these people more than my life."

W E CLIMBED THE DUSTY HILL at the refugee camp one final time. For a while I stood alone, looking at the band of gray mountains separating us from the country of Syria. Somehow I felt closer to the Syrian conflict on this hill than I ever had before.

Syria is my home . . . I cannot leave, the man on the plane had told me. I had heard those sentiments over and over from the people who had felt forced to leave.

I wish I would not have had to leave. My dream is to return. My first choice is to go back.

Most of them wanted to go back to that land beyond the mountains, whether to Aleppo, or Hama, or Homs, or Damascus.

Perhaps, across those gray hills, the kind man in the striped shirt was in his own home in Damascus, discussing the conflict with his wife and children.

We drove away from the dusty camps, the lines of laundry, the tires holding plastic in place on makeshift roofs. We drove on past the well-tended vineyards and apple orchards that had suddenly become the setting for hundreds of homeless people.

I remembered George's words in the dining room: "The main question with refugees is, 'Whose problem is it?' Anyone can say, 'Well, glad that's not my problem; I hope someone else does something about it.'"

I had seen the refugees firsthand and heard their stories. Whether I claimed them or not, they now had a claim on me.

The vehicle pulled up to a corner, and the turn signal ticked up front. We rolled up to a restaurant with an outdoor patio for eating and trees and sun umbrellas for shade. Traffic roared past as we climbed out of the vehicle and walked up to the restaurant.

A stand of shawarma welcomed us on its roasting pole by the front door. After having eaten it several times already, I finally got to study how it was made and served. Thin slices of chicken were piled on a tall metal stick which turned as the meat roasted. The chef cut down through the mountain of chicken slices, resulting in tender, moist chicken sandwiches, flavorful and juicy.

We sat outside on chairs of thin wooden slats trimmed with metal.

I turned to Nader, who had been interpreting for me that day and who was an employee of the relief organization that was hosting us. "What is your favorite part of your job?" I asked him.

"To preach to the Muslims about Jesus," he said without hesitation. "This is my gift from God."

He spoke to me in English, but often he had to pause to find the right words.

"Have you been able to lead people to Christ?" I asked.

"Yes," Nader said. "Most of my ministry is with them. And I studied the Muslim religion and continue to study it.

"I have a special question for the Muslim people. As we talk, I ask them about their relationship with Jesus Christ. And of course they ask, 'Who is Jesus Christ?' And from this question I can reach them. If somebody says 'I know about Jesus,' I ask them, 'What do you know?' "

"But they do know about Jesus, right?" Jana asked. "How do you get around that?"

"I start with them from this point and what is similar. In our book, the Bible, Jesus is the Son of God, and in the Quran it says the Spirit of God . . . *Ruh Allah.*"

"The Quran says that Jesus was a prophet. But in the Quran it also says Jesus is the word of God. You can't separate the word from the person. So how can we separate them? And so they often say, 'It is just saying that God tells the prophecy through Jesus.' But when I ask them more questions about this point, they start to think. This is what opens the door to understanding. Of course the big work is for the Holy Spirit, not for us. He leads us—every time He leads us.

"Every time when I pray I feel like the Muslim people are so very important to God. I love these people. I hate their religion. I hate the Quran because I believe this is an evil book. But I love these people more than my life, really. I love to see them come to Jesus, take Jesus as their Savior, and start a new life. You saw their lives! They're difficult. They don't like to learn new things. The women feel that whatever their husband does, they should support him. If he steals, kills, or takes another wife, they still need to support him. This is bad, especially for the women in the refugee camps. They are like robots sometimes."

"You weren't Muslim, though?"

"No, I was from a Christian background, but I became a believer only five years ago. Most people from Christian families can take Jesus as their Savior more easily. For Muslims, it's dangerous. They worry, *Maybe my dad will kill me, maybe my mother will kill me, or maybe my relatives will hate me.*

"When you see someone change, it's an amazing feeling. I live here to see the people come to Jesus and give Jesus their lives. Not one or two or an area or a village, but all of my country. In Indonesia, three months ago, three thousand Muslim people were baptized in one day. This is our dream in Lebanon."

"I love your passion," Keith told Nader.

"I know I am with Jesus, and I know He can do everything. By the way, I came to Jesus when I saw Him and He touched me."

His eyes took on a distant but glorious glow as he remembered.

"I studied the Bible for three months with some people, but I didn't believe in Jesus. But after these three months I came to Jesus. I asked Jesus, 'If you are really true, come to me, and show me yourself, and I promise you I'll give you all my life.' I read this sentence in Matthew 7:7, 'Ask, and you will receive.' One thing that bothered me in particular was my cigarette smoking. When I was twelve years, I started to smoke, and by this time I was twenty-five.

"So I asked Jesus, 'If this is true, I ask for you to come to my life. Change my life and help me to stop smoking cigarettes.' And then I slept, and in the morning, Jesus touched me. And then I woke up, and I saw Jesus. Not in a dream. There was a very white light, and I could see only His smile and His lips, and He said, 'I heard your prayer and I changed your life and you will stop the cigarettes.' And from that moment I stopped the cigarettes, which I had smoked for twelve years.

"After this, I lived all my life for Jesus. I started to preach to my family, and thank God my sister is a believer now, and she was baptized two months ago. My father and mother died before I was a believer. My father had a heart attack when I was nine, and my mother had an accident when I was nineteen, five years before I was a believer."

The food arrived.

"Please pray for us," our friend said.

Keith prayed in English, without translation, because everyone could talk at least some English.

"Father God, thank you for being with us this last day of our trip here. Thank you for the team here, their passion, their heart for you, and their love for the refugees. Give them continued strength, courage, endurance"—a vehicle roared past behind our open-air table— "bless their health so that they can continue, and I pray that many souls could be won for you through their work, through their ministry."

We left the Bekaa Valley for the last time, making our way back over the mountains to Beirut.

When we returned to the convent, I said goodbye to George, who would still be in Lebanon for a couple of months. I thanked him for all the things he had taught me about working with refugees.

I knew I should sleep to prepare for our flight back to Amman in the morning. But I could not imagine that I was leaving Lebanon and Beirut. I was sure Jordan could not be as beautiful as this country. I finally slipped out into the hallway and found a screen door leading to an open balcony. In the darkness, I climbed the stairs.

The Mediterranean Sea lay below, as dark as the sky above except for the boats on it. Boat lights and shore lights reflected deep down into the dark water, creating long, straight streamers of shimmering light. The September air was clear and warm and wonderful. A lighted white cross glowed on the hillside, and behind me, like a reflection, the lighted white cross of the convent glowed on its stone tower.

I thought about my life, about God's care and direction, and how blessed I was to be in Beirut and to have heard the stories of the refugees firsthand. I thought about how glad I would be to be able to go back to my own home, and how hard it would be to wonder if you ever could.

CHAPTER 26

Introduction to Jordan

"WELCOME TO JORDAN," JANA SAID to me as we drove away from the Amman airport after collecting our bags. I looked out the window of the taxi. It was still hazy, but I saw brown hills and flat roads. There seemed to be more space here than in Lebanon. But as we drove into Amman, I saw that this city was also built on hills. They were not as steep as Beirut's perhaps, but they still created beautiful scenery.

We had left Beirut early in the morning. The flight was much shorter this time than when I had transited through Amman on the way to Beirut, because the pilot took a different flight path. We landed in Amman before I had time to get sick.

After a taxi ride from the airport, we spent the rest of the day settling in. Keith and Jana showed me their second-floor apartment and helped me carry my things to a lower-floor apartment inside a gated courtyard. I would stay there for the next week. Jana took me to the corner store where I bought a few groceries for the week. She chatted with the owner, practicing her Arabic while he practiced his English. She helped me pick out yogurt, eggs, cereal bars, cheese, bottled water, and snacks. We went to a currency exchange shop, where I stocked up on Jordanian dinars, otherwise known as JDs.

"We will take you downtown for Jordanian *kanafeh,*" Jana promised. "It's different and sweeter. And there are places to shop."

Keith went with us on this venture. We went on foot, street by street, until we came to a hillside dropping in front of us.

"We used to wind around on the streets until we found these stairs," Jana said.

My eyes popped open as I looked at the stairway that dropped below us to a street I could barely see about ten stories below. Going down would be easy, but what about coming back? When we got to the foot of the stairs, we made a couple of turns and found ourselves at the top of a second staircase, as tall as the first. We went down it too. I tried to ignore the inevitable return.

The streets were packed with the approaching holiday. Apparently, Eid Al-Adha was to Muslims what Christmas was to Christians. People bustled around, shopping for gifts, children in tow.

I thought of the family from Aleppo who had hid in the well. Toward the end of our conversation, after telling us about the terror in the well, the father had lamented his inability to buy gifts for his family. *The holiday is coming up, and there are things that I want to buy for my children that they desperately need, but I cannot make a living. So I said, 'Forget about it.' I have no hope to be able to go and buy.*

We sat by the sidewalk, eating our *kanafeh* as people streamed by, many of them with children. The *kanafeh* was quite different from the Lebanese version, and even more calorie-laden, with thick cheese drenched in syrup. We boxed up what we couldn't eat to take back home.

Then we climbed those two flights of stairs. I focused on placing one foot above the other, my breath short before we reached the top of the first flight.

Back at Keith and Jana's apartment, we walked up to the flat rooftop. There below us, the city of Amman lay spread out on the hillside, similar to Beirut. At nighttime it was splendid, the carpet of darkness thick with jeweled lights. The lights of vehicles lit up the roadways below. Points of green light marked the minarets, the towers beside the city mosques. Loudspeakers at the tops of the minarets chanted out the Muslim call to prayer five times a day. We would hear this melancholy invitation much more in Jordan than we had in Lebanon.

Jana said that she counted all the green lights once. She could see twenty or thirty mosques just from her own rooftop. At prayer time, the chants from the different mosques created a plaintive chorus, beautiful and sad.

I had been sure I could never love Amman as much as Beirut, but it appeared that it might be a close tie.

The day after our arrival in Jordan, we met Fadi, our new driver. He worked with an umbrella organization that was providing relief items and support to Jordanian churches that were helping Syrian refugees. For the next few days as we traveled around Jordan, Fadi would take us to visit churches who worked with the refugees. Workers from the churches would then accompany us to visit refugees in their homes.

Fadi introduced us to the interpreter he had found for the day, a pleasant, bearded man in a black shirt and khaki pants. He was familiar with working with refugees and could speak both English and Arabic comfortably. When we got in the van, we discovered that Fadi had packed an insulated box full of snacks and drinks for us. There were Snickers bars, cookies . . . and pretzels!

After a short drive, we arrived at a church and were welcomed by the pastor. In the sanctuary of the church, on dark wooden benches with dusty maroon cushions, church staff members were scattered in a morning meeting. These people met with the refugees daily. The purpose of their morning meeting was to give them the strength to go on. A balding man stood at the front of the sanctuary with an open Bible in his left hand, gesturing with his right hand as he spoke encouragement in Arabic. The striped maroon curtain and dark wooden cross behind him matched the benches, perhaps chosen in a former day when they had time for interior decorating, before the refugee crisis hit and demanded so much energy and time.

"During these meetings, they share what happened during their last visits, and they encourage each other, and then they pray," we were told.

The pastor, a tall man, led us into the privacy of his office. The office had a tile floor, one whole wall of books and photos of workers, gold and white sheer curtains typical of the Middle East, and a heavy brown clock right inside the door.

The pastor seated himself behind his desk and asked the question we had come to anticipate.

"Coffee?"

An assistant hurried away to brew a pot, despite our words that we really didn't need anything. Another church worker sat with us in the office, listening and occasionally adding a comment.

"We have served refugees for eleven years,"[j] the pastor said. "We focus on discipleship, not just relief. Many churches started from this ministry, by God's grace. God showed us how to receive people, love them, share life with them, and share the Gospel with them. Then, even if they do move on, they take the Gospel all over the world.

"When I first decided to help Syrian refugees, I drove all the way to a church on the border and asked if I could help. And one man in the office said to me, 'Did you know there are refugee families that live close to you in Amman?'

"I went to a local organization and got the names of eight hundred refugees. I found more than seventeen families living right around my church here. So I realized this is what God wanted me to do. He wanted me to serve the refugees in my own neighborhood."

The door opened and the assistant returned with coffee. We took a moment to re-arrange with the drinks.

"Would you like coffee with sugar, without sugar?" the pastor asked.

"I'd take it black," I said.

"Sure."

There was a rattle of Arabic, and shifting of chairs and *Shukran* all around. As he poured our coffee, the pastor continued to talk. "I thought I would like to start with the seventeen families, but I didn't know how, because all of them were from different backgrounds. But at this time, I had a meeting for men once a month. More than eighty Christian men prayed in this meeting. But I wanted to invite the Muslims also, and I did. Seventeen of them came one hour early, and this surprised me. The meeting was at 10 a.m., and they came at 9 a.m., all of them.

"It surprised me that the Muslims came, because normally they would not come to a church. But as refugees, they came. And I can't forget their reaction at this meeting. Two of them came to me. One of them, a short man, said to me, 'Today I feel tall. I am fifty years old and a rich man back in Syria. I had three shops, a nice home, cars, everything. In one moment, I had to leave my country, walking, because I had to save my daughters because people

---

j *Before Syrian refugees flocked to Jordan, there was a large wave of refugees from Iraq. Many churches began their refugee outreach efforts by reaching out to Iraqis.*

started kidnapping girls. When I arrived in Jordan, I had a couple hundred dollars. I came to the camp after I came from Syria to Jordan. I walked for three days to arrive at the border of Jordan, and I thought I would find a life there. But when I came to Jordan I found that it was winter at Zaatari Camp, and it was a terrible life.' "

Zaatari Camp was a huge United Nations refugee camp in the northern part of Jordan. It was not far from the Syrian border and housed nearly 100,000 refugees.

The pastor continued. " 'I could not stay there,' the man told me. 'I tried to find any way to get out. I made some money, and they put me in the garbage truck. They promised to cover me with garbage and hide me for the forty-five-minute ride to Amman. When we arrived, we went to all the organizations here in Jordan and they dealt with us like beggars or like animals. But when we came to church, you didn't give us anything, but you smiled. More than twelve people came and greeted me, and this meant a lot to me. I felt, after five months, that I was human again.'

"So this man was one who really encouraged me to start this ministry.

"Another one came to me and said, 'I've been dreaming all my life to step inside a church. When you invited me, I was excited. I could not sleep last night, because I did not have this chance back in my country. When I listened to you, I was surprised, because I understood every word you said.'

"This man was an unbeliever, but he had a network of people to whom he was connected. Day after day, he took me with him to visit the new families. He introduced me to more than two hundred families by himself. And he said, 'Pray, pray,' and if I wanted to cry with him, he said, 'No, this is the time to pray.' He asked me to pray. So this was the second man who helped the ministry to start.

"For more than five months I worked by myself. I kept working as a pastor, but at the same time I visited Syrians. I pray day and night, every day at 10:02 a.m. and 10:02 p.m. to remind myself of Luke chapter ten verse two: *Ask the Lord of the harvest to send workers for his field.* I prayed that prayer twice a day, and God really answered it. Even up until now I set this alarm to remind myself to pray and thank God, because He sent workers from different nationalities all over the world.

"We have three sections—the evangelism team, the discipleship team, and the support team. These are mature people, committed people, who have a heart for the harvest. We have visited more than five thousand families from 2011 until now, and we never work out of the church building. We go to the homes. This is why you see the team here now. From 8:30 to 10:00 during the week they pray together, make evaluations, and get training before they go to the homes sharing the Word of God.

"We have started many home churches. Right now we have maybe fifteen or sixteen. But when you have a successful ministry for the Lord, Satan does not like it, so we have some attacks from Satan from inside the church or outside. The officials investigate my team one by one, especially the ones that focus on Bible study. Some of them are put in prison for a couple of days, even women."

"Why?" I asked.

"Because they work with the majority. They are sharing the Gospel with the Syrian refugees," he said. "Almost all of them are Muslim. We had just eleven Syrian Christian families, and they emigrated after a few months."

I began to understand that here *majority* meant *Muslim*.

"It is difficult for Muslims to come to Christ, of course, but here we apply the strategy from Indonesia. This strategy is never to try to change the Muslim culture. We hold the Bible study in their homes. Each one of them has the connections to start with his network. And we never try to reach a single man or a single woman or young person; we reach all the family. And it doesn't matter if they come Sunday before the Lord or Saturday or Friday. The main issue is that they have discipleship, and they are changed from the inside. The main issue is that they accept that Jesus Christ is Lord.

"We focus on the home, on the network. This is difficult, but we want to make new avenues for them to accept Christ. Just like in the beginning, you remember the struggle between Gentiles and Jews during the time with the disciples. We are in that stage here.

"Other Christians have different ideas about reaching Muslims. They invite them to church, and they think if they come to the church for one year, and they baptize them, everything will be okay. But my experience is, after three years, if they are there alone, they leave and return to their background. I have several examples."

"It sounds like you are busy. Do you find it exhausting, or also rewarding? How would you describe how you feel in doing this?"

"By myself I can never, ever do anything. Delegation to the right people really helps. We started schools for the Iraqis, and later on for the Syrians, and also for Jordanians. God led me to the right people to be responsible for these ministries. And when I started the ministry for Syrian refugees, I gave it to someone who is trained. He knows where to go and how to make a strategy, not just provide relief. Relief is easy. I can find many people to help with relief work. Our focus is spiritual life. I have to find the right people. If I didn't have assistance, I would be exhausted. God helps us and sends the right people. My strategy is to get everyone in his track and to use the spiritual gift God has given him."

I noticed a piece of artwork on the wall that I hadn't seen before. *Pray for America,* it said.

"And you are praying for us also, I see."

The pastor smiled.

"Last year I was in America, and I had several souvenirs that said 'Pray for Jordan.' So I wrapped one as a gift. After dinner I gave it to my friend, an American.

"He said, 'Can I open it?' and I said yes.

"Then he gave me a wrapped gift too.

"We opened the gifts. My gift to him said, 'Pray for Jordan,' and his gift to me said, 'Pray for America.' "

We all laughed.

"For America to say, 'Pray for us,' this is very new," the pastor said as the laughter died down. "But my friend told me that America is struggling. For maybe two hundred years, America prayed for and supported all the Christian workers, and they did a great job. But right now I believe we have one body. We have to pray for each other."

Changing subject, Keith said, "You know all the unrest that's going on in Yemen, Iraq, and Syria. Lebanon has some problems with their government too. What is going to keep Jordan from following in this path? I mean, is Jordan safe? How long can Jordan hold out against ISIS sympathizers?"

"You know, I want to answer this question in a spiritual way," the pastor said. "If you look on the map, you will see the fire around us, and we are a very small country. If you look at the politics, you see that Israel is building a wall between Israel and Jordan. That means they want to protect themselves and be ready for the big war, and they will include Jordan with the war. ISIS is getting bigger and stronger every day.

"You know we pray for the Christians to be strong enough. You know in northern Iraq there are thousands of Christians. If they start to do these things there, the Christians . . . where will they go? It will be a crisis. And you know, if ISIS has control of all of Syria and Iraq, that means it would be easy to take Jordan, because the border is huge between us and Iraq.

"So I look at it spiritually . . . and it gives me comfort. Jordan is a land of peace and also a land for refugees. When you have few resources but you have a big heart, I believe God pays attention to that. We are the fourth poorest country in the world in water, and we still welcome refugees. By now we have 50 or 60 percent refugees in our land. We don't even call the Palestinians refugees anymore; they are Jordanians. And they have all the things Jordanians have. The hospitality is good in Jordan.

"On the other hand, the biggest countries in the Arab world refuse to take refugees. Jordan has taken more than 1.5 million, but they take only a couple hundred. Jordan hosts all of them and opens the gate for all of them. So I believe God pays attention to that. He will keep Jordan a land of peace, a land of refuge. Because if some crisis starts here and we have a lot of refugees . . . where would we go? Israel is closed. Iraq and Syria are fighting. Where would we go? To the Dead Sea? Egypt even closed the border to the refugees, so God have mercy! We are afraid, and it's not easy to deal with that fear. In one day everything could be turned upside down. Lots of people here in Jordan support ISIS, at least in their thinking. But God will have mercy, I believe.

"If I would focus on how ISIS could take over, I would quit working with the refugees. I would prepare myself and my family to leave Jordan. But by the grace of God, we keep going. It's not easy. We have to have hope, that's all," the pastor said. "Our expectation is in God."

"Five minutes, if you have any questions," Fadi said.

Through the walls of the office, we could hear the team singing.

"So what do you think about the future of refugees?" someone asked. "Can they get jobs? Can they work?"

"No. For sure not. Whether Syrians and Iraqis, they catch them and put them in the prison. Two days later they send them back to Syria or outside. Yeah, it happens every day with the people we serve. If they work, they catch them and put them across the border or in the Zaatari camp, or if they are Iraqi they send them back to Iraq."

CHAPTER 27

"They kill them one by one."

Encouraged by the pastor's words, we left to visit a refugee family. A worker from the church went with us. After parking along the street, we walked down a narrow alley with walls on both sides, electric wires swooping overhead, manholes under our feet, and balconies and barred windows stuck into the walls. We entered a house where a good-humored argument arose about who should sit in the chairs. My interpreter and I settled on the floor.

We were instantly offered drinks.

"Coffee, tea?" my interpreter asked.

"Some tea would be great," I agreed to be polite.

The woman of the house looked at me critically as if she was disappointed.

"Tea is considered less honorable," my interpreter informed me with a smile.

The couple had five girls and no boys. The voices of the women and girls rose in the room as multiple people talked at once. This was not a family of quiet women.

The last family we had visited in Lebanon had been from Aleppo. This first family we were visiting in Jordan was from the same town.

"I used to work as a contractor," the man of the house said. "I would take empty land, build a building, and then sell it. This was my father's job, so it's a family business.

"When the war started in 2011, I had open heart surgery following a heart attack. At that time my wife took the initiative and she took me and my daughters to Damascus.

"For a month or so I felt a heavy pain in my chest or my back, and I would walk for fifty meters and then I would have to rest. I was getting really sweaty, and I could not breathe and they poured water on my head to cool me off."

"We didn't know," his wife said. "The symptoms were there, but they were not able to diagnose the problem. For about a month, he used to have attacks, but when they got him to the hospital, they wouldn't know why it was."

"Twice I took the ambulance to the hospital," the man continued, "and both times they did an ECG and nothing showed up. And the third time when they took me by ambulance, they felt that if they delayed treatment, I would die. They gave me shots, you know, that lets the blood be smoother or thinner. The second day they saw where the blockage was."

The man got up and walked to another room. He returned with a sheet of white paper with Arabic writing on it.

"This is . . ." My interpreter picked up the sheet and scanned it. I looked at it also and saw one familiar phrase: LIMA-LAD.

I was pleased with the familiar operative report. "I am so happy to see this. This is how they do it in America also."

"You can understand this?" my interpreter asked.

"This I can," I said, pointing to the one phrase, LIMA-LAD. This meant the surgeon had used the left internal mammary artery, which normally feeds the chest wall, to bypass the left anterior descending artery, a major blood vessel feeding the front of the heart.

"Over in the Arabic it says that they opened the chest and took out the breast artery," the interpreter said. "And they took . . . I can't understand the Arabic words."

"It was an emergency case," the man we were visiting said. "The blockage was 100 percent, and I was living by the grace of God at that point."

"The doctor told me it was a miracle from God that he survived," the man's wife said.

"After the surgery, everything was okay," the man said. "But I wasn't able to move for around seven to eight months; I had to rest. And there was a lot of bombing and shooting around there, so it was very difficult. But now everything is okay."

"I didn't leave him for one second in the hospital," his wife said. "Even when he got home, I wouldn't allow anyone into his room. Our daughters would come to this small window just to talk with him because I wouldn't allow anyone to come inside."

"How long after the heart surgery did you leave Aleppo?" I asked.

"Ten to twelve months," he said.

"Daraa was the town where the people started demonstrating—crazy people," the woman said. "But the town that was damaged the most was our town, Aleppo. Lots of people died there. Two major massacres happened in Aleppo. When they started bombing, the sheikhs in the mosques would tell the people to go to the lower floors of the buildings. They would announce this over the big loudspeakers that are normally used to announce the call to prayer. We used to live in one of the top floors of our building, so when the bombing started, we moved down.

"The violence had no warning. Although they said there were regulations on the war, no one actually followed them. People would be walking on the streets, and there would be a surprise explosion. Or, they did the opposite sometimes. They would send a small shell into an area and wait for people to gather to observe or help the injured. Then, once people were gathered, they would start bombing again to kill as many people as possible.

"Sometimes people were killed while walking on the street. This is what happened to my cousin. Two soldiers were walking and made a bet between each other if one of them could get a head shot. My cousin was even a government official, but he was a Sunni. The bet was on a drink, a kind of tea, nothing even valuable.

"We lived in the basement for some time. We didn't take any of our stuff to the basement because my husband was sick, and I had two babies. The two youngest girls were one year old and two years old during this time. At that point we didn't think about material things, just about how to survive."

Finally, they arranged a safe passage out of Aleppo.

"We didn't think about going back for our things," they said. "We left the house in our pajamas."

"We first moved to the suburbs more in the countryside, but there were threats coming to us and missiles coming above our heads. The people supporting the regime said, 'We will steal, we will kill, we will rape.' So because I had daughters, I had to take them away. We moved to Damascus. We were in Damascus for fifteen days. Then we went to Daraa for a couple of days. Then we went to a refugee camp for ten days, and then we came here.

"It was a coincidence that every step was on a Sunday. We moved out on a Sunday, we went to Damascus on a Sunday, we went to Daraa on a Sunday, and we came to the camp on a Sunday. From the second we moved out of our house in Aleppo until this second, although there was terrorism and fighting, we were protected by God for the whole period. Even when we were going from Damascus to Daraa, there was some conflict between two groups fighting. But when they were two hundred meters from us, everyone disappeared. Even that was easy for us."

"I was raised as being peaceful all the time," the man of the house said. "I don't want to hurt anyone; I don't want anything from anyone. Before the war, this kind of thing never happened. We never knew a difference between Christian and Muslim. It was all started when these events started. We used to have a church and a mosque side by side. Some children, Muslim and Christian, used to be side by side in the nursery, and a Christian woman would nurse a Muslim child. We would even share the same holidays and events.

"It's easy for us now to describe what happened, but there's a saying in Arabic: 'The person who counts the beating, or the whips, does not feel the same as the person who is receiving it.' So now we are telling you things, but you can't understand what we felt. The punishments, the fatalities all the time . . . although we are trying to describe, it does not come close."

"Even in the last few years in Aleppo," his wife chimed in, "the lack of food, the lack of fuel, the lack of electricity, the lack of water. Some young people used to arrange for some packages for the families, and I was forced to go get them myself because I had young girls, and my husband was sick. I could not walk. I had to run because there were snipers waiting to find people."

"Before the crisis, our situation was really good," one of the teenage girls joined in. "When the war started, we were surprised. I was in shock. Before I was happy; our life was nice. I would go to school alone; I would walk by myself. My father used to wake me up. He would go to his work, and I would go to school. We would eat together, and my grandparents would come to us and our life was normal and happy.

"After the crisis, I stopped going to school. At the beginning when I came to Jordan, we were in the refugee camps. It was awful and difficult. My dream was to be a doctor, a pediatrician. Now I want to become an interior designer.

"The Eid is coming," the daughter continued, meaning the holiday. "In Syria, we would have a countdown till when the Eid came. Now we don't want it to come because it's not the same. We used to give gifts, and money was exchanged between the parents and children. It is a huge difference, especially for the children. A lot of things used to be available. Education was available in Syria for everyone, but over here it's more challenging."

"I used to visit my grandparents," a younger daughter remembered. "They used to have a whole room for toys and dolls. They had a computer, and we used to play computer games. They are in Lebanon now, and we really miss them. Every time we talk to them, everyone starts crying because they were a big part of our lives, but now we are separated."

"A computer was something special, but they had one," the mother explained.

"When we first arrived, we didn't think we would be staying," the father said. "That's why we didn't send the girls to school. Thinking we would go back, we didn't buy a refrigerator or a washing machine. We would eat straight from the dish rather than using plates, because we thought there's no need to buy them. We thought it would be a temporary situation.

"But then after one year, we saw that things would go longer. The pastor came to me and he said, 'You're not allowed to stop your family from pursuing an education. No one will help you but yourselves, and you have to go and study.' "

"What made you realize you would be staying for a long period?" the interpreter asked them.

"I will tell you when the girls are gone," the father said. "They are getting ready to go to their tutoring session."

The girl who had been talking continued, "The teachers here treat me in a bad way because I did not complete my homework. They use harsh words. In school they have two different sessions. The first is for the Jordanian students, and the second is for the Syrians. And they have two ways of treatment. I have friends from the first session, and they all tell me that the teachers allow them to do things that we are not allowed to do."

Her father agreed. "If you want to tell something to a student, at least tell it separately, not in front of everyone. The teachers in Syria were respected, but over here it's different." Then he amended his thought by saying, "All of the teachers are good with the exception of two teachers."

"We are giving you the good side and the bad side," the mother said. "Although there are some bad teachers, the girls anticipate Saturdays. They look forward to the tutoring sessions."

"In Syria I learned Arabic and French," the girl said, "but now since the second language of Jordan is English, it's difficult for me to change."

"What kind of supporting courses do you need?" the church worker asked.

"I need English," the daughter said, "because sometimes when the teacher is talking, I do not understand what she's saying. If I had English courses, I would receive less punishment."

As the girls got up to leave, the one stopped to ask the church worker something.

"She asked for a backpack and sports shoes," my interpreter whispered to me. "She is saying, 'Right now we can't go ask our father for things because we are all in the same situation. The only people we can ask for help now are the church workers or someone from the ministry.' "

A young relative had arrived and now spoke up.

"You Christians are doing so much more than the Muslim community is doing for us," he said. "The Christians are coming and supporting us, and the other people are not even asking about us. From the second we came to Jordan, the Christians have been by our side."

Now that the girls had left, the father returned to the question of what they had heard that convinced them they would not be able to go back to Syria for some time.

"The news of terror that we heard. Da'esh, Da'esh,"[k] the father said. "We started to realize there's no way we are going to go back. The terrorists are beasts. The people we know in Syria who convey what's going on, they tell us that things are really bad.

"There are problems with both the terrorists and the regime! There used

---

k   *Another name for ISIS.*

to be three million people in Aleppo, but now they estimate that there are only 500,000," he said sadly.

"All the neighborhoods where there used to be demonstrations, all of these were destroyed and people were kicked out," he went on. "The shops, workshops or whatever, got robbed by the pro-regime people because they took everything, whatever they could get. Between what we heard and what we saw on the TV, we knew we couldn't go back. It's different for us to see something on the TV than it is for you to see it on the TV, because when you see it, you don't know what it used to look like. When I look, I know these neighborhoods. I understand the context of what happened."

"Thankfully, my parents are here, and his parents are in Lebanon. We stopped caring about the wider community. I only care about my parents and his parents. That's it," the man's wife said.

"Are they still manufacturing things and making food in Syria?" I asked, remembering the man who hid his children in the well, the one who told about the looting of factories and homes.

"Only in the areas where they are supporting the government regime."

"I know that I can't understand what you went through, but I want to write a book that will help the people in America understand a little bit of what you went through."

"In general," the man said, "Syria is going through a war, and this war destroys the poor and the common people. But the Middle Eastern people are some of the kindest people in the world."

Well-filled with caffeine and sugar, none of us argued.

CHAPTER 28

"Take off your shoes before stepping on Aleppo."

THE NEXT FAMILY WE VISITED was related to the family from Aleppo that we had just visited. Instead of having five girls, however, this family had five boys. We entered a room with a battered brown entertainment center and mats and pillows on the floor. We seated ourselves on the floor. The husband and wife seated themselves, the wife close to a white door leading to the kitchen and the husband and five boys in a row in front of the piece of furniture. We found out that the two-year-old boys were twins. The other three boys were older, the oldest probably ten or twelve.

"I was working at a poultry shop, selling chickens," the man said, as a twin wailed. "A supplier would supply us with the chickens on a daily basis. We were in the middle of the souk, the middle of the market."

The man's wife disappeared to the kitchen to bring us tea.

"The war was sudden. Suddenly there was no safety or security where we were living. The pro-regime military forces were in the next neighborhood, and we heard they were coming into our neighborhood. Everyone fled. We went to Damascus, and we stayed there for six months. In our last few days there, we lost all sense of safety and security. The pro-regime forces would come into our houses at night. We couldn't sleep because at any time someone might open the door."

"Whoever they saw, they would arrest," his wife said, "if it was a good person or a bad person, good-looking, bad-looking, they would just take whoever."

"I was going to my work on a normal day—what appeared to be a normal day—and we got to the security checkpoint. We stopped, and they opened fire toward us. My son wasn't with me that day. I was not hit, but I did not give them any reason to do that. One time I went out to buy some groceries, and when I came back I found out that the military had closed my neighborhood. I stayed on the street. It was 1 a.m. before I was able to get inside.

"The main reason we left were the massacres in the neighborhood next to us. We heard that many people were killed. We heard the bombing and saw the fighter planes going over our heads. That's why we were afraid. My wife and the woman you just visited who has five daughters are sisters. We went to their house and stayed there for three days. Even there, we could hear the shooting. We were not able to go out of the house to work or anything.

"Before they would start bombing in a certain area, they would close all the exits and all the entrances. So they would not allow anyone to go in or to get out before they started the bombing. That's how the pro-regime forces operate.

"Snipers would sit in the tops of the tall buildings. When we did go out at certain times, we moved quickly. My wife's cousin was killed by a sniper. He was in his pickup, hauling produce. And my uncle, a taxi driver, was taken out by a sniper when he was working in his taxi."

The man's wife had returned with drinks for all of us, which she passed around the room.

"Some people took a picture of our house. It was all burned down and destroyed," the husband said. "And we deleted the picture because we couldn't stand looking at it."

"My heart was burned to see it," his wife said. "His parents and most of his family are still in Syria. My family is scattered all over. Some of them are in Jordan, some in Lebanon, and some in Europe."

She handed me a phone with music and pictures playing of her cousin's funeral.

"Is that Aleppo?" I asked, looking at the screen of the phone. "Let me see."

I looked more closely at the screen. Arabic words were written across the picture.

"Take off your shoes before stepping on Aleppo because the soil of Aleppo is from the ashes of its youth," my interpreter read for me as mournful

"Take off your shoes before stepping on Aleppo."

Arabic music played. "Aleppo is one of the most beautiful places in Syria, but it has also been one of the most destroyed."

"What was life like before the war?" I asked the lady of the house. She was dressed in black from head to toe. She held one of the twins on her lap and seemed happy to talk with us.

"There are so many differences between here and back home. I used to wake up and clean the house and care for the children. It was safe for us, we could go walk, do whatever we want. There were lots of neighbors and relatives.

"Our twins were born here in Jordan. We say they are 'made in Jordan,' and if we go back, we will leave them here," she said with a weary but loving expression and a twinkle in her eye. "At the beginning we thought they would be a girl and a boy, but then we found out it was two boys. Taking care of twins is difficult. It's agony. They cry together, they eat together, they sleep together, and when they get sick, they get sick together."

"We want to go back to Syria," the father said. "But as long as President al-Assad is the leader of Syria, we would go to any other place in the world. It would be better than going back to Syria where he is. Our only dream is to live a happy and safe life. That's it."

The boys had sat quietly listening. When we asked them questions, they answered, telling us about football and swimming.

"In Syria on Fridays we always would go on outings for things like picnics, but here we don't have these options," the father said. "To be honest, I don't think we have a future in Jordan. I can't work. If I start working and they catch me, they will immediately send me to Syria. If I stay in Jordan, I will always be a refugee. I knew two or three men who tried to work, and they immediately sent them to Syria. If they catch you working, they will give you a twenty-four-hour warning and say bring your stuff, bring your family, and you will be sent back to Syria. Even the UNHCR told me they couldn't protect me if I work."

The church worker was sitting on the couch, the lace window curtains blowing around his head. The family turned their attention to him.

"He is always taking care of us," they said. "The church visits us, they call us, they check on us—we are family now. He is part of our family. From the second we came to Jordan, he took care of all of our needs. Even for the children, the church used to make breakfast for them, and take them to church and give them gifts. When we go back to Syria, we want to take this man with us."

"I would like to go to Syria sometime," I said, "but they say it's not safe."

"Don't think of it," the woman said. "They will think you are a terrorist."

CHAPTER 29

"Even the wiring was taken out."

NEXT WE VISITED A YOUNG couple from Aleppo. They had two children, a boy and a girl. The boy, black-haired and black-eyed, was brandishing a gold sword when we arrived. His older sister wore an American-looking blue top and had two thick black ponytails that fell around her shoulders.

The man of the house was clearly in charge, although he was a small bearded man, dressed in a white robe. His wife was dressed in black, with only her face showing. He insisted that we sit on the furniture, and he picked up a square plastic stool, most likely a child's chair, and sat cross-legged on it, facing all of us. In front of him was a square brown table, and behind his head a single light bulb dangled. He passed us glasses of cold water.

He explained that he had worked in a chicken shop before the war, deboning chickens. "We used to make shawarma," he said.

"I was happy. I was living in the city center. My work was not very far from my house. I had a hybrid bicycle. It had a small electrical motor, and I would pedal and use the motor for support as well."

He was a charismatic man, gesturing with his hands as he described the bicycle. His way of saying things in Arabic must have been funny as well, because from time to time, those who understood Arabic would burst out laughing.

"I had a full house with a full bedroom, a decent living room, a kitchen," his wife said. "One month before we left, we bought a new washing machine. We couldn't turn it on during the day because the electricity would be turned off, but at night we would turn it on and sit next to it and look at it."

Behind them, the plain white plaster walls showed the simplicity of the house they lived in now. A lace curtain and a plaid blanket had been hung. Yellow French doors with glass windows led into the kitchen. Beside those doors, a laundry drying rack was hanging full of clothes. A pink towel was hanging over the top of a door that I concluded might lead to a bedroom.

"I'm not good with dates because I even usually mistake my birthday," the husband said. "But we lived in our house in Syria for two years. That was our first house, and everything we accumulated those two years was in it. Both of my children were born there."

"How did the two of you meet each other?"

The woman laughed, embarrassed, while her husband answered.

"We lived in the same neighborhood. I wanted to get married, but I was in the military. I would call my mother and say, 'Did you find anyone for me?' Every time my mother would recommend a girl, there would be something about her I didn't like. Either she would be too tall, or too short, or something would be wrong. But then I saw *her* while I was riding my bicycle."

Everyone laughed.

"I was taking a break from my work and while I was riding my bicycle, I saw her at the back of her house. So I went to my parents and I said, 'I saw a girl over there.' I was crazy at that point; I just wanted to marry her. We usually arrange for a meeting, kind of a first date. The young man will spend some time with the girl. If he likes her, he will leave money or a gift. The second I saw her, I was putting my gift down immediately."

"Our wedding was the best day of my life," the husband said. "I didn't spare any expenses. We did the best things possible. We have two separate parties, one for the women and one for the men. I rented the best place for the women and a mansion for the men. My father knew the people who owned the mansion, so the owner told him, 'We want you to make the wedding at our place.'"

The ring of a cell phone broke the conversation, and the topic turned from joy to pain.

"The main reason we had to leave Syria was because of the arrests. They started invading houses and arresting people. They didn't need a reason to arrest people. The raids would mainly happen at dawn. The government army would stop all communication so no one could warn their friends about the raid. Land lines and cell phones were all cut off. You would wake up in the morning and see that your phone was not working, and you would know something awful was about to happen.

"This happened all the time. We were terrified because we knew that at any point someone would invade. But we never knew if it was going to be our house or our neighbor's house. Three or four times our house was invaded while I was gone, and only my wife was there. They weren't looking for any certain person.

"Usually when they searched homes, they would come in and ask the wife or mother, 'Do you have any men inside?' Regardless of how the woman would answer, they would search the house. If they saw something they liked during the search, they would just take it."

"It was terrifying," the young wife said. "They would suddenly come inside. The first time I had one of my relatives come and sit with me until they finished searching the house. After that I would stay alone, but it was terrifying every time. The soldiers would come inside, often about four of them, all heavily armed. Usually a huge number of soldiers would be in the neighborhood, but they would divide themselves among the houses."

"If they found someone they wanted," her husband added, "they would often arrest that person. The person would disappear and no one would know where they had gone. Or they would take the young people and ask them to stand in a line with their faces toward the wall, and they would start hitting them in the street. The main purpose was to humiliate them in front of everyone in the neighborhood. If anyone was caught looking out of the window during this raid, they would be punished as well. So you had to stay in your house until they left."

The man explained that the main reason for these raids was to search for men who had been involved in the anti-government demonstrations. But during the raids, the soldiers would arrest others as well. If they came to a house and they didn't like the way the person was talking to them or looking at them, they might arrest him. If they saw something valuable they wanted and the owner tried to keep them from taking it, they would arrest him. There was always a feeling of dread that at any point a man would be taken away.

"We lived in a high apartment building at the end of the neighborhood next to the checkpoint, so there were many raids. There was one particular case that I remember, although I wasn't at home then. They were shooting so much that bullets started coming inside the house. My wife and six other women and the children were inside the house, and they all gathered in the bathroom until it stopped. There were no windows in the bathroom so it was safer. They hid in the bathroom with the children for an hour. There was no time to explain anything to the children. They just opened fire, and we didn't know why.

"Another time, I was home when the raid happened. We were living in the third floor of our building. The armed soldiers went through the first floor and then through the second floor. I was terrified. I gathered my family. I was thinking this would be the last time I would see them. But suddenly the soldiers just turned back, and they didn't continue.

"We finally left Aleppo when we received news that the pro-regime forces were moving ahead. Around us, massacres were happening, people were being killed. All through the night, even sometimes in the daytime, we would hear bombing and shooting. So we were really afraid that it would come to us. For a time, I sent my wife and children away to a safe place, but I was always afraid for their safety. Finally, I got them and then we moved to Damascus and then came here to Jordan.

"I didn't think it would last for a long period of time. When we left, we took only enough clothes for two days. For our daughter we took only two outfits. We thought we would come back. When we left, the front of the house was damaged because of the incident when they opened fire. Since then we have heard that one of the side walls fell on another house, but other than that, we don't know. I'm sure everything was destroyed. One of my relatives went back to see his house, and even the wiring inside his house was taken out, and the doors were taken out. I am almost sure that everything is gone.

"If God wills, we will go back to Syria, but most probably it will never happen. If they gave me the option whether to go to the States or to Syria, it's a difficult question, but I think I am leaning toward the States. Lots of people I knew went to the States. They are living a decent life there, and they are able to work. I could have a better future for my children.

"Here, I'm not receiving aid from the UNHCR, and I'm not able to work. I wish they would either provide us with funds, allow us to work, or send us somewhere else. My daughter is supposed to be in first grade, but I cannot get proper documentation. When I go to the refugee camp for documents, they tell me to go to the police station. When I go to the police station, they say, 'It's your problem, manage it yourself!' I told them, 'I will give you whatever you want. I will go all over Jordan. Tell me what you want.' When I go to the Syrian embassy here for documents, they say, 'Go to Syria and get them.' So they will not give me documents, but they are asking me to bring documentation. It's so frustrating.

"I miss my neighborhood, my community," he said. "I miss the sea . . . in four years I haven't been to the sea."

"I miss my house the most," his wife said. "I miss not only the washing machine, but everything!"

"Hopefully when we get to the States it will be better than that," the man said. "My wife's uncle is going to the States today. Some other relatives have been there for the last three weeks. They rejected some people and accepted some. If I get rejected from the States, I would not stay in Jordan. I would do whatever I could. I would go through the sea to Europe; I would do whatever, but over here I can't work.

"Besides, yesterday I had a fight with the landlord, because we had agreed on 120 JDs, including utilities. Now she told me that, starting in October, we will also have to pay for utilities. Look at the house! It's a very bad house! They are asking for more money, and we don't have any resources. Our situation is really bad. I don't want anything from anyone. I just want someone to let me work!"

VOICES

OF JORDAN

CHAPTER 30

"It's His work, not ours."

AT THE NEXT CHURCH THAT we visited, a man welcomed us into a basement office. On the wall, photos printed on canvas were labeled with Arabic phrases. The man said he had designed them himself and had them printed as a reminder. One print with masses of people boarding a train was labeled with the Great Commission in Arabic: "Go ye into all the world and preach the Gospel."

It was wonderfully cool in the basement office. Our host invited us to sit on couches and watch a presentation his group had put together about their work with refugees.

A song accompanied the presentation. "Let it be Jesus, the first name that I call," rang out the words.

"We have a burden to reach Jordan for Christ," the man on the presentation spoke. "And our statement for ministry is that everyone in Jordan has the right to hear the Gospel at least one time. So we started to go to reach them for Christ. We started church planting and home groups. And with these home groups we teach the people how important it is to share with others. So God gave us the vision to multiply new churches through sharing the Gospel and training people and sending them to the world.

"When the Syrian crisis started, we did not think it would last long. No one knew how long it would last. That's why we started seriously thinking what we could do for these people financially and spiritually. We attended training seminars to learn how to deal with psychological issues and how to help those people who are suffering from the trauma of war."

"I want to especially thank a women's team," a voice continued in imperfect English, "who came many times to Jordan just to wash the feet of the Syrian women, who came from a long distance, walking from the borders of Jordan. When they came here and found these people loving them and willing to wash their feet, their hearts opened more to receive Christ.

"I want to thank our partners from America who are helping us to reach these people, the Syrian refugees.

"We are thankful for God and what he's doing for our ministry, and we are so excited because we are seeing the hand of God working in these people. We are following up with people individually, and home groups have been started with Syrian refugees. We baptized many of them, and many are waiting to be baptized also."

"For me to live is Christ," the music went on, as photos flashed across the screen.

"This is briefly what our ministry is about," our host said when the presentation ended. "We believe we have been called from God to reach the Muslim people. All of the people you saw are Muslims. None of them are from Christian background. So thank God, He gives us fruit, and the fruit encourages us to continue. We are blessed people because of what God is doing among us. And we know there is still more and more work. Nobody knows exactly how long this will last, but as long as this door is open, we will use it.

"Our ministry started with sixty Syrian families. Now there are over two thousand families."

"How many?" I asked, thinking maybe I had heard wrong.

"Two thousand," he said.

"So we reach out to many, but still there are many more," he continued. "So we try to work more with them. We try to hire more people, not as workers, but as people who are called from God to work for Him full-time or to be a volunteer part time, because the field is so big. We have eight people now working on our team. We go daily to visit people at their homes. We have at least two or three visits every day for each person who is visiting. So we try to always keep in touch with them and serve them. God is doing something with this door."

"The two thousand on your list," Jana asked, "are those on-going? Do you visit them every month, every two months?"

"Our strategy is we give a chance to each family. We are not a relief ministry. We do relief. But our ministry is sharing the Gospel. We use the stuff God puts in our hand to reach them. Our strategy is to give every family three to five visits, so that means a maximum of five months for each family because we go there once a month. And during those visits we share the Gospel with them. After that if they are not open to hear the Gospel or the message, we have to stop with them and start with another family. Because I can't spend two years or three years with one family just to give them food; there are a lot of people. We are so comfortable with this strategy because it gives us more opportunity to meet more people to reach them. We continue helping the people who come to Christ. We continue to help the believers because they are now brothers and sisters."

"I like that goal that everyone in Jordan should get to hear the Gospel at least once," I said.

"Of course, of course. We do our best, and we depend on the Holy Spirit, because it's not easy to be with the refugees every day. It's affected us mentally, emotionally, and physically. Yet we believe the Holy Spirit gives us the strength to continue with them because we believe it is our call to be with them. We don't know who is coming next . . . Iraqis, Palestinians, Lebanese? But as we did with the Iraqi refugees in 2004, we do the same with the Syrians. They were in need, of course, but it was a little bit easier, because most of them were already from Christian backgrounds, so it wasn't hard to convince them that Jesus is the Savior. But in either case, we believe that Jordan is one of the shelter areas, as the Bible says. As a Christian, I believe this is why God put us in Jordan, because we have many things to do. The harvest is great, so we have to use any door God opens."

"God bless your ministry and continue to give you strength," Jana said.

"You know, even though it is emotionally draining, we thank God actually that we are still human beings and can connect with people when they tell us their stories. Some stories are repetitive: we were living in Syria, they started shooting, we ran, we crossed the border, we walked through the desert for two days, and then we arrived here.

"But sometimes we are faced with a story that breaks our hearts, and we can't even sleep that night. We need you to support us with prayer because we are on the front lines all the time, under pressure all the time. Sometimes we take all these bad stories home with us. If we feel angry, or sad, or depressed at home, sometimes it's because of what we hear all day long, and it affects us. We need prayer to keep us safe and healthy so we can continue working in this ministry.

"But we believe that God is more powerful than any spirit around us, and He can protect us all the time. That's why we depend on Him. That's why we believe in praying."

"How did God call you to this work?" I asked.

"Actually, my friend asked me to help with a ministry outside of my hometown. He asked me if I would like to be a volunteer, and I agreed. I went with them for two weeks. I saw the needs, but I started thinking, *Why am I doing this away from home, when we have these needs in our own neighborhood?* I started thinking and praying, and God led me to the first Syrian family. So I felt the approval from God to start this ministry. I came to the pastor, and I shared my vision of having home groups among the Syrian refugees. Because he is a godly man and he believes in working among the Muslims, he encouraged me to start.

"We started to think how to extend our team, to have a team working with us. We started with one lady, and then another, and now we have eight people working. My wife is working with children. We try to cover all the needs: children, women, and men.

"Telling men and women about Christ requires different approaches. With women, actually it's very sad. They are so brokenhearted. They are so desperate. Many of them live without hope, without future. They don't know anything about refuge. They just wake up and sleep, the same routine every day for them. They don't have any hope in life."

As he talked, the Muslim call to prayer belted out over the city.

"So this is an open door for the ladies on our team to reach them with the hope from the Bible. They share the story. We had training about how to take stories from the Bible. You know there are many, many stories we can share about Jesus, and how He deals with many situations. And it's wonderful among the women. You can share whatever you like, whatever they need.

"Sometimes we share on the first visit. Sometimes we wait for another visit to share. We try to build their trust in the Christian church, the honesty of the church people. If we promise something, we should do it. These are small things, but they make a difference with them because they can tell who's honest and who's not honest.

"Usually the men are different. Even if they are not educated about Islam, they will start arguing with us. They will say, no, in Islam we don't have this, Mohammed said this, Mohammed didn't say that. We try to give them the reason why Jesus is completely different from any other.

"Last month I met a man for the first time. From the first visit, his face was angry. He was so angry I thought maybe he was a fanatic Muslim. I was a little bit afraid, and I didn't know if he was willing to hear. But on the first visit, I shared with him, simply, how I came to Christ, how I believe in Jesus, and how He changed my life. I told him how in the Bible, Jesus changed the life of everyone He met. And I asked him if he would like to accept Jesus. It was that simple! And he said, 'Yes.' So sometimes you need to spend hours talking, and sometimes it's a simple word. So we believe it is not our job. It is His job!

"I'm not saying everyone we share with accepts Jesus. It doesn't work like that. It is God's work, not ours. But we should put the seeds, and He will continue. It's His work, not ours. Our job is to obey Him and go and reach them. The fruit is His. It's not our job!"

CHAPTER 31

"They want to write a check and then forget."

ON OUR WAY HOME IN the darkness, our interpreter shared some of his thoughts on the refugee crisis.

"I've been heavily involved for the last two years," he said, "and that's about half as long as the war has been going.

"What I see is that everyone is trying to help the refugees survive but not a lot more. Even though they provide them with very little, the organizations, the countries, they are trying to help them survive. But unfortunately they're not giving them the opportunity to work or to make their own living.

"This is causing a serious shift in the structure of the households, the way that they operate and think. Now they plan how they can get more support instead of thinking how to work more, because they aren't allowed to work. This is creating two problems. First, it's creating the idea among the refugees that they're not supporters, but that they need to be supported. It enforces their need to be dependent. Second, no one is working and helping them thrive or get trained. No one is thinking about how to equip them to go back to rebuild Syria! Now Syria is destroyed, but things naturally get resolved after a time, and no one is equipping them to go back and start again! What will happen is they will have a country full of people waiting to be served, to be helped, to be aided by other countries!

"I think this same amount of money that is being used for aid could be used to help them with vocational training, education, and better equipping them to go back and build their country. They need to have the opportunity to work for what they earn. Even if you want to give them handouts, make them work! Help them feel like they are productive."

"And it sounds like a lot of the refugees want to do that!" I said. "That's what I'm hearing."

"Yes. Most of them want to do that," my interpreter agreed. "But you know when your hand or your leg is broken and you don't use it for a long period of time, it gets weak, and you need to go through rehab. It's the same way. They got broken, but now they are letting their muscles die. No one is thinking of five years from now. Right now they're on a track where every day is worse than the day before. There's no light at the end of the tunnel. There's a train that will hit them at some period of time, because there's no planning. No one is thinking about the big picture. There's this relief and response, but no one is thinking of how to help them survive and thrive in the coming period of time."

"But initially, that response of giving them things is what's needed, right?" I asked.

"Yes, at the beginning. But we have to help them to sustain themselves. We're not talking about adults, because adults will die soon. We're talking about the children.

"For example, at the first house we visited today, the girl asked the church worker for a backpack. So the children are getting the idea, *Ask! Ask for help from these people.* She doesn't have the idea, *I can earn it,* or *I can ask for it from my father who works.* This idea is getting reinforced in their heads. And I think this means they are going to go into much deeper struggles and challenges in the coming period.

"I know that this is more of a capitalistic point of view," he went on, "but instead of opening a refugee camp, the government could open an industrial city in one of the empty areas of Jordan and choose two or three light industries. You could provide the refugees with accommodation and provide them with food, and use the products that they are making to sell somewhere. It would be almost free labor, but you would also be creating a productive society that could easily merge into Jordanian society. Then they would not be considered a liability; they would be considered productive members of the community. They would help Jordanian communities instead of becoming a burden that we have to carry.

"They want to write a check and then forget."

"This is the problem," he continued. "People and companies don't care. They want to write a check and then forget what's happening. They want someone else to deal with it so they can forget about the whole thing but still say *Our Business Cares*, or whatever slogan they have. But no one cares about what happens on a country level, on a higher level, what will happen in the big picture. We were talking about at least four million refugees. You have *four million* people who came from a country where most of it has been destroyed. Damascus is said to be the oldest capital in the world! You are talking about a country that needed all this time to be built, and now it's down to the ground. And you will be sending back people that will be always looking out for handouts to rebuild their country. It will not happen! It will just be a bigger refugee camp."

CHAPTER 32

"It's a way to ignore Jesus' blood."

I TOOK A WASHCLOTH AND wiped the dust from the glass top of the kitchen table in my furnished apartment in Amman. The dust storm had affected everything, left its mark everywhere—much like the refugees. It didn't matter whether you tried to avoid them or not. There were ways to insulate yourself, to ignore them, to write a check and forget about them . . . but they were still there.

I spooned a little instant coffee into my mug and heated water. We had taken a quiet day on Sunday, sleeping in, having a meal together in Keith and Jana's apartment, and going to church in the evening.

But this morning was a new day. Fadi picked us up along the street. He had refilled our zippered "refrigerator" with glass bottles of apple soda, plastic water bottles, and chocolate and salty snacks in a separate zippered compartment.

We drove out of Amman, past a dusty KFC with both American and Arabic letters on its front, past a stadium that dated back to the Roman Empire, past green road signs with only Arabic lettering, past dusty hills of dirt. We drove by a truck with tarp over its bed for a roof. Two people were sitting in the bed, one on a plastic lawn chair.

We picked up our interpreter at a nearby school she and her husband had founded. The school now had more than four hundred students. A group of children chased each other through the playground and around picnic tables on a tile courtyard. A paper airplane spun through the air from the lunch area as our interpreter slipped through the gate and into our van.

"It's a way to ignore Jesus' blood."

The interpreter's name was Reema. She was a professional who had not only worked as a journalist at one time, but had also interpreted for such publications as the *Los Angeles Times.*

We headed north toward Syria on a sleek black highway that lay in a line between the brown hills. I saw sheep being unpacked from multilevel trucks. The shepherds would prod them forward and get them to jump down from the top level of the truck to the ground, a seven- or eight-foot drop. Pens of sheep lined the road in preparation for the upcoming Muslim holiday, the Eid, when each family would butcher and share a sheep.

"In a few days there will be a smell," the interpreter told us, "while they slaughter all those sheep."

Fadi explained to us that people were supposed to slaughter sheep only in certain places, not just anywhere in the city.

We also mourned the holiday's implications. Jesus, the Lamb of God, had taken away the sins of the world and relieved us of the need to sacrifice lambs. I remembered in the first tent we visited in Lebanon, I had been shocked by the boldness of our Christian guide. He had deliberately addressed the subject of the Lamb. *This is what I believe, that Jesus came for all people. He didn't come to certain people. He came for the Christians, the Muslims, the Druze, Jews, for everyone. The Jews didn't accept Him. They crucified Him. But whoever accepts Jesus and what Jesus did, he's the one who will be saved, because Jesus died to save everyone. As God prepared a lamb to die on behalf of Abraham's son, Jesus was the Lamb who died for all of us.*

"Eid Al-Adha," Fadi said, "It's a way to ignore Jesus' blood. That's why Christians often spent the day fasting and praying for the salvation of the Muslim people."

The Muslim holiday had also canceled one of our meetings for the week. The group in charge of an evening meeting had concluded that no one would come because of preparations for the festivities.

When we neared the Syrian border, Fadi turned to me and pointed to the right.

"Katrina, do you see those tents? This is Zaatari Camp."

Far away in the terrain of brown dust, broken white and red rocks, and clumps of dust-covered green weeds, a vast white camp of square tent tops pooled in the desert. It was the huge United Nations refugee camp. We were not planning to visit there because it required special government permission.

Instead we turned into town right after a blue road sign that said "Syrian Border" with an arrow. We were only a few miles away from the line.

CHAPTER 33

"I like to be downstairs and sit with people."

WE DROVE TO A CHURCH in town, a few buildings down from a chicken shop.

Syrian refugees were already congregated, this early in the morning, in the tiled church sanctuary with brown benches. There was a lot of black clothing, although only one of the women wore the *niqab*, the full face veil that only allowed a slit for her eyes.

The pastor welcomed us into his office. It was a new office, as the building was under construction, but he had requested that the pillars from the old church porch be integrated into the new building. So, in his office close to the door, two of the pillars stood in the way. He liked them.

"It's history," he said. "I have been in the church thirty-five years. We still have the church here. It was built in 1961."

In his office, the pastor told us that he and his church had a vision, before the refugee crisis, to turn their building into an outreach of some kind. He powered up a slide show to talk about their organization, flipping through the screens as he talked.

"Of course the Syrian war began as peaceful demonstrations, but it became chaotic. Demonstrations in Syria started in March-April of 2011. It was in the summer of 2011 that Syrian refugees began to arrive in our town. In August of that year, we met forty families. Now, there are 70,000–100,000 Syrian refugees in the city. Just in the city. There are thousands more in the villages around us and maybe 90,000 at Zaatari Camp."

As he talked, someone knocked on the door, asking to take orders for drinks. Although this had become routine, taking orders on a piece of paper was a new touch. I asked for something cold since the day was warm.

The pastor pointed to a map and then traced the wider border of the country of Jordan.

"It looks like a gun," he teased, "so be careful! When the British divided the area, they put their gun on the map and they said, 'This is Jordan.' "

We laughed appreciatively. I had thought that the outline of Jordan looked like a hatchet stuck in Saudi Arabia. But I could see his point about the gun.

"At the beginning of the refugee crisis, we focused on food packages, which we're still doing. We provided mattresses, blankets, pillows, gas heaters, and gas coupons for the basic needs of life. There are a lot of other needs we cannot cover. We still give food packages to three or four hundred families every month. The UNHCR cut most aid and the refugees are coming to us, but we cannot help everyone. We get thousands of people every month asking for food packages. If we wanted to help all of them, we would need a huge supply of money and volunteers.

"We are able to provide some people with food packages, clothes, eye glasses, and even speech therapy every month. We recently started a medical ministry which operates through home visits. We have a Jordanian medical doctor using his license, and we are organizing the team now. This is a huge need because the refugees are not covered medically. There are some hospitals and a big clinic, but they cannot cover everything. We would like to increase the medical ministry, but it's a huge thing. UNHCR is not able to take care of medical needs."

Our drinks arrived, and we sipped them gratefully.

"We started with a pickup truck, going to people's houses with mattresses piled high. Now we have warehouses and two trucks for distribution. But we still use the same method, driving from house to house. We don't ask them to come and carry the things to their houses. We like to get into their houses. We started with three people, but now we have eighteen. We have people from our church, people from Amman, and short-term volunteers coming all through the year. You can see the calendar here."

"Oh, wow!" we exclaimed, looking at a minutely complex wall calendar written full of tiny words and names and color codes.

"I like to be downstairs and sit with people."

"We have helped more than 5,000 families house to house, which is about 30,000 people. We continue to visit 300–400 families every month," he told us.

"It's important that our ministry was started by the local church and is still coordinated by the local church. This is important in several ways. For one, it is not an outside program that will stop in time. We live here. Also, we are not under investigation from the government, because we are a church."

Loud singing came through the walls from outside, along with knocking noises. The pastor seemed to be used to it and kept talking.

"At the beginning we had small donations, but now in 2015, our budget is $400,000. Most of the sponsors are Christians. Some of them are one-time and some of them continue. Once we had a donation from the Hungarian government, and once from the Czech Republic. And the minister of the Czech Republic came here and had breakfast on the roof with us. And a government official came from Hungary and signed the paper personally.

"One organization helped us buy a school building. We had a small school here at the church for two years. We had spent one year searching for a school building, and God gave it to us in one minute. I was driving down the road and God shifted my route and took me to the building. It was marked with a 'For Sale' sign. That was in January of this year. It was designed as a school, not as a house. We never expected to find a building that was actually designed to be a school! It is a building with two floors. We want to make a playground and a soccer field in the back. With the new building, we increased the capacity to ninety-one students.

"How much time do we have?" he asked Fadi, who had become the keeper of the clock, a difficult job in the hospitable Arab schedule.

"Fifteen minutes," said Fadi with a smile. "Fourteen."

"This ministry work is very taxing," the pastor said. "We emphasize vision, openness, and patience in this work.

"We had a vision, a church vision. It cannot be a one-man show. The vision for our building had been in place long before the refugees came. For twelve years we were planning, studying. We had the design and the blueprints since 2010. So God was preparing us. We were very involved in reaching out and helping people before the Syrian refugees came. Because God had put this in our hearts for a number of years, when thirty refugee families arrived, we were already prepared with vision and ideas. Quickly, the numbers swelled from dozens to thousands. We were faced with a crisis too big to help everyone. It's a moment in time. It does not happen every day. Jordan is a unique place, and this is a big chance to reach many people. Churches should rise up now.

"Next we emphasize openness. When you do physical relief, you can partner with anyone all over the world. When you do evangelism, you can partner with Christians all over the world. We do both: physical relief and spiritual relief. We do home visits, Bible studies, and Sunday schools. We have many volunteers who help us.

"And third, patience! Sometimes people come here and sit and drink coffee and tell us their needs. Even when we tell them, 'Sorry, we cannot help,' they feel helped because somebody listened to them. Many other organizations don't do relationships. We see people, not numbers. We know them personally, by name. We know where they live and how many children they have."

"One minute," said Fadi, then softened. "Five minutes."

The pastor finished his presentation, and we stepped out of his office for a tour of the addition to the church, which was still under construction. In the hallway, the pastor was immediately accosted by an aging lady in a red and yellow hijab. Even though he was busy, she demanded his attention, saying she was angry at him and that's why she hadn't come to church.

"Were you angry at me or angry at God?" he asked her pleasantly.

"At you," she said instantly.

"Well, then, if you are not angry at God, you should come to church," he pointed out, as he told her to wait a bit until he came back.

The pastor took us around and showed us the dynamic structure. There was a new sanctuary in process, a guesthouse for the many volunteers, a room for the medical team's director, and classrooms for the refugees to learn skills. He showed us where the old school had been before God provided the new building.

"This is the new sanctuary. I wanted one of these side rooms to be my office," the pastor confided. "Sometimes I need to be alone. But now there's a need for these rooms to be used for other things. And I like to be downstairs and sit with people."

"I like to be downstairs and sit with people."

Would I be able to sacrifice having a private room if I were him? I wondered to myself.

We tramped up cement stairs. He showed us kitchenettes and bathrooms and the community center. Four or five ladies gathered in the sewing room, making purses. A sewing machine hummed.

"These are from used clothes. Recycled," The pastor said, pointing to some of the projects.

There was a rattle of Arabic, and people laughing. On the wall, pretty aprons and children's clothes that had been made by the ladies were on display. A woman pulled a thread through a crocheted purse, securing a floral pattern to it.

He took us finally to the top floor, still covered with construction tools and dust, and showed us the view.

"There will be a guesthouse on the roof," he said.

"Can you see Syria from here?" I asked. I knew we were close enough that windows were occasionally rattled by explosions in the fighting zone.

"The Syrian mountains," he said. "But now I think it's not clear enough."

Off to the right, part of the refugee camp was visible.

"So where would Syria be?" I asked.

"Syria is there," he said, pointing off to the left of Zaatari Camp. "You see cars there, going close to Syria," he said.

We made the descent down a number of flights of steps.

The lady in the red and yellow hijab was still in the hallway but seemed to be back on good terms with the pastor. The pastor introduced her to me, telling me that the old woman was a nurse.

"And now I am seventy-eight and not working!" she said. She was from Pakistan, and had not only been a nurse, but also a midwife and a nursing instructor.

"I don't think I talked to any nurses before on this trip," I told her.

"Colleague," she said. Her pronunciation was poor, and I wasn't following. "You are a nurse, me a nurse, colleague, together colleague."

As Fadi propelled us on, she was still talking from beneath the checkered red and yellow hijab.

VOICES

FROM ACROSS SYRIA

CHAPTER 34

"There was so much light."

SAMIRA, A WOMAN FROM THE church, took us to visit a refugee family. She introduced us to the lady of the house, who was surrounded by a roomful of dark-haired, rowdy boys, and one quiet girl. The lady welcomed us, and we seated ourselves on cushions around the perimeter of the room. She began to talk.

"I am from a family that was financially secure. I have nine siblings total, seven girls, two boys. Our life was like any normal life; we were so happy. Then my husband and I were introduced to each other.

"I was married out of love," she told us. "We knew each other for seven years before we were married. It took seven years, because neither of our families approved of the marriage. After suffering through the disagreements for seven years, we finally got married. Our wedding was a good one, thank God. Two years later we had twins. The twins didn't feel like a lot of work, because my parents and sisters helped me. Of course it was a new life for me with my parents-in-law, and I had the normal problems that people face with a mother-in-law. But I adjusted myself. If there is love, everything else will be solved. My husband was always by my side."

As she talked, three dark-haired boys tumbled and tousled around her. Occasionally, she banished them from the room or told them to be quiet.

"My father was a government employee. He was the head of a public transportation company in the city. When the war began, our financial situation began to deteriorate because there were no jobs.

"First we lived in Homs. The tensions began between those supporting the government regime and those opposing the regime. But no one announced which side he was on because everyone wanted to keep his family safe.

"During the incidents," she said in a low voice, "I began to lose some of my siblings. First we lost our brother. The opposition took him. Then we lost my second brother, but he was taken by the government, not by the opposition.

"At that time in Syria, if I had problems with you personally, I would go and inform the other side about you. So the political conflict was used to settle personal issues. My family supported the government, but I was living with my husband's family, who was opposing the government. The opposition wanted to take me, because they knew my family supported the government," she explained.

"My husband and I decided to move from Homs to Damascus. Things were quieter there, at least for a time. We stayed for a year and a half. Then things began to happen like they had in Homs, the same problems between those who opposed and supported the government. So we found the best solution was to leave Syria."

The woman had skimmed over the details of losing her brothers. Perhaps it was just a cultural inattention to detail. But Samira whispered to our host, "Tell them about your family."

"I was trying to avoid it so I wouldn't cry," she said. "The holidays are most painful for me because I remember how I lost two of my brothers and my sister. I told you we are seven sisters," she said. "I don't know the whereabouts of all of them. I only know about three of them. Because of what happened, each one left her own way. Some found each other, but the rest . . . I don't know where they're at."

She paused again, as if she could not go on.

"I could try to say the details of how my sister was killed, but it's too hard for me to remember that."

Fadi reassured her in Arabic.

"In America," he said in his gentle voice, "they don't know what you have been through, the specific details, and the sacrifice. What you have been through wasn't simple, it wasn't normal. You don't have to talk about it, but know that it is important."

She gathered her courage.

"We feel that everything that is happening in Syria is because of the Gulf States like Saudi Arabia and the Emirates," she said. "They give the finances that support the extremist youth. One of these radical young men was my brother-in-law. The Gulf States provided huge amounts of money for them to use for arms and weapons, so they would go out and demonstrate against President Bashar al-Assad.

"My brother-in-law offered my brothers money to join these demonstrations. They refused. And because they refused, they were taken.

"My oldest sister complained about my brother-in-law," she said quietly.

A chill settled through the room.

"My brother-in-law was taken into custody, and he was in jail for five months. But then, with bribes and payments, he was set free. He wanted to get even with my sister who had complained against him. There was no good security at that time, no real authority, so he could do what he pleased. He sent people to my sister's home. She had a hairdresser salon, and that's where she was when they killed her."

The conversation had fallen into a hush. Even my interpreter whispered, a respectful echo of the subdued Arabic.

"The revolution was a big lie," she said intensely, her voice rising. "It was made by people to settle their personal affairs. The revolution was all for the sake of money. My brother-in-law would have killed me too, if I had stayed in Syria. My brother-in-law! And it was all for the sake of money.

"To us, President Bashar al-Assad was a very good president. The problem was inside the government. People inside the government were causing problems. Maybe it was his fault that he couldn't control his people anymore. It began in Daraa, when the teenagers demonstrated against the government. Then the government responded by killing one of the boys, and the revolution began right there in Daraa. He sent people to solve the problem, but they didn't, and it escalated. He should have interfered personally in that. That's all I have to say."

Our host's young daughter was sitting close to me, and I turned to her to give her mother a chance to recover from telling a painful story.

"I like to play girls' games," she told me. "I like to read stories. I go to school at 1:30 p.m. every day."

"This lady is a new believer," Fadi whispered across the room.

We had not talked about religion at all so far.

"There was so much light."

"This is also a long story," the woman told us, smiling. "When I first came here, I was in a miserable situation. I knew nobody here. I had no relatives, no relationships with anybody. We heard about a church that was distributing aid, and we went to register for aid. People from the church came to visit us, and on the first visit, they brought us full supplies for the house, because we had nothing to sit on, nothing in the house.

"They came to my house several times. I liked them. I liked their hearts," she said. "I felt I had a relationship now. There was someone who would knock on the door and ask how we were doing. Due to all the problems in Syria, I was having nervous breakdowns. But the church worker would always come and pray with me. I would be so tired and nervous, but whenever she would come to me I would feel free to tell her everything inside me, and I would feel stress relief. I would pray with the lady from church. I felt something behind those prayers, and my life began to change.

"Then one day, something bigger happened. My family was in Syria, and they told me that one of my sisters was trapped at the top of a building that was about to collapse."

"I didn't know what to do. I couldn't call them, because there was no service there. I had another sister in Syria, but she was in another area. Even though she was in Syria, she couldn't contact our sister who was trapped either. There was no way to know what was happening! We didn't know if we would ever find out if she had been killed, or if she was okay. We didn't even know if we would find out when the building collapsed. I felt completely helpless.

"The only thing I could think of was that the lady from church had told me I could always pray. So I sat in my room alone, and I began to pray to Jesus.

"In one hour my other sister called me. She told me that my sister had escaped the dangerous building. Ten minutes after she escaped, the building had collapsed. Someone was able to get word to the sister who called, and she was able to reach me to give me the news.

"Jesus was so real to me that day, and I felt on that day that He gave me His hand. I asked Him, and He helped me. I began wanting to know more about Him. And I began to pray to Jesus about everything—my children, my husband, even my work. Some days I feel weak and I draw myself away from Him. But then my friend from church comes and pushes me to have a stronger faith. Despite the weakness, I feel that someone is dragging me, telling me, *Don't stay where you are. Come.*

"One day, I wasn't feeling good emotionally," she said. "I was at church praying when I noticed light around me. I asked my friend if there was anyone taking pictures. There was so much light. Don't laugh at me when I'm telling you this! This is what I saw! There was so much light. The light was a message to me, and I felt in my heart that I'm not Muslim anymore.

"When we had Ramadan, I felt, *it's not mine anymore, it doesn't mean anything to me.* I began to tell Samira I wanted to know more, to be discipled. My children and I attended church meetings and discipleship classes and prayer meetings. My daughter is so much like me, even stronger in faith than I. She's even stronger than her brothers and her father.

"My husband needs more time. He has some fear of the community around him, and how they would respond if a Muslim became a Christian. However, my husband said that in a dream he saw Jesus. In the dream, Jesus gave him His hand, as if He wanted to bring him forward, and He told him, 'Go and talk about Christianity.'

"I told him, 'This means you are asked to become a Christian and to talk about it, to evangelize!' But he didn't comment. It's hard for him to share his feelings. He accepts everything I'm doing, and he sends me to church every Sunday. He doesn't oppose me. But he's still not sure."

"Do you read regularly in the Bible?" Fadi asked.

"No," she said. "I read but not regularly. I always pray, but many things, the children, distract me from reading."

"I want to encourage you to read because you said that many days you feel weak," Fadi told her. "If you read regularly, the Lord will talk to you through His Word. If you have a thirst to be closer to Him and to know His will directly, you need to commit to read His Word. Even if you read a little each day, you will not feel weak. You will feel closer to the Lord."

"I can tell there's a joy in your heart because it shows on your face," Jana said. "You have a very beautiful smile."

"I don't feel afraid," she said. "I want to be baptized but they are delaying because of my husband. They are hoping to have a family baptism. I always ask the Lord for my husband because I found relief in the Christian religion.

The Muslim religion was so stressful for me. All the Christian prayers are alive for me. I want to be a true disciple, a daughter!

"I want to tell you one thing," she continued. "A while ago at the church, they did a children's camp, and there was a class for the mothers. We prayed and talked and shared. The teacher said, 'I will give each one of you fourteen beads. For the next week, whenever you have a blessing, put one of these beads on the string.' When she gave me my beads, I laughed. I told her I would give them all back the next Saturday. I wasn't hopeful that anything good would happen. I told the teacher I have no trust in friends or people surrounding me. I had two big problems in my life right then and I could see no hope."

As she talked, the woman's daughter went to another room and brought her mother a bag of bright blue beads. The woman took them in her hands as she talked.

"The one problem was that we used to live in another house, not this one. I wanted to move to this house, but my sister-in-law tried to take it before me. She offered more rent than we did, so I knew she would get it, not me. The second problem was I really wanted my daughter to be able to go to a camp for children, but I didn't think she would be accepted. Some Syrian girls were working there and one of them was my friend. She told me that there was another child more qualified than my daughter, so she would most likely be accepted for that spot at the camp.

"I'm going to say honestly what I prayed. I told God how tired I was of the battle. I said, 'Jesus, I want you to intervene in my life.' I'm the kind of person that doesn't want to harm anyone, but people like to harm me. I always face harm from people around me. I received so many phone calls, 'You lost the house, you lost the house. There's no way you'll get it.' I had lost trust in everyone. I could only turn to Jesus. I said, 'You know, it's up to you, Jesus. You either give me that home, or no, because I can't rely on humans anymore.'

"The owner of the house called me and he said, 'Your sister-in-law offered more to take the house. But I decided I prefer you, and you are the person that's going to take it.' So this was the first bead to be put on the string!

"The second bead was when my friend called me. She said the girl that was more likely to take the camp spot from my daughter was not accepted. This was the second bead!"

She looked at the shiny blue beads in her hand.

"The most difficult part of my whole journey has been family disagreement," the woman said in conclusion. "It's so difficult when you have war surrounding you, but you find your family is not in agreement. All the brothers and siblings of my husband are in Jordan, and there are so many problems because they are not in agreement. They harm each other and talk about each other. I was so tired because of everything we passed through, and they didn't support us or help us. Instead of family being a support, it was completely the opposite. That is why I was so stressed and had nervous breakdowns. For a long time I couldn't be a real housewife, I couldn't be a mother. I couldn't help my children. I couldn't be a wife for my husband. I was so stressed and broken down."

"Why are you supporting your mom in her faith?" Fadi asked the daughter.

"I want her to be stronger," the little girl said. "I know that when she prays she will feel better and have relief in her heart. So I want her to be better. At church they take us upstairs and we have games together. And I love Christian songs."

As we wrapped up the discussion, the Muslim call to prayer began, ringing out loudly from the nearby mosque. The lady we were visiting requested in Arabic that we pray for her. At the same time, Jana asked our interpreter, Reema, if it would be okay if we prayed with her.

Reema laughed and explained that there had been a request for prayer in both languages. As the Muslim call to prayer sounded, we stood to our feet, formed a circle, and began to pray in the name of Jesus.

CHAPTER 35

"The worst night I have ever lived through."

WE PARKED NEAR A RAMSHACKLE place and stepped off the curb into an unshaded valley of dust. A stone wall bordered one side of the path, and a bank of trash lined the other side. We knocked on a tin door that promptly fell off one of its hinges.

A Muslim woman with a welcoming smile answered the sagging door. She was dressed entirely in a maroon fabric with small white polka dots that seemed to be continuous from her head to the floor. She carried a chubby baby.

The lady began to tell us about her baby. When he was an infant, she had taken him to the hospital because his kidneys stopped working.

"He stayed for twelve days in the hospital, in the ICU. After twelve days he urinated for the first time. His kidneys began to work again. Each day it got better, and he began to eat. He is now eleven months old. And every two months we go and make a medical checkup to make sure everything is okay."

The conversation continued. "So what about your life in Syria?" I asked.

"We were living in a safe place. But my husband's construction work did not provide good financial resources, so we were poor. Whatever salary he got, we would live from that, and that's it.

"As a housewife, I would wake up in the morning, clean the house, and prepare food. I would never go out of the house unless I was visiting my family. My son went to school, and when he came back I used to sit with him to help him with his homework.

"I have five children. I had four in Syria, and then this new baby was born here. His sister, the youngest before he came, was born when the problems began to happen in Syria.

"When I went to the hospital, due to give birth, there were many roadblocks and checkpoints on the way to the hospital. I was in labor, but we could not get through. Finally, we reached the hospital and after that everything went smoothly.

"From that time on, we began to be afraid. Every Friday there would be demonstrations, rockets, and bombs."

The baby with the miracle kidneys fussed as the lady talked on.

"There were injustices in Syria before the children were arrested in Daraa. All the Sunni students who would finish and graduate would not get good jobs. All the good jobs went to the family and the relatives of Bashar al-Assad, who were Alawites. So, although they had college degrees, the Sunnis often had to work as day laborers. If a Sunni did manage to get a good job, it was only with great difficulty. So the people were upset because of what happened to the Daraa children, yes, but they were already angry because they were not being treated fairly.

"When the demonstrations began, the government put tanks in the streets. Even in peaceful demonstrations, they would shoot the people. We had so many martyrs, young men and children. But the deaths didn't make the demonstrators scared. The opposite happened. They became angrier. They began to go out more for demonstrations, in bigger numbers.

"My brothers-in-law, my brothers, my family, and my husband's family all went to the demonstrations. The people went out peacefully in demonstrations, but because President Bashar al-Assad ordered the army to shoot at the people, the people began to use guns. The young men began to shoot back at any government checkpoint. My brother joined them, and a sniper shot him and killed him.

"The day my brother died, they invaded our suburb, at 7 a.m., with tanks. They surrounded the whole area, and they went through the streets shooting the houses and the buildings. Women and children began to run away in the streets. Young men were helping them go to safer places. My other baby was little at this time," she added, as the baby in her arms cried and squirmed.

"Both my sister and sister-in-law, with their children, couldn't leave their houses. The government army took both of their husbands and interrogated them in their homes. They asked them many questions, and then they took them out to the checkpoint to where the blocked roads were. They didn't kill them, but they beat them there in front of everyone. After torturing them, the men were almost bleeding to death and they wanted to shoot them, but an officer came and said, 'No, that's enough, send them back.'

"After that the two families were not allowed to leave the street, although everybody else left. The army kept them in custody there and did not allow them to leave their homes. They stayed for three days inside the house, surrounded with tanks.

"My sister couldn't bear it. One night she and her husband took their children, and they left, just holding the children, running away in the street. My other brother-in-law saw them holding their children, running away, so he decided to run with his family. They followed them, running, but the police noticed them, and they began to shoot at them from far away. There was another suburb close by, known to be the Christian area, so they hid there. My sister knows one of the Christian families. They stayed there until everything calmed down, and then they fled to one of the villages.

"After they left, there was not a single person left on that street, nobody living there. The houses were left empty. They even demolished many of the houses so nobody would come back.

"When we left our home, we went to a village where we had one room only. There was no job for my husband, no school for our children. Whenever it would rain, it would rain inside the room. It was not even a completed building. We stayed a year like this, but it was so difficult. After a year, we came here.

"It was a scary journey. We came the ordinary way through Damascus, but there were so many roadblocks and checkpoints. They would often take young men into custody, so it was a scary journey, but we made it. They would shake our luggage, which was nothing, only some clothes for our children. They checked the ID of my husband. They were so serious in checking his ID. They checked and re-checked his name. At one checkpoint they stopped us for more than three hours. I thought they were going to take my husband, but thank God they let him through."

"What was the worst part of this whole experience for you?" I asked her. She grew quiet before slowly beginning to talk.

"When I had my baby, the problems were beginning, but we still lived in our own house on our street. One night my husband went out around 9:00 with his friends. It was the worst night of my life."

She began to cry.

"My husband and his brothers and friends began to call *Allahu Akbar*, the Islamic prayer, in a loud voice. They heard them at the government checkpoint, and they began to shoot them. They moved the tanks to attack. My husband and his friends began to run away. They ran back into our house. They locked the door, and they went up to the roof and they jumped from our roof to the next roof. They jumped from roof to roof to escape.

"The tank had followed my husband and his friends, and they saw which house they entered. They broke into our house, around twenty of those military men and two officers. I was with my three sisters-in-law and our children. Our brother-in-law who had had a back problem stayed in the house because he couldn't run. They caught him and began to hit him.

" 'Where are they? Where are your brothers? We need to know,' they yelled. They said, 'You need to give us the guns. They shot at us, and we need to see where they hid their guns.'

"They broke into everything—the bedrooms, the mattresses, everything we had. They held guns in front of the children and threatened us. We began to cry for my brother-in-law. They were beating him so hard."

She was sobbing and could barely talk.

"They wanted to take him into custody with them. We followed them and begged them not to take him. 'We have no guns, believe us, we have no guns,' we said. They didn't believe us. They went into the kitchen, and they threw all of the food on the floor. They went into my brother-in-law's house above us. They broke almost everything; they threw everything on the floor; they stole things.

"I followed the officer, begging for the life of my brother-in-law, asking them not to take him. He pushed me and told me, 'Stop it or I will take you with him.' "

She stopped talking to control herself.

"The worst night I have ever lived through."

"They threatened my brother-in-law and told him, 'If your brothers don't come tomorrow morning at 7:00 to our checkpoint, we will come to take you.'

"Later that night, my husband and brothers-in-law came back, using the roofs of the buildings. My husband broke his leg that night jumping onto a roof.

"When the men came back, they saw the situation of the house. They saw how harshly the officers had beaten their brother and what they had threatened. They heard how they told him they would come get him in the morning. They knew that they had a clear view of our roof from the checkpoint, and they were always monitoring us.

"We didn't sleep at that house that night. My sister-in-law and I went to our parents' homes, but my brother-in-law who had been beaten and his wife stayed at the house. In the morning, my oldest brother-in-law and his friend went to the officers, the military men at the checkpoint, and told them, 'Here we are. We came to you. We have no guns; we have nothing.' They interrogated them for long hours, but then they let them go. But they still kept watching us.

"This was the worst night I have ever lived through.

"And when they took my father into custody, we couldn't see him, and he died in prison. Nobody could reach him. He was there for fifteen days but nobody knew what happened to him. Did they torture him? Nobody knew. I called to ask about him multiple times. Finally after fifteen days they told me, 'He's dead. Here's his stuff.' I asked where they buried him, or where his body was, but nobody seemed to know. They didn't tell us. Many people we know who left the jail said, 'We saw your father. We saw how they were torturing him. But we don't know where they took his body or what happened to him.'"

"You must be a very brave woman," I said.

"We thank God for this. We should be patient. We have nothing else to do. The only thing we wish is to have peace in Syria and to go back to our home and country. My older children still remember the conflict. But they are passing that period. They are forgetting what happened."

"Can we pray with you before we go?" Jana asked. "Your story touched my heart."

She crossed the room to sit with the woman, and she prayed as Reema repeated her words in Arabic.

"Dear God, thank you for the opportunity to be with this family today. Thank you for giving our friend courage to share her story. Thank you that their family is safe. Would you bring peace to their hearts? Keep the rest of her family safe wherever they may be. Would you give their children a good education and a good future? Most of all, please allow them to know that you love them very much. I pray this in Jesus name. Amen."

CHAPTER 36

"No one could leave the house."

A COURTYARD COVERED BY A ceiling of grape vines growing on an arbor greeted us as we made our way to visit another refugee family. Light bulbs dangled from the wooden slats of the arbor, and I could imagine it must be a beautiful place after dark. Jana remembered that there had been clusters of grapes dangling there when she had visited this family earlier. An indoor carpet was spread out to dry in the courtyard.

The man of the house was not home, but his wife, dressed in pink, greeted us with a smile. She seated us on couches and chairs.

"Syria was known, before the troubles, to be the country for everyone. The rich man can live there, people would say, and the poor man can live there. My husband's work was good. Our first child was born a year before the crisis. We had our second child during the crisis.

"In the beginning it was hard for us because we couldn't get used to the idea of having a war. The Lebanese are used to having war all their lives. But as Syrians, we couldn't imagine having a war. The first time we heard a rocket, we wept. We were not used to that.

"Even though we were Christians, we did not have problems with our Muslim neighbors. We knew them, and they would never harm us. But when foreigners began to come, like from Libya or Afghanistan, they didn't know us and we didn't know them.

"When I gave birth to our second daughter, we were afraid for the safety of our children. You could forget about yourself, but you would worry for the children. And then my husband could not find work, and everything was so expensive. We couldn't even afford bread. So even though we stayed through much of the crisis, we finally came here. We have been here a year and three months.

"I miss my house in Syria. We built it ourselves, and my husband did some of the construction work. It was bigger than this house. It had three bedrooms, bathrooms, and a kitchen. We did everything with the best materials and took a loan from the bank. We were building it as the home we would raise our family in, the home we would live in for the rest of our lives.

"We painted the rooms with our favorite colors. First we painted the children's room light blue. The bedroom for the second child, we made light pink. Our room was peach. But we hardly had any time to live in it after it was all finished.

"I liked everything about my kitchen. I liked to cook. Arabs in general are known to be good cooks, but especially Syrians. My favorite dish to make is grape leaves. We stuff them with meat and rice. I don't put in many spices, but I like to season them with black pepper and salt. Then at Easter, we eat *shakrieh.*"

"And now you will want to know what *shakrieh* is?" Reema asked, laughing at the difficulty of explaining food in English. "*Shakrieh* is lamb stew in yogurt. You cook the lamb, then you cook the yogurt in the broth of the lamb, and you add garlic and dried mint. The stew is a white color, which is why they make it for Easter. When I make *shakrieh* I make it the Syrian way," Reema added. "The Syrian way is better. My American friends tell me this must be food from heaven!"

Our host began to talk again. "She's telling me her recipe," Reema told me. "She's telling me not to use . . ." her English trailed off, and she spoke Arabic to the lady we were visiting.

"Okay, I will try this," Reema conceded.

"Were you doing it wrong?" I asked.

"No," Reema said. "But there are two ways of thickening it. She is telling me to use egg rather than starch to thicken it. So I said I will try it."

"That's a nice tradition," I said. "In America, people usually have ham, or something like that for Easter, which isn't very symbolic. The lamb is nice."

"It's a tradition from our grandparents," our host said. "The color white shows our joy. We cook it, we go to church, and we come back and eat *shakrieh.*"

Pausing, she began talking about the war again.

"Besides our house, we also lost my husband's family home. It was all demolished. His parents had left it to us for an inheritance. After the terrorists left the suburbs, his parents went back to check on the family home, and that's when they found it demolished. It broke our hearts.

"And of course the hard thing is the children. I feel that they haven't had a childhood. They were born in the crisis. For a period I couldn't even afford milk for them. Now we can at least cover the basic things. But not being able to buy milk for them was so difficult for me.

"Perhaps if it would have just been us, we would have stayed in Syria longer. But having children sped up the decision. You can bear more if it's just adults. One whole winter I didn't have enough gasoline for heating. We had to sleep together on one couch to stay warm. It was such a shock for us, because in all of our lives, we had never had problems like this. We always had gasoline. Everyone had affordable heat during the winter. My sister in America called me, asking, 'Do you need money?' and I told her, 'It's not about money! There is no gasoline to buy! If you go to the store for gasoline, you will wait there from 7:00 in the morning until late at night, and you still won't get any.'

"When I came here, I came on the plane. My parents came at the beginning, but at that time we couldn't come with them because we didn't have enough money. But my sister sent me the money for the plane ticket. We flew because all the desert roads and the main way were filled with ISIS."

Jana asked how her sister was doing in America.

"Very good," she said in English, before reverting to Arabic. "They have a good life there. My sister was there before the war. She was married there. But now my parents and my brother are there. And I heard that the States will allow 10,000 refugees in. I'm praying I can go there because I haven't seen my family for four years."

She paused.

"I want everybody to know, though, that Syria was not like this before the war. Before the war, we were all living in peace with each other. Nobody imagined this would happen to Syria. Syria doesn't deserve this. Even in the last years, we as Christians had so much freedom. Christians in Syria were treated better than Christians in all the other Arab countries. We could celebrate our religion freely with no pressure.

"At Easter we would have a procession. Someone would hold a big cross, and we would all carry candles. Everybody celebrated freely, dressed as they wished, and went out in the streets. We were never persecuted as Christians. Even the Muslim friends we had were moderate. We didn't have any extremist Muslims in our neighborhood."

The Muslim call to prayer rang out across the town, permeating the living room through the windows.

"Tell me about Christmas," I said.

"We decorated the whole house with red candles. Different people had different decorations, but I used red candles. We made sweets for Christmas."

There was an exchange of Arabic that was not interpreted. "Forgive me, but we were having an argument," my interpreter finally said. "She's saying that the Syrian sweet that they make for the holiday is better than the one we make. It's called *gras*. It's a dry sweet made with flour. It's soft, a cross between a cake and a biscuit."

The Syrian lady continued, "We got gifts for the children. We would only get gifts for the children, not like in America where everyone exchanges gifts. For the first three years of our marriage, my husband used to bring me a gift at Christmas, but after I had the baby, he stopped," she said, laughing. "Then he began to bring gifts for our children, because they are more important. They would wait for Christmas and wake up that morning and run for the gifts.

"But the year in Syria when it was so cold, we didn't celebrate," she said. "We couldn't afford anything. Usually we would celebrate together as a family. We would get together for dinner. But that year we were scattered. And we couldn't go out for dinner anyway, because we weren't allowed to be out at night. And we couldn't have a sleepover because it was too cold, and there was not enough space. So we had Christmas huddled on our mattress, and we spent the night crying."

Outside the windows, birds chirped merrily, but her memories had the power to transport us to her dark and difficult past.

"We have ten minutes," Fadi said.

"Oh, good, then I can ask about her husband. How did you meet your husband?" I asked.

"I worked in a pharmacy for four years. He knew me before that because his older brother is married to my cousin. But he saw me at the pharmacy and used to stop in to talk to me. We wanted to get married, but he couldn't afford a house.

"He's such a good man. Despite everything we have been through, he's still so good. He has a kind heart. We finally had our engagement party at Christmas. Then our wedding was the next year on September 30.

"We invited the family and friends to the wedding. My wedding color was light blue. The tradition is to have three evenings of celebrations, but it was such a good time that everyone wished it would go longer. My husband had twenty friends to celebrate, and a Syrian band with pipes and drums. Of course, that was before the crisis, so we had money to afford a celebration. I have pictures also if you would like to see them."

She paged through the photos in the little book, pointing out family members and celebrations.

"Our son was born at Christmas, so we got him a cake," she said. "Here we are with family. We always gathered together to eat and spend time together. Here we are celebrating Palm Sunday. We would walk in the streets and celebrate with music. This is a huge balloon full of balloons. They put it up on the church on Palm Sunday and when the children come out holding the candles, they release the balloons down on top of them."

"They did celebrate Christmas and Easter in an amazing way," Reema said to us. "I lived in Syria at one time, and even after I lived here, we would go there to celebrate Christmas and Easter."

Horns blared outside as we talked. Our host's young daughter arrived from school. Her husband walked in as well. He was a pleasant-looking man who took a seat inside the front door.

"I think your wife told most of the story," I said. "But what would you say has been the worst part of the story for you?"

There was silence as he pondered the question. The birds chirped on outside.

"The hardest thing is when, as a man, you don't have money even to buy

191

bread," he said his voice full of pain. He got up and walked out under the grape arbor.

"It's hard," Remma whispered to me.

I felt terrible. I wished I had not dived into such a difficult question.

"After 4 p.m., no one could leave the house in Syria," his wife added. "It would be foolish for even the bravest man to go out. It was so dangerous."

In a few minutes, her husband returned, blinking back tears.

"It's not safe anymore, it's not secure," he said. "I do tile now. Sometimes I find work, sometimes not."

"Nice work," his wife said in English. "He's really a professional decorator. He's talented."

"Thank you very much," we said, beginning to stand.

"Stay for lunch," the lady offered.

We declined politely and stepped out under the grape arbor.

CHAPTER 37

"Jesus Christ gave me the strength to forgive."

OUR LAST VISIT FOR THE day was at the home of an elderly couple. There were no extended family members, just two of them in the house. They had furniture, which was wonderful after a day of mostly sitting on the floor. High on the wall of the living room hung a cross.

"First of all," they told us, "we are not Muslims who converted to Christianity. We were born in Christian families, but we just recently became born-again Christians. We want everyone to see, to hear, to record, and to take pictures because we really wish for everyone to know what's happening, what's going on, what radical Islam does to people. Yesterday, four of our relatives were killed in the bombing in Damascus.

"Our life in Syria before the war was good. There were no beggars in the street. We were a stable country. There was love between families and love between people. On the Christian holidays, the government would clean around the churches to make things look good for the holiday. The officials would go to the churches to give their greetings to the Christians. This was how the government treated the Christians at the beginning.

"In the last ten years I was working in a contracting company that was owned by the government. I was working with the general manager. I was his assistant and driver. We were happy. Whatever I say about what happened next, I will be selling it short. We experienced a huge drop in our quality of life when we had to leave.

"First, people started to act differently, especially in the way they treated Christians. The neighbors that used to greet us and treat us warmly started to become cold in their treatment, sometimes even ignoring us in the street.[l] Radical Muslims were going through the streets at night, especially when the police were not present. It was something unusual to see them so frequently. They used to go and visit houses, but nothing was obvious. It was not clear why they were doing it. They started painting and spraying messages on the Christians' houses, like 'There's no place for you, cowards.'

"Then the real problems started. The radical Muslims would go demonstrate and they would chant: 'The Alawites to the *tabout*[m] and the Christians to Beirut.'

"They started swearing on Jesus Christ at that time. On the morning of Easter Sunday 2011, a huge demonstration started going toward all the churches. They were saying offensive slogans toward Jesus Christ. And they tried to cut off all the roads leading to the churches so Christians couldn't attend church.

"Our area used to have a population of 1.2 million people. And out of those 1.2 million people, 250,000 of them were Christians.

"At that time, we started being terrified. We felt that danger was near us. We started to see armed forces in the street. The radical Muslims started killing the police. It became more frequent to see demonstrations, tire burning. The opposition forces wouldn't allow us to go to work. If I went to work, they would see me as an accomplice with the regime, the government. Gunfire was a daily routine for us. The most terrifying thing is that these events escalated on Fridays after they leave what they call the worship houses, the mosques. The sheikhs that would preach the sermons would pump the people up with hatred. The targets were minorities: Christians, Shi'ites, and Alawites. So we knew the danger was increasing. We already had two daughters who had married and come here. So when I saw this going on, I sent my wife and daughter as well. But my two sons and I stayed longer.

"We lived on the second floor of our building. Underneath, under the back of my house, it became a center for the armed Muslim people. Under my house! These were the young men that were raised with my children. They suddenly changed and became almost different people.

---

l   *Things like this happened because many Muslims assumed that the Christians were*
supporting Bashar al-Assad and the government regime.
m   *Casket.*

"Jesus Christ gave me the strength to forgive."

"The radical Muslims started pushing my two sons to carry arms and join them. They forced me to bring water, coffee, tea, and alcohol to them. They wouldn't trust a Muslim to go get them, so they would ask a Christian. My younger son is a bit hot-blooded. I was worried he would do something in anger and get himself in trouble, so I sent him to my sister's village, still in Syria, but a safer place.

"One day, my son was coming from that village to visit me. When he passed by the place where the armed radicals were camped, he ignored them and kept walking. But the leader stopped him and told him, 'Today, it's your responsibility to help us guard this checkpoint.'

"My son started to swear and shout at them. He knew they had some evil plan in mind. But somewhere in the conflict, they remembered that his father—me—was bringing them their drinks."

"They're not supposed to drink alcohol," Jana said.

"They're not supposed to, right! But that doesn't keep them from doing it; they just might do it privately so they aren't seen. Anyhow, when they remembered that this was my son, they slowed down a little and let him go. But when I heard what had happened, I told my older son, 'Your younger brother is in danger and needs to leave today.' At that point there was still some kind of public transportation, even though it was expensive. I told my older son to get my younger son out of the country, regardless of the cost. I felt danger coming, a huge threat to my son. That same night we got him here. Sure enough, they came to me, asking, 'Where is your son?'

"Right after I sent my son out of the country, I saw a man get beheaded in front of my house. It was a man they considered to be an accomplice with the government. Until this day, I have nightmares about this. Many other Christian people were killed that night. At that time, all of the police and the people who were responsible for security left the town. The only power and the only authorities were the radical Muslims."

"For example, if they announced that no one is allowed to move or leave their houses, no one would be allowed to leave," his wife inserted.

"If you remember, there was a clip that was circulating on social media," the man said, "where they were killing the ex-soldiers and throwing them into the river. That happened in our town. Churches were robbed, people were killed and murdered in their houses, especially Christians. It was no longer possible to escape easily. Later on I was able to escape to a Christian village with my older son. It was not far away, less than ten miles. My son and I were trying to come here and were not able to because of the daily bloodshed. There was agony, there was terror, and there was blood.

"Christians were being abducted and ridiculous ransoms were being asked—millions. If the relatives could not deliver the sum, the militants would send their loved ones in small pieces in bags and drop them at the houses of their parents or their friends. One of the people that was abducted was one of my relatives, a doctor. This doctor lived in the village for five years, and he used to work for free. They kidnapped him and asked for five million. The same people to whom he had provided free medical care kidnapped him. The five million is only 100,000 U.S. dollars, but for them, that's huge. All the Christians whom he knew gathered this amount of money, and we got him out after forty days.

"We finally managed to flee and come here. We came and lived with my daughter for a period of time. We thought when we went to my daughter's place that we were staying a month or two months at maximum, but we stayed there for seven months with seven people living in that house.

"We saw pictures of our house being destroyed and claimed by ISIS. Our house was at a strategic location. So they took the house, and they opened all the walls to make it more of a base for them.

"My sons are in Brazil because they weren't allowed to work here, and our youngest daughter got married here. And I am living here with my soul mate," he said with a fond glance at his wife. "We knew each other since we were thirteen years old."

"Did you like each other since you were thirteen years old?" I could never resist asking these questions.

"Yes! We used to love each other from thirteen. Please don't embarrass us!" they laughed. "We got married when we were twenty-two. We are only seven months apart."

"But something tragic happened in Syria that I haven't told you yet," the man said. It was clear that he was uncomfortable talking about this. "My sister was murdered. They sexually assaulted her before they killed her, and then they threw her body in the street. Whatever we say, whatever we describe will not even come close to describing what happened to the Christians and what is still happening to the Christians in these areas.

"When I remember my sister, I feel like I will suffocate," the man went on. "I am not able to express myself very clearly. My sister was fifty years old when she was attacked, and the one who killed her was a young son of the neighbors, a boy who was raised with her children. After he killed her, he went to her family and said very rudely, 'Go there and see your sister. I assaulted her and threw her in the street.' They couldn't go there immediately because there was bombing at that time, but when they got her, they put her in a wheelbarrow, a wheelbarrow that was used for concrete. But Jesus gave me the strength to forgive. Jesus Christ forgave the people who crucified him. How can I do otherwise?"

In the darkening room, under the cross on the wall, there was a hum of Arabic without interpretation. Then Reema explained.

"I said to him, 'I envy you. I heard the story, and I'm not related to her, but I can't even forgive at this point.' "

"The agony I have in my heart," the man went on, "makes me consider myself dead. Especially my sister . . . I'm still in pain and agony about what happened to her, although I forgave them, because this is what Jesus Christ asks us to do.

"God had a plan for us when we came here, because when we came here, we met Jesus. In Syria, we were Christians only by name. I would go to church every Sunday, but sometimes I would miss a Sunday or two. Here we became believers and accepted Jesus as our Savior, and we were baptized here. This is what gives me the power to forgive. In the Syriac church, I used to lead the choir. I know how to sing in the original Aramaic, in the language that Jesus spoke. Now I help in worship and discipleship courses."

He quoted some lines in Aramaic and also gave the translation in Arabic. Without understanding anything, I could tell that he was quoting poetry.

Faithful Reema gave the English: "We kneel in front of the Person on the cross, and we sing with the thief on the right, Accept us in your kingdom!"

Our host hummed a starting note, leaned slightly back, then began to sing from the depths of his body and soul, first in Aramaic, then in Arabic. The haunting beauty of the tune and the power of the voice, after this long day of listening to sad stories, electrified us.

We all sighed when the song was done.

"When we came here, we were struggling on a financial and social level. One of the Muslim people told me, 'Why are you struggling? The Christians are helping us, they should be helping you.' I called the number that they gave me.

"It was Sunday. Once I called the man, immediately he took our address, and he came and visited us. We had nothing, and we were sleeping on the floor. He told us 'Let's go to church,' and I didn't know where I was going. I was surprised to find myself going to an evangelical church because initially I had something against evangelical churches.

"Once I entered the church, I found I was sweating. The song that they were singing described my life. I love music, and I started to feel something pulling me more than usual through this song. My old ideas of religion were so different. I listened to the sermon, and I was really quiet. After that, I committed my life to Jesus Christ and the church. I said, 'I need to be baptized.' I took off my old flesh, or my old man, and I wanted to be new.

"When I accepted Jesus Christ, I felt that I became a new person. I felt overwhelming happiness. I started to look forward to meetings, singing, and worship. I became braver, and I learned to know God personally. I had the strength to proclaim my faith, to announce it loudly. I thank Jesus Christ that I had the courage to even enter a dangerous path, being involved with Muslims who were coming to faith in Christ. At every stage I pray for more strength to continue this work.

"I want to share something that I consider a miracle that happened. I am a heart patient already, and I had two stents in my heart in Syria. The symptoms increased when I came here. I went to one of the hospitals here. After they did tests, the doctors told me that I needed open heart surgery. But after the prayer of the brothers of the church, I went for a checkup after three months, and they told me there was no need for open heart surgery. They told me that if I took medicine, I would be okay.

"I always ask Jesus Christ for strength to bring peace to other people in the same way it was brought to me. The Lord brought me here to become a new person. All glory be to Him. He changed me; He liberated me."

The church worker who was with us said to us, "He is the key to reaching many Syrian families. He opens his home, and they have many Bible study groups here in their house."

The man disappeared and returned with a certificate he had earned in a church discipleship program. He stood holding the paper, framed by the white lattice bars of the open window behind him. He set the papers on the pink table which also held our tea and glasses. We sipped tea, and the Muslim call to prayer began as our hosts talked on in Arabic. Darkness had fallen since we entered the house.

"Shukran," Fadi said. This was a sign that it was time to go.

"I'm really happy and glad that you are here, because I really want our voice to reach as far as possible, for people to feel what we are going through."

We stood in a circle and closed the evening with prayer.

VOICES

FROM DAMASCUS

Damascus

Damascus is said by Josephus to have been built by Noah's great-grandson Uz. Certainly by the time of Abraham it was an active city. In Genesis 14:15, Abraham headed toward Damascus to rescue his captured relative Lot.

Nicknamed the "Pearl of the East," Damascus has always been the leading city of Syria, even before it was really the capital. Mark Twain visited Damascus, traveling on horseback through the mountains and deserts from Beirut. "Leave the matters written of in the first eleven chapters of the Old Testament out," Twain says, "and no recorded event has occurred in the world but Damascus was in existence to receive the news of it. Go back as far as you will into the vague past, there was always a Damascus."[29]

It is a fertile oasis of about 60,000 acres, with rivers watering its gardens and fields. "Damascus is simply an oasis—that is what it is," Mark Twain said of his first glimpse of the city from the top of the mountain they had just crossed. "For four thousand years its waters have not gone dry or its fertility failed. Now we can understand why the city has existed so long. It could not die. So long as its waters remain to it away out there in the midst of that howling desert, so long will Damascus live to bless the sight of the tired and thirsty wayfarer."[30]

In 2 Kings 5, when the Prophet Elisha told Damascus native Naaman of Syria to "Go wash in the Jordan seven times" to heal his leprosy, Naaman lost his temper. "Are not Abana and Pharpar, rivers of Damascus, better than all the waters of Israel?" After Naaman had a change of heart and was healed of leprosy by dipping in the Jordan, he tried to give Elisha gifts. When Elisha refused, Naaman asked for dirt from the land of Israel to take back to Damascus to build an altar to the one true God.

A few chapters later in 2 Kings 16, Israel's King Ahaz went to Damascus to meet the king of Assyria and saw an altar in the temple that impressed him. He sent its pattern to Urijah the priest, who had it reproduced in Israel.

In the New Testament, the Apostle Paul was headed to Damascus to arrest Christians when he was converted. The Street called Straight, where Paul waited for Ananias, is still a well-known street in the Old City of Damascus. There is a site said to be the location where Paul escaped in a basket through a window. The Chapel of St. Ananias is an underground structure which is possibly the room where Paul met Ananias and was baptized.

Probably on the same site where Naaman worshipped and King Ahaz admired the altar, the Romans dedicated a temple to the god Jupiter. Some of the massive foundation and columns from this time are still there today. Later, when Christianity became the religion of the Roman empire, the building was redone as a church, dedicated to John the Baptist. Still later, when Islam became the official religion, the church was remodeled into a huge mosque. Now called the Umayyad Mosque, it stands today. It was ravished three times by fire, but was restored each time. It is considered one of the most important mosques in Islam, along with the mosques of Mecca, Medina, and Jerusalem.

Interestingly, over a little-used doorway in the Great Mosque, a Greek phrase is inscribed in a beam. It says, "Thy Kingdom, O Christ, is an everlasting Kingdom." [31]

In 2008, Damascus was a great place to shop, eat, drink coffee, and spend the night, all at affordable prices. Although people were disappointed that President Bashar al-Assad had not made more reforms, "there [was] certainly a feeling of optimism in the capital."[32] Initially after his rise to power in 2000, President Bashar al-Assad made a show of permitting private newspapers and freedom of speech and internet use. However, this "Damascus Spring" began to fade into autumn as people were frequently arrested for anti-government sentiments, and economic policies favored the Alawite group. In 2005, Syria lost favor with other nations when Lebanon's prime minister was assassinated and the Syrian government was assumed to bear responsibility. In 2007, President Bashar al-Assad was re-elected with nearly 100 percent of the vote, but he was the only candidate.

When anti-government demonstrations began in 2011, President

Bashar al-Assad did nothing initially. Then, as the riots spiraled out of control, he sent tanks to the hot spots to control them. At the same time, huge crowds gathered in Damascus in a show of support for the president.

Because the president lived in Damascus, it was a safe place to flee during the earlier stages of the war. However, soon the conflict came to certain areas of the capital as well.

In August of 2014, much of the world was outraged by news of a chemical attack in areas of Damascus. Although no one claimed responsibility for the attack, it seemed evident that it came from the al-Assad regime. As family members escorted choking victims to makeshift hospitals and splashed water on blue-skinned children, many people made the decision to leave Damascus. In Ghouta, another area of Damascus where supplies were cut off by the government and people were starving, "some sheikhs allowed the residents to eat cats."[33]

By 2015, many people in Damascus were living in poverty. Still, life went on. People were getting accustomed to war and the constant inflow of refugees from other areas of Syria. People still tried to cling to some semblance of normal life."[34]

CHAPTER 38

"The war is complicated."

I HAD MET MY FIRST refugee from Damascus while I was in Lebanon. He was well-educated and could speak English.

"In one month, everything changed," he said.

"Do you mean it changed at the time of the incidents in Daraa?" I asked, referring to the anti-government graffiti that teenagers had written on a wall at the beginning of the war.

"I don't believe that was really the start of the war," he said. "There was something bigger and more mysterious behind what happened.

"I lived in Damascus, and I didn't think the conflict would come to Damascus. Everyone knew there was fighting in other towns, but for a long time it was peaceful in Damascus. But when the conflict came there, we decided we would move before anything worse happened.

"We decided to leave when a bomb dropped close to our house. We heard the voice of the bomb, a very strong voice. The crystal in our home broke. I had a young child, and he was scared. 'Why stay here?' my wife and I asked ourselves, when every morning we risk our lives by leaving the house?

"The war is complicated because a lot of terrorists are coming to Syria," he added. "Everyone wants to fight in Syria. In the Muslim religion, if you die while you are fighting, you will become a martyr and go to God. If you want to fight and die and go to God, then why not go fight in Syria? That's why Syria is becoming a very dangerous country.

"It's not just ISIS; it's more complicated than one group. And the people who are coming to fight are foreigners. Many are not Syrian, or even Arabs. Nobody knows who they are. Some of them don't speak Arabic. But they all have one thing in common: they want to kill you if you are a Christian.

"You could do any crime in Syria right now and get away with it," he went on. "I know of a man who was shot in his head just because someone wanted his car. The man who did it was a criminal, and he wanted a car. There are no police, so he killed the driver and took the car. Very easy! No one will go after him.

"It wasn't even a very good car," he reflected sadly.

They had concluded it would be better to live in Lebanon, and so they moved before anything could be destroyed besides the crystal.

CHAPTER 39

"If we laugh, it's not from our hearts."

In Jordan, I again met refugees from Damascus. The man of the house was balding and wore a gray zippered outfit that reminded me of a jumpsuit. His wife was dressed in an elegant black dress with a striped embroidery pattern on the cuffs of the sleeves. She walked to the window as we settled on the low cushions, twisting the curtains into a knot to let in more breeze.

"Inside the house I am able to walk without a cane," the man told us. "But outside the house, I use a cane."

From the way he was resting his leg on the cushion, I could tell he had been injured.

His wife went to a cupboard and began setting out glasses on a tray.

"Before, we would be scared to talk about our story," the man said. "We would be afraid to show our faces. We would refuse to take pictures or anything because we were afraid for our families still living there. But now we don't care anymore. Whatever has happened, has happened. We are not afraid anymore of the government or the system.

"It has been chaos. Even before the incidents, it was scary. We would be anxious, wondering if someone was watching us.

"We have no children. I had my own car. I worked within farms, transporting fruits: apricots, pears, grapes. I would take them from farms to grocery stores or the central market to sell them. I lived a very good life. I needed nobody, thank God."

But that all changed with the war.

"One day after the war had started, I was driving my car, going to work.

My brother-in-law and I were going to a farm, and we came up to a checkpoint. There were snipers in the top of a building close to the checkpoint. We would always go to this village, because they knew us there. They knew that we went back and forth with fruit.

"When I drove up to the checkpoint, I noticed that there were no people out in town. I thought it was strange, but I thought maybe there was a strike, and no one was working that day. We went through the checkpoint. The guard asked us where we were going, and I told him. I told him I was working, and that I would be transporting fruit and visiting family. I had already called the man who owned the farm to make sure it was safe to travel on that day. 'Yes, there's nothing going on. Come on out. It's fine,' he had said.

"So I simply told the guard what I was doing, and he seemed to accept my explanation. 'Okay, bring some cigarettes with you when you come back,' he told me. I told him, 'Okay.'

"I pulled away from the checkpoint. We had hardly left the checkpoint when the snipers began shooting. The people at the checkpoint had not told us the truth: there was a lockdown and nobody was allowed to leave their houses.

"The first bullet hit my leg. The second went through the door of the car and again hit my leg. I was telling my brother-in-law, 'I have been shot!' and 'Please, throw yourself out of the car, because you have children.' So my brother-in-law began to scream, 'We are only guests here! We are coming from Damascus to buy fruit.' He couldn't see the snipers, but he screamed to tell whoever might be listening that we were harmless. But it had no effect. They kept shooting and more bullets hit my feet.

"I threw myself out of the car and fell between the sidewalk and the main street. I tried to crawl away to safety. But they kept shooting, and the bullets would hit the car and come back to me while I was on the ground. I took three bullets in my back. I saw something on the ground made of metal, so I put it on my chest. I remember thinking that if I die, the metal shield will keep flies or dogs from eating me until someone comes to remove my body.

"My brother-in-law ran into a house close to the checkpoint. The people in the house took me in and cared for me. I only told them my name, and then I fainted. I woke up the next morning. I found myself here in Jordan at King Abdullah's Hospital, having no idea what had happened. My nephew told me I was screaming during the night because of the pain. But I remember nothing. I had seven bullets in my body. Two in my feet, two in my legs, three in my back. There is still one bullet in my back; they can't take it out."

The man's wife had brought us drinks, but I sat in rigid stillness.

"I'm not the only one with a story like this," the man said. "My oldest brother was the chief accountant in the education department in Daraa. He had a check with him for 250 million Syrian pounds for the department of education, and he disappeared. That was two years ago, and we haven't heard anything about him since.

"We weren't rebels! We didn't concern ourselves with anything happening with the government or the Free Army. We only cared for our work, our families. So who began it? How did it happen? No one knows. It's chaos, and it's getting worse. Now we even have Russian checkpoints in one of the cities. The Russian forces are supposed to be there now to help the government fight against ISIS. But they didn't come to fight ISIS, because the Russian forces are four to six hours away from where ISIS is. It's only protection for the president."

The man continued talking bitterly in Arabic. Reema stopped interpreting. Then she leaned toward me.

"He's cursing Iran and the Shi'ites," she whispered.

"They're the ones that support all that," the man went on. "When there was the war in Lebanon, we opened our houses for the Shi'ites of Lebanon. We were so nice to them. We paid for their electricity, their food, everything. Look how they treat us back, the Shi'ites. They're not dependable!"

The man's wife spoke briefly. She was a quiet woman.

"The hardest thing for me in all of this was the day he was shot. I didn't know how he was doing. I was in Damascus at my home," his wife said. "His family called me on the phone and told me he had been shot. Seventeen days after he was shot, I followed him to Jordan. I couldn't get there before then because of all the checkpoints. It was so hard for me to be able to leave. I could only find out how he was doing through his family, because he was in a coma and couldn't talk to me. But now I have another hard thing because I haven't heard from my family for the last three years.

"I heard I was in a coma for eight days," the man said. "For a year or more, a year and a half, I couldn't sleep at night. I would keep screaming because of the pain. When the doctor discharged me after twenty-nine days, I asked the doctor, 'Where will I go?' I had thought I would leave and go back to Syria, but I found out it was so bad I couldn't go back. The doctor told me, 'This is a hospital, this is not a hotel.' I lived with my brother for a couple of months before coming here."

The man paused before beginning another story.

"When we were still in Syria before I was shot, one night we went from Damascus to Daraa to visit my family. We stayed there for the evening, and then we headed back to Damascus. It was my wife and I and her mother. Around 10 p.m. we were about thirty kilometers away from the city. It was a cool evening, and I had the heater on in my car. I was a little nervous about being on the highway so late at night, so I was driving fast. I saw lights up ahead, and I thought it was an oncoming car. I moved to the side to give plenty of space for it, and I kept driving. But then I saw there were officers, men standing on the road. There were five of them, and they pointed their guns at our car.

" 'Stop, stop!' they were screaming. I stomped on the brake and brought the car to a stop. The five men with guns surrounded the car and pointed the guns at me and my wife and her mother. We began to sweat. I opened the window.

"They asked me, 'Where are you going?' I said, 'I'm going back home.' The leader said, 'No, stay here.' I said, 'Let me go back.' He said, 'No, you will stay here.' I asked him, 'Can you ask the officers to go a little bit away from the car, because the two ladies are terrified,' and he said, 'No! Nobody will move, and if any of you move, we will directly shoot you.'

"I couldn't tell what was going on. Some cars came up behind us, but they saw the officers and backed away. The other cars turned around and left, and it was only me. I was angry, and I wanted to react, but my wife held my hand and said, 'Please stay calm; please stay calm.' Her mom fainted, because the gun was facing her. We didn't know what was happening.

"We stayed there for an hour, from ten to eleven. We didn't know why they kept us there, but it seemed as if they were waiting for someone, and indeed they were. We were there when they caught him. They stopped him, as they had stopped us. But they took him out of the car and they took him in front of us and shot him. He was bleeding, but they put him on the ground and they hit him, over and over.

"Do you wonder what it was like? It was a night of horror. We couldn't believe it when, after that, they let us go.

"I never felt safe after that. We felt we couldn't do it anymore. So many other incidents happened with people that we know. They would suddenly stop a car and take the man, and his family would never know where he was after that. You couldn't ask where they were taking him."

He pointed to his twisted right ankle. As he went on, his wife began talking at the same time as him, in a dramatic voice.

"It's so hard," the man said. "It's so difficult! Even I know of people who are in prison right now suffering because of how they torture them. They would prefer to die than be tortured! Or even suicide; they would rather kill themselves! It's better than going there and being taken into custody in the prisons, because they will have no mercy. Before the incidents began, we were living well. We were surviving, but our main problem was the government itself."

Again, everyone was talking at once.

"Even before, the government wasn't good, but we were avoiding it. If you had money in your pocket, and an officer stopped you, you gave him money and went on. That's just how it was in Syria. So it wasn't good for us, but we were avoiding it."

"That's right," Reema told me later. She had grown up in Syria. She remembered her mother getting stopped for a traffic violation and paying the officer personally, to keep him from citing her. "It was common," she said.

"If you had the choice, would you prefer to have things stay as they were before, or to go on with the revolution?" one of the men in our group asked him.

"No, of course, before was better. If you had money, you would pay. You would bribe. At least the government would take your money in an ethical way. If you did something wrong, they would take your money. If they complained against you, you bribed them with money. If you crossed a traffic light, you would pay money.

"It was safe back then. I would go to sleep at the farm, even outside. We never felt unsafe. Our life was secure. I didn't care about the government, so we were avoiding it and living perfectly. But that changed. Since the war, even though I didn't cause problems or do anything wrong, I was still attacked and shot. We can't ignore the problems anymore. Maybe our American friends will know, because they are more advanced. In the United States, if two people die, the president needs to give an explanation of why. But millions are dying in Syria, and he's still in his office there as a president.

"I'm not debating, I'm not supporting King Abdullah, but if President Bashar al-Assad had a quarter of the smartness and wisdom of King Abdullah, he would have avoided all this. All he cared for was his office, his state. He didn't care for the people. What if, in the beginning, he had gone to Daraa and solved it peacefully?! They prepared for a visit from him, and they prepared to solve it peacefully. It could have been solved in ten minutes! But he promised to come, and he didn't."

The man's thoughts strayed to the possible future.

"I had my first interview for America. We might be accepted for going to the States. A year and a half ago, I was supposed to be in France. I and my family were accepted. They told me as soon as I'd arrive in France, I would have a house, and everything I needed. We only needed to pay the air ticket, and we would leave in two months. Then I had another surgery here. After three or four months, they called me and asked, 'Why didn't you leave?' I told them I couldn't pay. So now we don't know if we will be accepted to the States or not. We have relatives in Germany; maybe they will help us. I can't bear it as a man, to only be sitting in the house. To not be able to move is just killing me.

"I went to a hospital, and a doctor looked at me and said, 'You need the surgery and you will pay half of it, which is 1,500 JDs. We will not cover it all because you were wounded a long time ago, so we will only pay half of it.' I have nobody to donate or to help me. This surgery was supposed to be for my leg, not for my back. I used to do physical therapy, but now I don't do it anymore. For a year and eight months I went every day. And it would cost me 10 JDs to go and come back. Now they stopped the center because there are no donations to keep it going. Since I stopped the physical therapy, it's affecting my leg."

"If we laugh, it's not from our hearts."

"We are trying to start a medical service," the person from the church who was with us said. "I will try to ask if they can help you."

"In the sufferings of Syria," the man said, "there are many people who have been suffering more than me. Thank God that we are living here and surviving. Others are facing terrible situations. But there was nothing good about all of this. I won't lie. Since the problems began, we have nothing good to remember. If we laugh, we are laughing to be polite, but it's not from our hearts."

He leaned on the three pillows positioned to support him, his wife silent beside him. He seemed to be blinking back tears.

"Every night before I sleep, my eyes will tear up. I will remember my old days and our old life. When we see the news and see how it has changed, we cry. You can't hold yourself back from crying, because you are helpless and can't do anything. It's only God we pray to, because nobody else can help us."

"Thank you," I said. "I'm sorry for all the things you have been through."

"God bless you for this thing that you are doing. The only thing we hope for is to release the pressure that's on the population, the normal people. I consider the president and the people he's using to be terrorists. He is using people to kill his own people. Why don't we solve the problems between us without guns?"

CHAPTER 40

"God will be with us wherever we go."

OUR NEXT VISIT THAT DAY was to the home of some Syrian Christians. They brought us plates of grapes and a banana, a knife on each plate.

"It was a very good life. We were just living normally," the husband told us. "Syria was a good country for poor people because everything was cheap. Everything was available, even for the poor people, and it was safe for everybody. We never felt endangered or threatened. And we never felt any difference between the many sects: Christians, Muslims, Alawites, Sunnis, Shi'ites. We never felt any persecutions between them. They always lived in love.

"We lived in Damascus, the capital, but all of the areas of Syria were peaceful and safe. We had our own house which we owned, two floors."

The family had two daughters, bright-eyed girls with dark hair, about eight and ten years old. The one with dark-framed glasses told us what had happened to her at the beginning of the war.

"I was at school," the little girl said. "After we finished our school day, we went outside to wait for our parents to pick us up. Then the cleaning person who works in the streets came to take the trash. When he was looking inside, he saw an explosive, or a bomb, in the trashcan. He called the police. So the teachers took us to a safe place, and they closed all the doors around. We hid under the tables and desks. I waited for my mom and she came and took me, and after that I never went to school."

First, the family tried to wait it out.

"Then the bombs began to be so close to where we lived," her father remembered. "The explosions, the snipers . . . There would be snipers on top of many buildings, and they would just shoot people. We had a Christian neighbor who was going out of his home to a market next to our building, and a sniper targeted him and hit his shoulder. Our oldest daughter was in first grade in the first semester in November, and a rocket flew above her school and hit the area next to it. The rebel groups would plant explosives and bombs next to the doors of the schools, because the area where we lived was all Christians basically. One time a rocket fell two blocks away from our home. It didn't explode, and the army came and de-activated it.

"When we decided to come here, it was not an easy journey. From our house to the bus station is usually a fifteen-minute drive. But because of the checkpoints, it took us two hours. Every couple of minutes there was another checkpoint, and they searched us. They asked, 'Where are you going? What do you have in your bags?' They would open the bags and take everything out. At one of the checkpoints, a Muslim officer opened our bags and threw all the stuff in the street. We told him we were going to visit our family in Jordan, to spend Christmas there. Another officer close by said, 'Okay, Merry Christmas,' and let us go. We picked everything up from the street. At least it wasn't much because we didn't bring much, but it was very cold."

"I wish I could have brought my old clothes with me!" one of the daughters said.

"She wanted to bring her school backpack," the mother explained, "but we couldn't bring everything they wanted."

"Your daughters are so sweet; they make me smile," Jana said. The girls were playing a card game, sharing an arm chair, one sitting on the arm of the chair, one on the seat.

"Ever since the bomb was discovered at their school, they haven't gone back to school. When they hear fireworks for celebrations, they get scared," their father said. "They were used to an extended family environment. Now they don't sleep if they can't sleep in the same bed with us. When my wife and I would go out, they would stay with their grandma and their aunt. But after the incidents and the explosions they became too scared, and they would only stay with us and sleep with us."

"A month ago we went on a visit and took our daughter to a friend's house to stay," his wife said. "She wanted to stay there, but as soon as she arrived, there was a big explosion at the border and the window glass was shaking. So she was scared and came back with her father. At that house, you will often hear the bombs and explosions from the border."

"When we got here, we couldn't celebrate Christmas," the man went on. "We attended church, but our heart was hurt and we couldn't celebrate when our family was in danger. My sister and my mom were still there alone.

"We had to leave everything and come. My mom followed seven months later. But she suffered a lot until she reached here. She had to pass through seven villages until she reached Jordan. When she arrived at the border, they had a strike and were not working. She had to walk across the border to the Jordanian border, by foot, until she arrived.

"Now we are trying to pull out my sister," the man added. "When my mom decided to leave, my sister didn't think it would escalate. She was an employee of the government, so she didn't come. Also, she has never left Syria because she has no passport. Government employees don't leave Syria. So now in the suburbs, there are only women left, because men and sons and brothers have left so they won't be killed."

"So the government job she had won't protect her?" I asked.

"No," the husband and wife replied together, both providing pieces of the story. "Nobody can protect her. She's not married, and she's living alone in the house, and we are trying our best to bring her. Now, she has electricity and water only one hour a day. During the one hour of electricity, she needs to charge her phone, wash everything, fill what she can with water, and then the electricity shuts off until the next day. We need a paper from the intelligence office in Jordan to allow her to come in, because now they have stopped accepting new people."

A horn blared outside the window.

"So far, she can't come unless it's the illegal way, and that wouldn't be safe for her. She would have to walk for hours through the desert. But it's also hard for her to stay where she is. She's not working. She's living alone among all the rockets and the explosions.

"When I call my sister now, she's always crying. She says, 'If you could see Syria now, or our suburb, or our building, you would cry! Everything is destroyed! Nothing is here! Everybody left. Most of the men, brothers and sons, have died or fled. They will never get to be fathers! After 6 p.m. you can't walk out of the house.'

"It's so different from what it used to be! We used to stay out late at night, or go out at two or three in the morning. It was so safe.

"My brother-in-law fled to Germany," the man said as horns blared outside the windows of their house. "Even while they were fleeing across the water, their boat capsized. God saved them because they swam until they reached the shore. His son swam to the shore, and he called for help and then they brought boats. Many people died trying that. I was shocked when I heard that my cousin and her husband with her three sons also fled to Greece, the same way. They know they are doing something dangerous. But they are dying anyway from explosions and bombs, so why not?"

I remembered George's words, back in the convent cafeteria in Beirut, amid the clang of knives and forks on dinner plates. *Anytime you have people who consider themselves dead unless they cross the border,* he had said, *I don't know what technology or what infrastructure will stop them.*

"The hardest thing is to decide to leave your life, your job, your friends, your house, everything you have worked to build for years. We never intended to leave. On Friday, there were so many rockets and explosions around. My mom came and said, 'Pack what you can and leave now.' We talked about it on Friday, and on Sunday we left in the morning.

"We had a very close explosion. Our daughter was sleeping, and she fell from her bed because the explosion was so strong. We just kept saying, 'It is Jesus who will protect.' In Syria the blessing I look back to is that my girls were safe many times. And that until now my sister is still safe. And here without the church I would never be living normally again. They are the only ones who support us. We are doing better than others because they help support us."

As we talked, the church worker with us was taking apart the family's fan to see if he could fix it. He had some praise for the man we were visiting as well. "And he's very energetic about helping to serve other refugees," he said.

"I've heard that when people go through hard things, if they help others they do better themselves," I said.

"Yes, because you will feel with others," the man agreed. "You will feel with others, and you will be glad that you have the chance to help.

"Our dream is to leave the country and go to Canada," his wife said. "We don't have family there, but God will be with us wherever we go."

CHAPTER 41

"It's such a pity to end like this."

THE NEXT DAY, WE MET more people from Damascus.

In the morning, we met Fadi along the street close to our apartment. He had already picked up Reema. We headed south out of Amman, through a commercial section of the city. There were tall white-walled skyscrapers, one with palm trees growing in a balcony on the twelfth floor. We passed the Syrian embassy, which already had a crowd of people standing beside its doors, and we passed Petra University.

We passed fields of olive trees and rows and rows of green plants with giant metal hoops over them as if they were to be converted to a hundred greenhouses at a moment's notice.

We saw a sign for Mount Nebo, the mountain our Biblical refugee Moses had climbed in order to see into the Promised Land. Moses, the refugee who had not quite made it to his promised home, but whom God had so lovingly laid to rest.

We pulled into town and met up with a pastor, who led the way to the home of the first refugee family. We stepped down steps made of speckled tile and into a cool, walled alleyway. We were welcomed into a block house by a tall young man and two adorable young boys. The room we were invited to had mattresses stacked around the perimeter, giving us ample places to sit. One of the mattresses looked almost like a quilt from America. A typical wax-like reed mat was spread across the floor. One of the boys was dressed in a yellow shirt, the other in a blue shirt. Jana and I referred to them as the blue boy and the yellow boy after that. There was also a yellow curtain in the doorway to the next room, pulled back with a yellow cord and tassel to allow traffic.

"We lived in Yarmouk, a Palestinian refugee camp in Damascus,"[n] the man told us. "I owned a computer shop there, and I sold pieces for computers, hardware and software. Even though most of the people in the camp were Palestinians, I'm a Syrian and I used to live there," he explained. "The Palestinians were my clients, my friends."

Despite being tall, the man was strikingly gaunt, dressed in a small, white T-shirt that still seemed big on his frame. He had a bit of a goatee with a minimal beard and mustache. He sat with an elbow on one raised knee, and the other leg folded beneath him. Knowing he had lived in the Palestinian refugee camp and owned a computer shop made him seem unusual. He spoke with quiet calm, giving an understanding nod to Reema.

"At first, they began demonstrations in the outside suburbs, far away, but we began to sense that something was wrong. We heard about the demonstrations through the news channels. But nothing was happening around us. Then the war began to affect us. Electricity used to be cut off for long hours. People started to sense fear. There was some kidnapping and theft. Then they attacked our area, Yarmouk.

"I didn't leave until the last stage. I tried to stay in my house. But they began to attack and there were bombs and rockets that hit our building; they were that close to us. For a month we stayed in the same area, going to public places in Damascus, moving around. Then we said, there is no way other than leaving the country. I couldn't legally enter Jordan, although I had passports, but they didn't allow me to go legally, so I had to go the illegal way, through the desert. My sons went with my mother, before me. They came the legal way."

"Tell me about your journey here. How long did it take?" I asked.

"At the time I came through, there was a huge fight between the Syrians and the armed forces. And the day I entered, there were thirty-five civilians still lying on the ground, because they had been shot. Some people from that

---

n   *Yarmouk is an unofficial refugee camp that housed Palestinian refugees and descendants of refugees who fled Palestine when the state of Israel was created. Before the war, Yarmouk was home to the largest group of Palestinians in Syria.*

village were helping us through that stage. They helped us through the last stage they could help with, and then they had to hide. We had to go alone.

"At some points, the Syrians might even shoot the Jordanian soldiers, although it would be by mistake, but because they were shooting randomly. At my time, it was still much easier. It was faster than what happened later with everybody. I moved to one point in the morning, then at lunch I reached the second point, and from there I headed to Jordan.

"There is like a little hill or mountain. When you go up that hill, you see the Jordanian side. They began to receive you and call you. Really, they were so kind, the Jordanian Army. They helped with our luggage, they helped with children, and they put us on the buses. There were temporary mobile homes on the border to receive the people until the Jordanians could take them safely on the buses to the Zaatari camp.

"I first went to Zaatari. I stayed there for a month. The medical situation there and the health situation was so bad. I couldn't stay there, so I left.

"The thing that made me decide to leave Syria was the voice of the helicopters and planes and rockets. This is what made me send my children, even before I left. My children used to run to hide behind things, thinking it would protect them. Seeing them do that broke my heart, and I didn't stay any longer."

Fadi looked at the young boys sitting on the mattress.

"Now in Jordan, when you hear the airplanes, the voice of the airplanes, what do you feel?" he asked the one boy.

"If it's too close, I am scared, if the voice is too close," the boy said. "If it's high, high, I'm not scared; if the voice is not so strong.

"I'm sad for the toys I had to leave behind," he added. "I had a small couch for me to sit on, just my size. I would sit on the couch and put a chair in front of me and play and imagine that I'm selling."

"Computers?" I asked.

"Candy," he said. "But when I grow up, I want to be like my dad and have a computer shop."

"I had a car with a remote," the other boy said. "I used to sit in that car and drive it," he said. "It was an electric car."

"Did you share it with your friends sometimes?"

"Yes, I used to pretend that I was a taxi driver. The car took four people."

"Wow!"

The man of the house laughed, indicating that the car was not designed for four children.

"They used to *fit* four," he clarified.

The conversation switched back to the father's work.

"Here I can't work," he said. "I'm always at home. It's so difficult, the situation here. The Syrians now have more than financial needs. They need psychological help. The pressure, the stress, the situations they have been going through. They need the psychological support more than the financial support, especially the children.

"I already had an interview with the UN for the States. I'm praying to be accepted. The women in my family, my wife and my mother, are not doing okay. My wife is seeing the doctor now. My mother is an old lady and has knee problems. She used to live with us, but recently we had to get her a house along with my brother.

"My brother is depressed, so we had to take him away from the children. He is twenty-four years old and used to work as a tailor, making school backpacks. But he witnessed a horrible day at the beginning of the conflict. There was a clash between the government and the people of the camp. They continued shooting for twelve hours, from noon to midnight. For twelve hours, they were shooting in the camp."

"I heard about it; I remember," Reema said to me on the side.

"Nobody was allowed to go out. We were stuck, and this caused a huge fear inside of him. After that, there was more fighting and conflict. He deteriorated from only depression to a severe psychological condition, schizophrenia. I miss the brother he used to be. He was so wise; he was smart. I look at him, and it's such a pity to end like this. But he faced many things that he couldn't handle.

"We both had depression, but each of us has his own personality, and we received it differently. Then my father died in a car accident in front of him as well, here in Jordan. So everything has happened in front of his eyes. Sometimes he's peaceful, but suddenly he'll switch characters. He will love you and feel sorry for you, and suddenly he will be scared and angry. He has medication now, but he's not stable. We rented a small house for him and my mother."

There was knocking on the outer door, and a tall woman in a denim dress entered.

"Here's my wife," the man said.

She wore a white hijab with blue embroidery, and though the dress looked like American jeans, it had long sleeves and a long skirt, with buttons down the front. The man's wife wore glasses and carried a black purse. She had a beautiful smile.

"We wanted to know the gender of our baby," the husband explained. No one would have suspected that his wife was even pregnant. "But everything is a blessing from God, either male or female."

"Is your wife hoping for a girl?" I asked.

"We hope the baby is in good health," the man replied. "It is from God."

The woman left the room and came back with extra pillows, which she handed around to us. She was tall, slender, and graceful, with high cheek bones. She began to talk, and the interpreter began to talk and everyone laughed. She was trying to press drinks upon us, and Reema was trying to tell her we were fine. She seemed to be alarmed that her husband was entertaining us without offering us refreshments. We assured her it was fine, and she sat down and told her perspective of what they had been through.

"The hardest thing is to lose your loved ones, and to have to leave your home and your country. What we saw wasn't easy. If affected us a lot. To make the decision to leave wasn't easy; it was the hardest. We still react—if one of our sons hurts himself or we see a little blood, we panic. I am here, but I am always thinking of my family, still in Syria. I am only here in my body, but I keep thinking of them. Now a baby is coming, still inside me, and I'm scared for its life. I'm scared that we can't provide for it. If we get sick, we can't afford medication.

"I just went to this doctor who offers free checkups for me. She prescribed medications for me, but I told her I can't afford them. My blood pressure is going up and down, and she said, for the baby's sake, you need vitamins, you need antibiotics."

The men with us asked her what the medications were, to see if they could help.

The woman reached into the black purse for the prescriptions. Her movements were elegant and smooth.

"It doesn't seem like they would be very expensive," I said.

"Medicines in Jordan are expensive," Reema told me, "even for me. If you don't have insurance, you will pay, between the doctor and the medication, 50–75 JDs."

"I think first of my children," the woman said. "They need milk and food. Usually adults will hold their pain and sickness for the sake of the children. But even when my children get sick, we don't take them to the doctor. We can't!"

"We use glasses to help our vision, me and my son," the father said. Neither of them were wearing glasses. "But we can't afford them, and our old pairs have broken."

"Everyone thinks I'm in my third month of pregnancy," the woman said. "No one will believe I'm already in my seventh month. Perhaps the infections are affecting the baby."

I really doubted if the woman's baby would ever be healthy, since there was almost no sign that a baby even existed. Between the infections and the woman's health conditions, I was skeptical. Like the man had said about his brother's situation, "It's such a pity to end like this." But on January 11, 2016, I got a text from Jana: "Remember the computer shop man and family? We just visited them and got to see their month-old baby girl!" She even had a picture to prove it, and the baby, dressed in white and black with a yellow cap on her head, appeared to be healthy and strong.

It hadn't ended "like this" for the miracle child.

Voices from the Mosques

Throughout the conflict in Syria, mosques have played a key role. Many times, Islamic religious leaders would use the loudspeakers from the mosques to incite their people to violence in their Friday sermons. Yet the mosques also served as a source of information and a means of warning the people.

If someone died while crossing the border into Jordan, the names of the victims would be announced at the mosque. Family members would listen to the names that were read. Even though they hoped they would not hear the name of the person they had been separated from, the mosque was a source of information.

The mosque loudspeakers also warned the people during bombings to move to safer places, such as the lowest floor of an apartment building.

CHAPTER 42

"Some people died of hunger."

WE CLIMBED THE STAIRS TO the fourth floor of an apartment building for our next visit. The windows in the cement stairwells showed us a beautiful view of the tree-lined city.

The woman of the house was wearing the *niqab* with only her eyes showing. This was the first time we had spoken with a woman covered so completely in her own home.

Seated around the room on the floor were four big boys in jeans and T-shirts. The pastor pointed out the boy in the white shirt, saying he had come to church and helped him with the projector, when the pastor had been leading hymns. The pastor praised the family for being well-mannered and intelligent.

"We had a good life before the war," the lady said. "We had a home and a car. I had my children at the school. My husband had a job. I would stay with the little children, the two youngest, in the house."

I looked at one of the boys seated on the floor and asked him what his favorite subject had been in school.

"Math," he said. "I was in grade ten, in the commercial section. It's about accounting, mathematics, even practical things like IT problems."

The conversation turned to the conflict. Two people talked at once.

"In the beginning, we heard about the problems and the crisis," the mother started. "It was not in our area of Damascus. But then we were attacked with chemical bombs."

One of the boys continued.

"Some people died of hunger."

"That's when we left, after the government dropped the chemical bombs. It was a massacre. Almost 1,700 people died. People would inhale the chemicals and suffocate. Their lungs were damaged. Right in front of us, we saw them bring people to the hospital. They would admit them to the hospital for a day or two, and then they would die. The last injuries were only about a mile away from us.

"Of course, the areas close to the government weren't attacked, so the government wouldn't be affected. But we were between the government area and the other area."

"We left three days later," the mother said. "I went first with some of the children, and then my husband followed with the rest. Twenty days after the first chemical attack, we arrived in Jordan. At one of the checkpoints we stayed from 6 a.m. to 6 p.m., being checked for twelve hours. Sometimes they would shoot in the air to scare people. Sometimes they just put us on the side of the road for a long time. The soldiers at the checkpoints used civilians as a human shield. If they had a big gathering of people around them, terrorists were less likely to attack.

"Next we came through the desert. We started crossing the desert at 5 p.m., and it was 6 a.m. when we arrived in Jordan. We had hired a driver, and the first time he lost his way in the desert. He was taking us toward Iraq instead of Jordan. So we had to turn and come back.

"Then we heard planes coming. The driver told us to scatter with our families. There were some empty factories and abandoned buildings, and we hid there until the planes were gone. By then it was dark but the car drove with no lights, so nobody would see us.

"Each of us had an extra pair of clothes and two blankets in that duffel bag," the mother said, pointing to a bag in the corner of the room. "That bag is the only memory we have from our house in Syria, so we are holding on to it."

The woman's face was covered completely, but I noticed that her eyes continually traveled to the local pastor's face rather than looking at any of us.

One of the boys added that they also had a video camera with them. "At the Jordanian border, they wanted to take it, but we said, 'Please leave it for us.' We took pictures of everything that happened—the desert, the way we came—but they took it and erased everything on it, for security reasons. So we also lost our family pictures and everything about our life."

"I lost my brother in Syria," the woman said. "He was shot fifty meters away from the government officers. His body stayed there on the ground for a month. Nobody dared to go close and pick up his body.

"For a month—a month! And they would take pictures of him, how he was lying down dead, as if it was a story! After a month they burned the area with the bodies and the plants and everything.

"My husband was in great danger as well, because he used to work with the security police. I was in constant fear that they would take him into custody, but he made it here safely. He tries to find jobs here, but they are not allowed to work."

"If they find us working," one of the boys said, "they will catch us and send us back to Zaatari Camp. They ask us not to work, but they are not giving us any aid."

"I was prevented from going to school," said a brother with a head full of thick black hair. He was wearing a gray T-shirt and seemed to be the oldest. His tone oozed bitterness. "I stopped my education. We had to leave our country. So now here I have no future, other than to work and bring as much money as I can to help my family. I was planning to be a doctor, but the president has ruined our hopes for the future."

It was quiet for a bit.

"Why don't you continue school?" Fadi asked.

"I can't," the boy said. "If I stop working one day, my family will not have enough money. Each JD I earn is to cover basic things like rent and the food."

The boy in the white shirt, the one who helped the pastor at church, spoke next.

"I can't forget the voice of the rockets and the shells and the bomb explosions," he said. "I'm in high school, and I want to be a geography teacher," he said.

Reema laughed. She was a teacher herself. "That's the first time I've heard that," she said.

"Since I was in grade nine, I liked geography," he said. "If my sister or anyone asks me about history or geography, I can help them and answer them quickly."

"They always were smart," the mother said from behind the black *niqab*.

"They always had high scores at school."

I asked the family if there were any good things that happened along the way, amid all the bad.

"We escaped safely with all the children," the mother said. "Nobody was left behind. It was really hard there when they wanted to eat and drink, and you couldn't afford it. My sister is still there, and now she can't afford to buy milk for her children. She said, 'I have only two children, and I can't even afford a quarter of a meal for the day. How would you survive with your seven children?' It's so hard there. So I'm so glad we were able to leave safely. All my family is still there. None of the basic living conditions are available for them. Some days they had to eat leaves from the farms outside, any green thing to survive. Some people died of hunger because they couldn't afford food. And they are surrounded, and they can't move. Sometimes, even when we were sent aid, the government wouldn't allow it to come in."

I asked if there was anything else they could tell us that would help people in America to understand better what they had been through.

There was a distinct silence.

"Here we are suffering," the older boy with the gray shirt said. "We have no rights in any of the Arab countries. We call our relatives in European countries. We are called refugees and they are called refugees, but they are being treated better. Here we walk in the street and people say, 'Hey, you are a refugee,' and they humiliate us. It's hard, but I try to ignore them to not make problems.

"But it's not fair, because Syria always took care of refugees from other countries. And they didn't make camps. Syria was the only country where they built houses for the refugees. They didn't put them in tents. The first time I go back to Syria, and I meet a Jordanian, I will get back at him and treat him like I have been treated here."

Everyone started talking at once.

His mother agreed, at least in part.

"Some people tell us, 'You are living very good. You get coupons and you can have food for free,'" she said. "But they don't know how we are suffering. We are only surviving; we are not living as human beings."

"And they don't treat us right," the boy in the gray shirt continued angrily.

He squatted on the mat in front of a tray of orange juice that had been passed around to us. "We work for a day for a Jordanian, and they will give us less than we deserve. The first day he won't pay me, the second day he won't pay me, and then the third day when he owes me for three days, he says, 'No I'm not going to give you anything. You are a refugee, and you are not allowed to work. I will inform about you if you complain.' Or then they will offer the Syrians half or even less than half of what other laborers are paid.

"So then when I began to work, I would have conflicts with other workers. They tell me, 'You are taking our jobs, because you are accepting less money.' They don't realize that I'm in a terrible situation to have to work for half price, when I'm trying to support the family and basic things. I worked one day for eighteen hours and I took only 6 JDs. I didn't even have time to sleep. One man made me open his shop at 5:30 in the morning, even in the snow. He made me call him every morning when I got there so that he would know I was there."

"So we came to this location," his mother said, "hoping for a better opportunity for him, but it is the same. He will work the work of three people and get paid very little. The problem that we face is the rent for the houses keeps increasing. Our other problem is medical treatment. We used to get treatment from the UN, but now they stopped it. In Syria, we were used to having a salary that was always enough."

Reema had something to say now. "There are many Jordanians, too, whose salary is low, and they also pay high rent," she said. "It's an expensive country. My neighbor used to always complain about not having enough money. This is the situation for the normal Jordanian family."

One of the boys piped up with another complaint.

"If I want to get married, here I have to pay 4,000 or 5,000 JDs," he complained. "In Syria, for only 1,000 JDs, you could marry a beauty queen."

We laughed. Reema agreed that people would go to Syria to marry because their families would accept lower prices. "It's an Arabic phrase: Marry a Syrian wife to live a good life," she said.

A little daughter arrived home from school. She walked straight to the pastor, and greeted him with a kiss, then circled the room, giving everyone a three-stage kiss.

"Some people died of hunger."

"Don't look for justice," Fadi told the family, focusing on the boy in the gray shirt, as the girl made her kissing rounds. "Yes, there's injustice in this world, but don't live in anger because of that. Many people have hard circumstances in this world, but the only One we can depend on is God. Everything else will change. Only God is stable and fair and just.

"Life might change, and I may become a refugee. So try to depend on God even when you feel you are being treated unfairly. You are working for eighteen hours and taking a low wage, and you feel how unfair that is. But at least you are healthy to work. Others are not even able to go out of their houses to work. Everyone looks for better things, of course, but if you can't have the better now, just depend on God, and pray to Him."

We thanked the family and descended the stairs.

––––––––––––––––––––

After getting into our vehicle, we began to thread our way through the busy traffic. At one point, Fadi stopped to point at a dumpster.

"Look!"

Rising from the dumpster were four horse's hooves. Someone had thrown a dead horse into the trash.

We discussed where we should eat lunch, and we opted to drive back to Amman. It was the last day Fadi would be with us, and I was sad to have to part ways with him. I could tell he was a beacon of light in the darkness. I thought of the days of labor he had been through and would continue to have in a crisis without an end. I thought about the church workers and the huge task they faced as they worked with refugees. I thought of the old saying that one death is a tragedy, but 100,000 deaths are just a statistic. To the people who were working with the refugees day after day, however, they were not statistics. Each person was still an individual. Time and time again I heard myself say, "I'm sorry" or "I will do my best to help people understand what you've been through." But those words felt limp beside the lives of the church workers.

The refugees often pointed to the local Christians and said, "I had no one to help me. Except him. Except her."

VOICES

FROM DARAA

Daraa

Before 2011, Daraa was just another little town in Syria near the Jordanian border.

This area near the border had seen bloodshed before, however. It was here that a battle fought by Muslim general Khaled ibn al-Walid in 636, turned Syria into a Muslim state. The Muslim general did away with the remnants of Roman rule, killing 50,000 soldiers.

For hundreds of years, Daraa received little notice from the rest of the world. But when a small group of teenagers painted "the people want to topple the regime" on a school wall, Daraa reappeared on the world scene. People across Syria began to claim the story, chanting "Daraa is Syria."[35]

As the conflict spread to other areas, Daraa maintained a pivotal role in the war as a gateway through which refugees escaped the country across the nearby border to Jordan.

CHAPTER 43

"I just want peace."

ON THE JOURNEY OUT OF Amman on our last day of visits, we stopped at a roadside store for water and a few snacks. Our bill was five dinars, and our driver handed a ten-dinar bill to the clerk. By mistake, the clerk handed back a ten-dinar bill.

The driver handed it back, saying it was too much. The clerk took it and replaced it with the correct change.

"You must be Christians," he said.

We discussed this when we got back in the van. The Muslim clerk had identified our driver as a Christian because of his honesty.

We arrived at a church and stepped into a cool, tiled basement. It was a sanctuary with brown wooden chairs instead of benches. A maroon curtain was hanging behind the pulpit.

As our driver and the pastor spoke Arabic, I sat and watched their hands. I felt removed from the conversation because I could not understand. But my other senses were sharpened: my eyes toward watching gestures, and my ears toward picking up tones of voice. Both were abundant in the Arab world.

It was now the day before the Muslim holiday, or Eid. Schools and business were closed, the sheep market was booming, and the Muslim people were fasting. One of the church workers that went with us seemed tired, and I felt bad that we were keeping her busy on a day she might otherwise have been off. Even though Eid-al-Adha was not a Christian holiday, everything in Jordan, including the schedules of Christians, revolved around it.

It was now, near the end of our journey, that we began to hear from people from Daraa.

First we entered the home of a thirty-three-year-old former soldier. He was wearing a black T-shirt. He had a hard, determined face and a muscular frame. His wife was a plump woman who wore a brown dress and a pink and black plaid hijab. Beside the husband, a ten- or twelve-year-old boy sat silently. Beside the wife, a younger girl with frizzy black hair and a mouth full of bubble gum sat mischievously on the cushion.

"I was working in the military," the man said. "Before the persecution, we were living a very good life. I built my own house, and I bought my own car."

"In Syria it was peaceful and normal before the war," the woman said. "My favorite thing was visiting with other friends. We liked to go out. We used to live in a village. We didn't have restaurants, but all of the relatives would visit in each other's houses."

"I'm from Daraa. I worked with the ministry court for fourteen years," the man said. "In 2011 when the crisis started, things started to become more difficult. Everyone knows the story about Daraa and the teenagers. But the problem is not what happened; it is the government's reaction. One of the officials there was a police station officer, and he was President al-Assad's cousin. Instead of talking with the children and their parents, he put them in prison without any consideration to what could happen. And they kept delaying the resolution of this issue, which meant that every day it got deeper and extra towns and villages would join the demonstrations. And so it was getting wider and wider. It became deeper from both ends, because more people were joining, and the response of the government became more severe and more brutal. Both were making mistakes. It became more complicated because more people and countries were getting involved. It was not an issue of tens of people, it became villages and towns and principalities.

"In the first period it should have been easily resolved, but people were not able to act and make the right decisions. Although I was working with the military regime, many times the government would take people like me and arrest them. I was targeted by both parties. Because I was working with the military, the people thought of me as pro-regime; at the same time the regime did not think of me as one of their own since I was from Daraa, where the protests had started. So I was targeted from both sides.

"The bombing started in my neighborhood. I had to move to another place. I started receiving threats from the Free Army, saying, 'You have to leave the military and come and join us. This is an unfair regime and there's a lot of oppression, and you need to leave them and come to us.' It was really hard for me because if you leave the army you will be targeted by the army; if you leave the state, you will be targeted by the state. And at the same time, just living there, there might be random bombing.

"It was difficult to live there because you had to choose a side. If you didn't choose a side, you would be killed by both of them. When the first bombs fell, I made my decision; it was obvious for us. The children became terrified by the bombing, they could not sleep. That's why I decided to leave.

"When I looked at my children, it was terrifying because they couldn't cry. I could see all of them were afraid and terrified. They started to be afraid of the night because usually the bombings happened at night. My younger son was always anxious, even in the day, that there would be bombing. He would have nightmares about these kinds of things."

The man's son entered the room carrying a silver tray with glasses and a silver teapot. As he lowered himself and the tray to the floor, his father reached up and helped him steady the tray. The boy then poured the glasses full of tea and passed them to us as his father continued talking.

"My brother also died from the bombings. He was in the garden outside the house. We were all sitting in the house, but my brother was outside, and he was killed there."

I sighed. Sometimes as I sat and listened, the endless repetition of grief overcame me. I could say "I'm sorry to hear that," a dozen times, but how did that help?

"Was the bomb that close?" I asked.

"They were bombing in a nearby area, but not exactly where we were. We were all inside, and only my brother went out to see. When he went out, he was hit by a fragment. We took him to the hospital, but he died on the way to the hospital. He was twenty-two years old when he passed away. The day he died was the most difficult day of my life.

"I'm from the countryside of Daraa, so when I went to the city of Daraa itself, people asked, 'Why are you leaving your country? Why?' People asked, 'Why don't you protect your country?' But I was not thinking about my country or myself; I was only thinking about my children because they were terrified.

"When we left we didn't take even a plastic bag with us. Nothing. We had to walk very long distances. We had to walk from the last village to get to Jordan. There's a valley between Syria and Jordan. We had to cross it with the children, with the women, with everyone. It was March, and it was very cold. And the regime started to shoot at us. The whole trip from our town to Jordan took five days. But the border crossing took twelve hours, all night. If there had been no war, before the crisis, it would take us between one to two hours to get from my town to Jordan."

As the man of the house spoke, his wife and the children fell into an almost palpable stillness, their faces drawn and silent. The boy who made the tea sat with one leg bent at the knee, his elbow resting on the knee, and his face full of the darkness of the memories.

"Some people were called smugglers. It became their profession to move people from one place to another. These smugglers told me that I cannot use the bus, so I had to walk while my wife and children went in a bus because I could not pass through the checkpoints. I had to walk for four days to meet them, before the one-day trip across the border. I couldn't go through the checkpoints because there were two types of checkpoints: those that belonged to the Free Army (the opposition) and the regime. So whoever would catch me would think I was with the other side. And if my family would have carried anything with them in the buses, the people at the checkpoints would have understood that they were fleeing, so they would have been detained."

Suddenly, the reason no one took anything began to make more sense.

"Whoever would catch you leaving the country, regardless of which side you were on, would create so many problems. Either you would be detained, or you would be killed, tortured, whatever. We had to look for a smuggler at each village we got to. And every time I had to pay different payments. It was not free. Some of the desert areas could not be accessed by cars. Not even the military people would go there because it's rough terrain. Also, everything had to be done at night. The smugglers would provide you with a place to stay during the day, and then they would move you at night. There were certain areas where it was known that anyone going there was escaping. That's why we had to wait until night.

"We had to cross the Yarmouk River. We tried to cross it multiple times, but sometimes they would shoot at us, and we would have to go back and go to another area. A lot of people were killed on this trip because the pro-regime forces would shoot at night at these areas because they knew refugees were there. So they would shoot without even seeing individuals, because they would anticipate that there were refugees there. We had to take some wounded with us. During the trip some people were shot and killed and we left them where they were, and some people were wounded and we took them with us. When we finally crossed the border, we felt safer. We were relieved that we got to Jordan. We knew we were across because the Jordanian Army received us.

"They separated us in Jordan; my wife and children went to Zaatari Camp. But then my wife and daughter got sick in Zaatari Camp, so I had to take them out. I rented a house. That was two and a half years ago, so this is the second house.

"In Syria they missed half a year of education because of the crisis, but here they're getting a good education. What is a man's goal, other than to see his children safe and getting a good education and a better future?

"My wife's leg is broken. She fell down the stairs. There were no organizations that helped us with health care, but other people assisted us. At the beginning we used to be receiving health benefits through UNHCR, but now they stopped everything. Things became a bit tight, but then we got introduced to the church people, and they will be standing by for whatever we need.

"Some things are affecting us negatively here in Jordan, but all of my children are smart, and they are pursuing a better education. When they started school in Jordan, the things that they went through made it difficult for them to achieve, but now it is getting better.

"All of the neighborhood where we lived in Syria was destroyed. They sent me pictures of my house. If there were one thing I would want people to know, it is that we are living a tragic life, with a hard situation. We die a hundred times every day. We don't ask for more funds. We just ask for peace, to get back to our country, and live a normal life. This whole thing started because people wanted freedom. I don't want freedom anymore; I just want peace."

CHAPTER 44

"Death was surrounding us."

"I HAVE FOUR BOYS AND a girl and my husband," a woman dressed in black told us as we settled into her apartment. She held a baby in her lap, and her daughter, perhaps nine or ten, sat beside her. The two oldest boys had bandages around their fingers, both on the right hand.

The family was fasting today, so we were not offered drinks. The woman did not want her face to be photographed.

"We were living in heaven. There is nothing better than what Syria was like before the war. I will never forget my memories there. I am originally from Daraa. Everything is good in Syria: the weather, the families, the food, the fruits. I remember my furniture, my pillows, my kitchen, basic things like that. Everything was affordable there.

"At first my kitchen wasn't that nice. But my husband helped me, and we made it like an American kitchen. Our house was old, but we renovated everything. We made it the way I wanted it to be. I put my touch all over the house. I love colors. I love plants and natural decorations. My kitchen was brown. I also like dark red and beige. I am an artistic person, but here it's hard to be artistic when you don't have much.

"It was always safe before the war. I could leave at night and come back. But when the war started, death was surrounding us. There was shooting and rockets and many buildings were attacked around us. We couldn't go out because we were afraid for the safety of our children. Before we left, there was continuous shooting and attacks and rockets during the night. It didn't stop. We stayed awake all night, moving from one room to another.

"Death was surrounding us."

If the sound was close to the bathroom, we would go to the other side of the house. If it was next to the bedroom, we would move again. After so much suffering, we made the hard decision to leave.

"It wasn't like when the attacks began, we immediately decided to leave. No! We kept saying, 'It will get better; it has to get better. Surely we can stay! We will not leave our country.' We went and stayed in other villages for a while. But it just didn't get better, and we had to leave. And even when we left, we thought it was just for a day or two. I left everything in my house. I had a mattress on the floor, and I didn't fold it because I thought I was going and coming back.

"This boy, my little one, he used to be so scared. Even now when he sees a police car, he will scream and run away. A while ago, he saw some fighting in the street, and he got scared, and he had fever all night."

"Do you remember these things?" I asked the oldest boy who was wearing a blue shirt.

"Yes, I remember the fear. We used to be afraid to move from one room to another. But I also remember going out with friends and playing soccer in the streets. I would move and play different positions. I'm not a goalkeeper though. I enjoy the offense better."

"They were playing soccer, you can see!" The mother pointed to each boy's bandaged hands with a tired smile. "That one has a bandage because he hurt himself playing soccer. The other one went through the door too quickly and hurt himself that way.

"We left on the third day of Ramadan in 2012," the woman went on. "We were fasting, and it was hot. Smugglers helped us find a safe way. We would move forward, then they would make us wait if there was fighting. Whenever the clash was finished, we would go on. These smugglers were people in the Free Army, the opposition army. They took some money from us for the car, and to ensure we would arrive safely.

"I tried to bring clothes for my children. But because the way was so hard, we dropped many of the things we had along the way. We arrived at the camp with no shoes. We had walked most of the way. We walked about four hours through the desert from midday to around four in the afternoon. When we heard shooting we hid among the pomegranate trees and the olive

241

trees until it calmed down. Then we walked again.

"Walking through the desert like that was known to be dangerous. They even told us to turn off our mobile phones, because they said we might be discovered through the mobile signals. The smugglers stayed with us until we reached the border. They said 'hello' to the Jordanians, and then they went back.

"The Jordanian Army was the first thing we saw when we arrived. My children were scared when we crossed the Syrian border. The soldiers all came to help us, but the children were afraid. They began to cry. But I saw what the Jordanian Army did. With their right hands they would shake hands with the children, but they would hide their weapons behind their backs. Then they also gave us water and juice."

The Muslim call to prayer began to sound out.

"We stayed in the camp for a while, but my son got an infection, so they took us to a hospital. Then someone sponsored us so we could leave the camp. The camp was dirty and dusty, and the bathrooms were awful. There were twenty-two of us in one *caravan*.°

"But even though the camp was awful, the worst part was having to leave Syria," she said. "I heard that our house was attacked by rockets and is half destroyed, but you know, I don't care. I just pray for the crisis to finish, so I can go back to my country. If I have to live on the sand, I will live on the sand. I miss everything, even the wind.ᴾ

"Every night we keep praying to go back. Syria is my life. My country is everything to me. I can't describe it. No matter how much I talk, I will never be able to describe how I feel.

"When I was in Syria, my dreams were to educate my children and give them a good education. But here it doesn't seem possible. Now my son is in grade one, and I'm trying to help him in reading. I'm trying to help my children with their education and their learning. I wanted them to go to college, to study in the universities."

One of the church workers spoke.

---

o   *Metal buildings similar to small mobile homes that are used to house refugees in Zaatari Camp.*

p   *"It's an idiom in Arabic," Reema told me. "It expresses how attached you are to your country. Even its wind will revive you."*

"You should have hope!" she said. "When the Palestinian refugees came here, their situation was worse, and now look, they are the best people in the country! They have businesses and jobs. At least you have people helping you. But at that time, there was nobody. The Palestinians left their country on donkeys or walking with nothing, not even their IDs or their passports. So you have hopes and God is faithful."

The woman went on.

"I don't dream about a house, a car, or a dress. My only dream is to give a good education to my children. I'm trying to help them in their learning. I refuse to send any of my children to any of the European countries. I want them always to be next to me. I'm so cautious. I refuse to travel outside, even if it would mean a better future for them.

"At least here I feel I'm close to Syria."

CHAPTER 45

"If you were in my place at that time."

AFTER A LUNCH OF CHICKEN shawarma sandwiches eaten hastily from paper wrappers in our hot van, we drove to a new subdivision. Most of the block wall houses were under construction, but we pulled up in front of one that already had a planted garden complete with a scarecrow.

As usual, we all took off our shoes and entered the sitting room and seated ourselves on low floor cushions. I was beginning to like the corner, where two cushions intersected and I could sit at a right angle with my interpreter. Jana sat beside me on the left, so she could also hear the English version.

The man of the house was tanned and muscular. He apologized that the electricity in the neighborhood was off, so his fan would not work. He opened the window in the room to let in a breeze before sitting cross-legged on the cushion. He wore a dark shirt and blue jeans. We discovered he was the gardener.

"Thank you," I said, as I was offered a drink. "What do you have in the garden? Cucumbers?"

He said something that sounded like "lokia," and Reema said something back that made everyone laugh.

"It has no translation. It's *mulukhiya*," Reema said, "and I found out it has no translation in English. It is a vegetable with green leaves that literally has no equivalent in the States. I've been trying to find the word for the last five years. So I just know it's *mulukhiya* and that's it."

The man continued.

"In my garden I have *lubia*, a kind of bean," he said. "I had the seeds from

Palestine, the original seeds. I planted them, and I'm taking care of it. They told me it doesn't work here in this environment, but I am taking care of it. I can even show you the beans it is producing. It has produced so well that we have put some in the freezer to save for later.

"I also worked with produce in Syria," he said, "because the area where we lived was basically dependent on farms and farmers to produce food.

"I am 34 years old. I'm originally from Daraa. We were living normally; it was safe. Almost everyone there was involved in farming."

The husband's story followed a familiar pattern of a normal life that became unstable when the war started, and they decided for the sake of their children to leave Syria. I didn't expect to hear anything different.

"The first thing that told us something was wrong was when they began to kill the people," the man said. "It had already begun in Daraa. All of Syria's problems began in downtown Daraa when fifteen children were taken into custody, and one of the boys was killed. After that the incidents began to escalate and they began to kill people. We began to see what the government was doing to the people, and we opposed that."

The church worker with us whispered that he had worked with the father of the boy whose death had marked the beginning of the civil war. The father had come to Jordan as a refugee.

I hadn't really noticed the man's wife, sitting off to my left, until she began talking.

"Those were little boys," she said, "but they used to watch on TV what was happening in the other countries, in Iraq and Egypt and Tunisia. They were just children imitating what they had seen, but the government took it so seriously."

"We decided to leave because we were afraid for the safety of our children," he said.

"Everyone has a wife, a daughter, a sister," his wife said. "We wanted to save our honor, because they would go and attack them.

"I am a nurse and I used to work at the hospital there, so I saw lots of incidents," she continued. "I used to work in a hospital close to Daraa. So when they began to shoot people, they brought the injured to our hospital. We were so busy with all the injured people. We had no time for everyone.

Someone would bring an injured person in. We would treat them quickly and then discharge them.

"We had to discharge people so quickly for two reasons. First, there was no space, and new injured people would come in and need the beds. Second, we discharged them quickly because the government soldiers were known to come to the hospitals to find people to arrest.

"There is one day I cannot forget," the nurse said. "I was in the hospital and there was lots of shooting. A head trauma patient was brought in with a bullet in his head. It was clear that he could not possibly live through the injury. Half of his brain was out. It was clearly a fatal wound.

"The injured man was a government employee. His friend, an officer working with him, brought him to the intensive care unit. His friend told us, 'If he dies, I will shoot the whole hospital.' He parked his tank in front of the hospital and pointed it toward us.

"So, to save our lives, the doctors told him, 'We don't have the capabilities to treat him. You need to move him to another hospital.' They knew he was going to die. But to save us they sent him to the other hospital.

"Before the war I worked in the dialysis unit, helping to clean the blood of people whose kidneys failed. People needed to be connected to the dialysis machine for at least four hours at a time, so I got to know the people. I would sit with them and talk to them," she said. "I was really close friends to many of them."

But when the war started, everything changed, and our nurse friend had to assist the injured who began to come through the emergency room doors.

"Even if we were at home, they would call us in, and we would go in immediately. We would stay for days helping there with the wounded people. Sometimes, I had hardly gotten home, and they would call me again. So I would go back.

"Once they brought a fifteen-year-old boy who was shot by mistake because he was caught between the opposition and the government. We had hardly treated him when the government officers were at the door. They wanted to arrest him. We didn't know whose son he was. But one of the nurses kept crying and begging the officer . . ."

Nursing school teaches that nurses are supposed to be advocates for their patients. They are supposed to voice their concerns for people who are unable to voice their own. In all my years of being a nurse, I had never heard such a story of nurse advocacy. I wanted to cry. I was afraid the story would have a bad ending. How could a nurse stand up to a Syrian army officer?

But the lady finished the story simply.

". . . She kept crying and begging until they left him." My eyes widened in surprise and relief.

"We were witness to many horrible things," the nurse went on. "We would hear shooting while we were working, and several times they bombed the hospital. My kidney patients who needed dialysis got into trouble. It wasn't easy for anyone to reach the hospital anymore, and they were supposed to come for dialysis three times a week. Only the ones who were close came, and even then they wouldn't come on the right day or time. Most of them couldn't live for more than three days without being hospitalized. Many of them were supposed to be on a special diet. But because they did not have access to the right food, they would hardly survive the normal two days. Then the army would call curfews, and no one could travel, so there was no way for them to make it to the hospital. I kept calling to check on them, but they told me many of them died because they couldn't reach the hospital.

"Finally, it became so dangerous that I couldn't reach the hospital either. My husband would normally drive me, but it became too hard to go there. Every time I would leave my home," the nurse said, "I would go to my sister-in-law and my family and tell them, 'If anything happens to me on the way, please take care of my children.' There were checkpoints on the way to the hospital, and they would stop us and humiliate us. At some of the checkpoints, they were nice because we were Sunni, and they were from the same village. But at the security checkpoint there were Alawites, like the president, the Shi'ites, and they were not nice to us.

"I had to stop working three months before we came here. I took a no-salary vacation. Many other people left the hospital too, especially after the hospital was bombed. Now they are telling me that it has become a field hospital. The dialysis unit has been discontinued because there's no way to do it anymore."

I had heard the nurses' training programs in Syria were very good, so I asked her about this.

"When I studied nursing, it wasn't that strong, but ten years later, they began to really focus on nursing. Even when I graduated, I didn't know much. The trainer at that time didn't care if I knew or not. But I learned by practice at the hospital."

"Did they teach you to put in IVs in school?"

"Yes, basic things," she said.

"Because I didn't learn that in America," I said. The first IVs I had placed were in a blue tarp cholera hospital in Haiti.

"That's good," she said.

Everyone laughed, pleased that the Syrian education had been superior in this case.

"Now when I look at the new nursing section," the Syrian nurse said, "and I look at how they are teaching them, I realize I learned nothing. Now it's so strong and focused compared to ten years ago. The newly graduated nurses can now manage many patients alone. They trained the trainers recently, and the whole curriculum became stronger. At my time it was only three years of study, but now it's five."

Her husband began to talk again.

"The hardest thing was when we went out for peaceful demonstrations, we would receive gunshots and shooting," the husband said. "They wouldn't accept even a peaceful demonstration. Many of the demonstrators were taken into custody. Or they would just shoot the demonstrators in some cases.

"The only thing we could bring along when we left Daraa were my IDs, the family book, and passports. All the memories are stuck in my mind. I can't describe it. I left my country and my family. My parents are still there. They can't go out; they can't leave. My mom is a Palestinian, and my sister-in-law is an Iraqi, and they are not allowed to leave Syria. We communicate with them. We call them, but there is not good coverage there. They still live in the same place where we used to live."

"Maybe this is a dumb question," I said, "but what is a family book?"

"The family book is an ID for the whole family that lists the husband, the wife, and the number of children," our driver explained. "The main reason for the family book is because people here can marry more than one spouse, and so it's easier if they keep the records all in one book. You will find it in these countries, for statistics. They can keep track of births and number of wives and everything."

"My dream for my family is just that they can live in a safe place," the man said. "To live safely and securely is important. Now I have to pay for my children to go to school. I don't have a salary. Our older daughter was burned three months ago with hot oil on her hand. It was a serious burn. I took her to the hospital here, but they didn't help her. So I had to go and buy medication for her. It's her right hand, and now she feels so sensitive about going to school because when she writes with her right hand, the burn will show. She's embarrassed and wants to cover it."

Our hosts served us tea. I tasted mine with surprise, recognizing the fresh taste of mint from my childhood.

"I am facing problems with the education of my six-year-olds in grade one," the nurse said. "Their teacher doesn't teach them well. She doesn't explain the letters. She doesn't care if they learn it or not. And they are twins. I have twins in grade one, a boy and a girl.

"Raising the twins was as if I was in a dream, and now I'm awake! I was still working at the hospital when I had the twins. My sister and my parents-in-law tried their best to help me. I worked at the hospital almost every day. I would take Friday and Saturday off and replace them with other week days. That time of my life seems like a fog. When did I have my children? When did I raise them? How did it happen? I can't remember. It's as if I just woke up from a dream, that I had those children and I raised them.

"I would tell everybody, 'Don't leave your country. It's better to stay in your own country!' If I had the chance to go back, I would. It's our fear for the safety of our children that keeps us here. Now my priority is to teach my children well, and to help them have an education, which is so hard here. So, although they go to school, I make it a priority to teach them at home as well.

"In the hospital so many things happened to us. Many times it would be time for us to leave our shift, but there was shooting between the government and the opposition on our route home, so we would stay at the hospital overnight. We would stay until it was safe."

"Were you getting paid more if you worked extra?" I asked.

"No," she said, and everyone started laughing at my question. "Nobody cared. The duty control manager who managed the schedule, the one who would ask us to work extra, was the first one to flee.

"If you were in my place at that time, you would be so overwhelmed by the many injured people and the blood around you, that you would forget your children for three or four days. We became so focused to save those injured people. Almost any nurse who could make it to the hospital would come as soon as they were called. Some nurses who couldn't make it would treat people in their own homes."

We stepped out to take another peak at the man's garden. He had a black tarp pathway that allowed a person to walk down the center aisle of the garden. He had carefully-tended fencing around the edge.

The gardener was particularly proud of his bean plant that had defied prediction. He had built a wooden trellis for the beans, and they had long beans hanging on them still, although the main harvest was past.

Besides the beans, cucumbers, and greens that clung to the brown dust of the garden, a row of young trees had been started along the side of the house. There was a pomegranate tree, an olive tree, and a pear tree.

I felt certain that, like the transplanted Palestinian bean, this family would prosper in their new land.

The Last Hospital in Daraa

On the 1,571st day of the Syrian conflict, an article was posted on a Syrian war website,[36] attributing the destruction of Daraa's last hospital to the al-Assad regime. It was the summer of 2015.

Before the war, patients with kidney failure had a choice of hospitals to go to for dialysis. Finally, there was only one hospital still functioning, the Busra Hospital. For a year it served all the dialysis patients who could reach it. It also was the only remaining hospital to provide neonatal care. Although medical care was already strained, the Busra hospital was a last lifeline for patients in the Daraa area. Dialysis patients will die within days or weeks if not treated.

On a Monday night in June at about 11:00, the hospital was attacked by four barrel bombs, breaking doors and windows. With helicopters drumming overhead, staff evacuated patients before six more bombs were dropped that destroyed medical equipment and most of the building.[37]

CHAPTER 46

"I don't know who was asking for freedom."

WE ENTERED AN APARTMENT WITH red hand prints stamped as a border half-way up one wall. There was a sad-faced Muslim woman in black and a man in a striped robe who was her husband.

"We had our own apartment before the war," the man said. "But we heard it's been destroyed by rockets. I used to be a delivery driver for a construction and tiling factory in Daraa. I got to know the streets of Daraa very well."

"He is a good driver," his wife added.

"My children would go to school, and we were glad with our lives. We were safe and free! All our relatives were around, our friends. Now we don't have anybody around us. We don't know where they are."

"Each one of us had his own apartment," his wife said, "but we all kind of lived together, cooked together, stayed in the evening together. My sisters-in-law and I would often cook together."

"In Syria, even in the city, this is the way they do things. They are so social," Reema said. "It's not like Jordan. Relatives get together for evenings, dinners, and lunches. They have a constant social life."

"I used to be a driver," the man said, "so every night I would be in Homs, or Damascus, or Daraa. Whenever I would have free time, I would play cards with friends or meet at a coffee shop.

"Then we began to hear about the fighting. We thought it couldn't last long. But they began shooting, not only bullets, but rockets and bombs. Then they began to use airplanes to shoot rockets. When they started shooting rockets out of airplanes, I came to Jordan. I was worried about my son; he was so scared, that multiple times I thought he would have a heart attack!

"The worst part of the rockets and explosions was the noise. You would hear a whistle and then a huge thunder. It's much louder than a fireworks explosion," he waved his hands in the air, tracing the imaginary sights and sounds. "Fireworks are only a light version. You have to imagine something much louder, with a huge thunder.

"There was no warning. You would be sleeping at one or two in the morning, and you would hear the noise beginning, and you would know there was a rocket or a barrel bomb behind it. We would grab our children and try to run away to our friends' house next door, or our neighbors, or relatives who lived in buildings with three or four floors. Those buildings were safer because you could retreat to the ground floor."

"I felt like I was in a horror movie," the girl in the teal hijab said.

"The worst thing for me was when the security officers broke into our house," the mother said. "There I was with my children, and they broke in with their guns."

"They wouldn't knock on the door," her husband added. "They would break it down. They searched the whole house for guns and weapons. They had intelligence about who had been joining in the anti-government demonstrations. But even if you hadn't been part of the demonstrations, they would still break into your house.

"Also, it got to where we had a hard time finding food and water. They used to cut off the electricity and the water. And of course the bombing harmed the generators and wires, so even when you had the electricity back, it would work in some places and not in others. We were living in these conditions almost a year.

"When I finally left my house, my brother moved into it, thinking it would be safer for him. But one night they were hit by a rocket, and his wife was injured. The rockets fell into the house through the roof. His wife had forty stitches in her head and lost four fingers. Her whole body was embedded with shrapnel, little pieces all over.

"When we came to Jordan, we all came together the illegal way across the desert. It was dangerous. We came through the night. Of course the way was not paved. We had to walk across stones and rocks, which was hard. We also knew that at any moment, they would begin shooting us.

"We crossed the desert with a huge group of people, about eight hundred families in one day. We started at midnight and walked until about 6 a.m.

"We first saw the Jordanian Army at the border. They were the first ones to meet us. They held the children in the night. They were so sweet and so kind. They gave us everything we needed. They put us in *caravans* when we arrived at the border, and they gave us food and water."

"I'm dreaming of going back to Syria and finding it the way we left it before," the woman said. "We don't want freedom. I don't know who was asking for freedom and democracy. Without the freedom and without democracy, we were living a great life.

"What's the freedom they say they want? We were free. As ladies, we could leave the house at 2 a.m., and we would never feel scared. The water, we used to drink from the tap, it was so clean. The food was cheap. So what do they want more than that?"

"I have no mind to think anymore," her husband said. "Why would we dream, when it will probably all be in vain?"

CHAPTER 47

"We are suffering in Zaatari."

ONE OF THE REFUGEES WE met was a thirty-six-year-old grandmother, a despondent woman who normally lived in Zaatari Camp.

"I have two married daughters," the woman said. "One is in Syria and one here. I am living in Zaatari Camp, but the situation there is so bad. There is no electricity and no water. And it's very hot. So I left for fifteen days, because you can't bear it there with the heat."

"She's their mother too," our guide from the church said, pointing to three little girls. They sat on the floor in identical kneeling positions, their hands in their laps.

"We were living in Syria, in heaven. We wish we could go back. I have only good memories. It's enough to have your own house to live safely with your children.

"We had an extraordinary house," she said simply, her eyes welling up with tears. "I had a refrigerator, an automatic washing machine, a freezer, a vacuum cleaner, and all electrical machines to clean the house. The kitchen had high-quality tiles and ceramic.

"We left Syria because a rocket hit our house. It was in the night. We were sleeping, and then we began to run to the streets. The shrapnel injured my children."

"We were sleeping, and we heard a big sound," the girl said.

"When the first airplane dropped a rocket, my older son stayed in bed for a week, sick and fearful. We stayed on for two months, bearing the rockets and the barrel bombs. But when it began to be continuous, every night, we knew we had to leave.

"I didn't even think of what I should pack, I was so scared. I saw the airplanes flying above our heads as we were leaving," she said quietly.

"We fell multiple times walking across the desert because we couldn't see, and it was all stones, rocks, and sand. There were five hundred to a thousand of us because there were so many rockets and barrel bombs that many people decided to leave.

"My daughter is still in Syria, and she has a daughter, my granddaughter. It's rare to have coverage there, but when we can, we'll talk on the phone. She lives in the same area where I used to live. My daughter is sixteen years old, and her daughter is now nine months old.

"Both of my daughters got married here in Zaatari Camp. We needed money, and I had daughters. I needed them to get married so their men would help me. So they got married in the camp. We had a wedding with the sheikh. Then this daughter's husband went back to Syria, so she had to follow her husband. She was fourteen years old when she got married."

"According to the law," the church worker said, "the sheikh can't marry a girl under eighteen years old. It's against the law!"

There was no answer.

"My husband is still in Syria. He didn't leave with us. He's serving with the opposition, the Free Army. He came once to visit us. Sometimes my daughter gets to see him. When he has coverage, he will try to call us. He saw our new grandchild."

"I'm sure your daughter is happy to have her father there," I said, grasping at the one positive thing I could hear. The woman seemed full of despair, and her response was tepid. "Of course, she will see a member of the family."

Reema asked a question of her own, and the woman replied, "My daughter's husband is twenty-three years old, and he's good with her. They knew each other before. They were relatives, but they got married in Zaatari Camp."

Maybe it was the pronunciation of the letters in Arabic, but whenever someone said "Zaatari," the word spit forth as if it had been shot out. The letter Z at the front came out like the tongue of a poisonous snake.

"This is the major suffering," she went on. "There it's miserable. We have no electricity. On the TV they tell you we have electricity twenty-four hours a day, and that's not true. We have it only five hours in the night. And during July and August, it's so hot. It's torture.

"They tell you there are donations, there are funds—but we see nothing of that. And we can't leave, because we can't pay rent for a house. So we only came for the sake of the children to take a breath during this heat, and then go back. And the camp is in the desert, so it's too hot. The *caravan* is almost the size of this room or less, but it's from wood and plaster. When there is no electricity we go to sit outside. Imagine, when it's 7 a.m., the heat is like the middle of the day.

"The hardest was to decide to leave my home, my house. We dream to go back to Syria as we were. But now it's only dreams. We are suffering in Zaatari Camp."

CHAPTER 48

"We'll die in our country."

OUR LAST INTERVIEW WAS WITH a refugee woman who had been a teacher in Syria. We climbed a flight of steps to get to her. The white walls of the stairways were defaced with graffiti. We were exhausted and hungry.

The teacher wore a brown hijab. She had intelligent eyes and a calm, comfortable manner. She was holding a baby with a head full of black hair. We talked about the baby, and she said she also had an older boy, in grade one.

"I have a bachelor's degree in teaching from Damascus University. I taught for nine years before coming here," she said. "I taught elementary school, students from seven to fourteen years of age. I would teach all the subjects: Arabic, English, and math," she said.

"My husband was studying, finishing his Arabic language studies. He was depending on my salary. He would keep postponing the university and keep delaying semesters so that he wouldn't have to enter the military, but then at the end after four years he couldn't anymore, so the military took him. My husband wanted to be a teacher as well, but he never had a chance to do that.

"My husband went into the military service in July, and the crisis began the next March. I was teaching at the time the crisis began. And on the way to school I was harassed multiple times with the checkpoints. I was supposed to be finished with teaching at 1 p.m., but sometimes I didn't get back until 3:00.

"At the checkpoints, they would open the vehicles to see if there were males, basically. They took the females out, and there would be a lady to search us, and they searched our papers. Schoolteachers were searched in particular because they were afraid that we were giving out brochures or propaganda.

"It was scary because they suddenly appeared in front of the van with guns.

And many times they would attack or shoot the school without any alarm or warning. They didn't intentionally shoot the school, but the random shots were dangerous.

"The students used to be scared. They would run to me to hide behind me. We would go under the desks. There were no places to take refuge in the school because it was only one floor. We could only hide under the desks. As soon as it was quiet, I would tell them to go home, because they would be safer with their parents than at school. The school had a huge number of students; it would be a disaster.

"Then we would all leave. We would send the children, make sure they would all make it home, and then we would directly move to our own homes, because we have our own children. The one school I used to teach in was hit by barrel bombs; they came inside the bathrooms. Nobody was injured, thank God.

"The children could not learn as well after this began. They began to recognize the sound the rocket makes when it's shot. They knew that a rocket was coming. And they began to recognize the sounds of the airplanes. They would hear the sound of an airplane and know there would be an attack. And whether it would shoot or not, they were scared. They were paralyzed in their places and unable to express themselves.

"My husband left the military, and we came to Jordan in February 2013. After we left, our house was intentionally bombed because my husband left the military. Every soldier who left the military had their house targeted.

"I stayed here in Jordan until August 2013. Then I went back to Syria from September 2013 until March 2014."

"Why did you go back?" I asked.

"I couldn't live here. It was too hard, although the decision to go back was hard too. Only my son and I returned to Syria; my husband stayed here. I didn't have this little girl yet. My son and I went and lived with my husband's family."

The teacher's son bounded into the room. His baby sister was playing with a crumpled paper, and he snatched it from her.

"I went back and taught grade one. This return visit to Syria was the hardest period. Now, when I looked at my students, I could see how they had lost their childhood. Dealing with them was so painful, completely different even than the earlier part of the war.

"Classes that used to have thirty-six to forty students had hardly eighteen students. And in the winter there was no gasoline for the heaters. So the students used to bring their own fuel with them: papers, pieces of wood, cartons, cardboard, anything to burn to heat themselves.

"By this time, the first graders could identify the kinds of bombs and the kinds of guns they heard. Even their drawings in the classroom reflected the war. Or in math class when I tried to teach the number two and I asked for examples, they would reply with two tanks or two guns. If they drew a person, they would tell me, 'This is not a government officer, this is the Free Army officer,' as they wanted me to know which side they were on. Even as friends talking to each other, one boy would say, 'Ah, you love Bashar,' and the other boy would reply, 'No, I don't love Bashar.' This is what they got to know!

"They were still children, so they still tried to play. You can't erase childhood completely. Sometimes if we were having science class, they would ask, 'Can we have science class outside on the playground?' They wanted to go out, even though they knew it was dangerous. They tried to live a normal life.

"But whenever they heard a noise, they would be terrified. Some cried and some wet themselves, like first graders do when they get scared. Some put their hands on their ears to try to block out the sound.

"Finally, I decided that it was too dangerous for my son and I to stay in Syria. I still didn't want to go to Jordan, but it was different coming the second time, because by then I had seen death multiple times. It was so much worse in Syria than it had been when we left the first time. When my son heard the rockets shooting, he would tell me, 'It's all your fault; you brought me back here.' He went to school with me. When he would hear shooting or explosions, he would be paralyzed with no expression. Now he's better here in Jordan, but still, whenever he hears a loud noise, he is scared. There in Syria he was so limited he could barely move or play. Here, it's like he exploded. He won't sit still. He will keep moving all day, as if it's a reaction."

A child screamed outside the room.

"Maybe the thing that traumatized me the most was what I saw when we used to go pick up our salaries at the city center. The worst thing I saw is when they used to make the college students go in front of the soldiers to create a human shield. The soldiers would make them go down in front of the city center to fill barrels with sand. They wanted the young students in front so they would be killed and the army would be protected."

There was a moment of silence.

"Most of the children in my class had at least someone in their family die. I had one student named Mustafa. His father was a dentist, and his mother was a psychiatrist. They were living in a one-floor building, and the barrel bombs attacked their building, and Mustafa died. The parents lived, but the mom's leg was injured. I found this out because they were neighbors to my parents. My parents knew he was my student, so they told me about it.

"In September this year, my co-teachers began school again," she added. "Only until 11:00 in the morning, only basic subjects. No sports, no art, just basic things. No amusement, no time out, no break. The situation is so scary, so they can only teach basic things. But my dream is still to go back to our country and continue teaching."

The woman's son came into the room, and our team tried to engage him in talk. He was noisy and restless, as his mother had said. The adorable baby on her lap was starting to cry as well, apparently tired of our visit.

"My husband is now trying to work at Zaatari Camp," the mother said. "He is helping in construction. Whenever the head of the camp allows him to take a day off, he will come to visit us. It costs a lot for him to come to visit me and go back."

The woman produced a paper like a receipt, as the baby wailed.

"He will take a day of vacation, and they will give him a paper that gives him permission to leave," she said. "They take his UN card to make sure that he comes back."

Before we parted ways with the teacher, I asked her if there was anything she would like to share with the world about what was taking place in Syria, anything that would help Americans understand what the Syrian people are going through.

"I want them to know," she replied, "the situation of the people who are still in Syria, like my family and my husband's parents. They are facing difficult times and shooting, but they don't want to leave Syria. It's a big achievement just to be able to charge your cell phone, but they want to stay. They want to die there. Especially the old people say, 'If we're going to die, we'll die in our country.' "

We walked out of the building, down the flights of stairs littered with cigarette butts, candy wrappers, and shells from seeds.

I couldn't believe we were finished with interviews. The teacher, our last source of information, had echoed the words of the first Syrian man I had met on the plane. *Syria is my home. I cannot leave.*

REFLECTING ON THE

VOICES

CHAPTER 49

Crossing the Jordan River

OUR TRIP TO JERUSALEM STARTED badly when our taxi driver announced that he was taking a friend with him. This meant that Keith, Jana, and I would be packed, with our bags, into the back seat of his small, hot car.

It was a blistering hot day, although the scenery was beautiful as we slid down the mountains of Jordan and into the Jordan River valley. I didn't think I had ever seen so many greenhouses, rows and rows by the hundreds. We were north of the place where Moses had climbed the mountain to see into the Promised Land. But if it was like this view, what a view it must have been!

Keith and Jana visited Jerusalem about once a month, and I wanted to go to visit a friend who lived there. This was basically designed to be a relaxing weekend with some socializing after our heavy days of interviews. However, exhausted both emotionally and physically, I felt that I was beginning to get sick. I didn't know if I would have the energy to enjoy our time in the City of David.

The Jordan River itself, shrunk in modern times by irrigation, was the size of the creek along the country road where I grew up in Wisconsin. It was hard to picture the band of Israelites, refugees themselves at the time, fording it as they had in the book of Joshua. But, although crossing the Jordan River was now easy in 2015, actually receiving permission to enter Israel was not. Instead of the walled city of Jericho, we found ourselves up against the glass window of the border patrol.

When we reached the border, we first stepped out of our taxi onto the baking roadside. We waited in several lines and finally found the line to the windows where we would be questioned. Keith arrived at the window first and for about twenty minutes, they asked him question after question. *Why are you here? What other countries have you been in recently? What organization are you working with?*

From his time spent living in the Middle East, Keith's passport was cluttered with stamps. But even though this passport had no Lebanese stamps in it, the border official asked Keith point-blank, "Were you in Lebanon?"

"Yes, we were," he admitted.

As it was, we spent a total of about six hours at the border. The officials rifled through our luggage, questioned us, and mostly asked us to sit and wait. We witnessed a screaming match between the vitriolic manager of the border crossing and a woman who had been traveling all day to reach the border, only to be turned away for some reason. I tried to block out the unpleasant conversation, but it was impossible.

This was something I had never experienced before. Only in reading had I encountered an atmosphere like this, where guards screamed at people, officials asked parroting, repeated questions, and personal belongings were treated roughly.

Finally, an official slid our passports under the window without an apology, and we were dismissed.

By the time we got out of the border crossing building near closing time, everyone else had gone, and the buses were no longer running. We managed to find a taxi to take us halfway to Jerusalem, and Keith called one of his friends to pick us up near Jericho.

When we arrived in Jerusalem, we went out for non-kosher pizza on a busy street. The pizza was good, but I felt that I was coming down with a cold, and I was eager to get to bed. I was in a near-daze from the whirlwind of two weeks of interviews and twelve hours of travel.

That night I wrote a sarcastic article titled "Border Crossing in 25 Easy Steps," beginning with a recommendation: "If you've not been through many border crossings by land, I have a brief, bleary-eyed recommendation for you: Don't."

CHAPTER 50

The City of David

AFTER LEBANON AND JORDAN, ISRAEL seemed cold and unfriendly. With my mind so full of the stories of the refugees, I found the irrelevance of my new surroundings almost frustrating. I spent most of the first day inside napping or sitting at my computer, sneezing.

Things improved, however, when I met up with my friend Laura at a coffee shop that seemed very much like America. We shared our spiritual journeys and encouraged each other, having been apart for a number of years.

Later, Keith and Jana escorted me through the Old City. In a stone café, I ordered lentil soup, which felt wonderful to my sore throat, and hummus with pita bread. I bought a few scarves and stepped around the tourists and cats striding through the maze of archways, stairways, and doorways. The Old City was like a giant castle, parts open to air, parts not. We visited the Church of the Holy Sepulchre, where I watched pilgrims bending before the stone on which Jesus had supposedly been laid in the grave, kissing it and rubbing objects over it, as if to infuse them with supernatural power. Their adoration was okay, I supposed, but somehow my recent experiences made their acts seem shallow. How much more worship did Christ receive by the tireless, faithful work of the Christians I had met in our visits to the refugees!

Keith and Jana knew several shop owners personally. Three times we ducked into shops to talk to someone. I bought two scarves from one of their friends. Another man showcased a collection of antiques and stone jewelry.

I was most captivated by his wall of old keys. They were thick metal keys with ringed handles, most of them rusty. The shop owner said he asked people to bring him keys from the countryside, and every week he would receive four or five.

"I've heard that the Palestinian refugees would take their keys with them when they were evicted from Palestine by the Jews," Jana said to me quietly. "I don't know if that's part of the significance of this or not. It was a symbol to them that they would return, if they took their keys with them."

"Help me pick one out," I told Jana.

She helped me look through the keys on the wall. Some were short and some were long. Each one had a slightly different shape. I finally selected one of the shorter ones. I wanted to have one in memory of the many people I now knew who had fled their homes.

I had heard the stories of so many refugees! Now, in the city of David, George's words, back in Lebanon, seemed fitting.

"David was a refugee. Jesus was a refugee, according to Matthew. Paul was a refugee. Adam and Eve qualify as refugees. Moses and Abraham were refugees, and Daniel got captured and taken to a foreign country."

I thought about my sarcastic list, "Border Crossing in 25 Easy Steps." In between sneezing into toilet tissue the last twenty-four hours, I had been convicted about my complaints. I probably would not have made a good refugee. After all, there had been no gunfire at the Israeli border, no hiding in pomegranate trees, no picking up the wounded to take with us—and I still had written a sarcastic review.

We walked on to the Western Wall and onto the balcony where non-Jews could stand to watch those praying by the wall. Female ushers walked among the visiting women, offering veils to anyone who walked up immodestly dressed or with uncovered hair. As we stood there, the Muslim call to prayer began to sound from Al-Aqsa, the famous mosque behind us.

We kept going, ending up in the Muslim quarter. I found it fascinating that the city was truly so split that they had to divide it into four pieces: the Jewish Quarter, the Christian Quarter, the Muslim Quarter, and the Armenian Quarter.

In the Muslim Quarter, I prowled among the sweets shops. I wanted to take sweets back to my friends and co-workers, so I would need a huge package. I finally selected a shop, and the owner piled a square foam tray full of diamond-shaped baklava, glistening with sticky glaze. He put another foam tray on top of the baklava, facing down, and wrapped the plate sandwich in shrink wrap. Pleased, I carried the package with me out of the Old City. We purchased some falafel, the hot spicy balls of fried chickpeas, and ate them with hummus on the wide steps that formed an outdoor arena facing Damascus Gate.

I sorted through my wallet. I now had four currencies: U.S. dollars, Lebanese lira, Jordanian dinar, and Israeli shekels.

We ended the night by winding our way back through the maze of arches and stone hallways to the home of my friend Laura and her husband Todd, whose bedroom ceiling was an arch made of rock.

As we walked to and from their house, I thought that the Old City was like a giant, ancient hotel, with a thousand doorways, hallways, stairways, and cats. Despite my first suspicions and my bad experience at the border, I was warming to Jerusalem. It had authenticity and beauty and history. I hadn't had time to see much of it, and that wasn't my goal on this trip, but it was really quite nice. And who got to tour it for free with people who knew it well?

One thing was left on my list of things to do. I wanted to climb the Mount of Olives and visit the Garden of Gethsemane.

CHAPTER 51

Gethsemane

All those who journey, soon or late,
Must pass within the garden's gate;
Must kneel alone in the darkness there,
And battle with some fierce despair.
God pity those who cannot say,
"Not mine but thine," who only pray,
"Let this cup pass," and cannot see
The purpose in Gethsemane.
–Ella Wheeler Wilcox

I HEARD THE EXPLOSIONS AS I was gazing down on the city of Jerusalem, catching my breath from the steep climb up the Mount of Olives.

I had walked there alone. Jana had thought about going with me, but she was meeting a friend that morning, and I thought it might be good for me to go alone anyway to spend some time in prayer. What could be more fitting in this place? Keith gave me directions, telling me how to skirt the Old City of Jerusalem and then cut down through the Kidron Valley and up the Mount of Olives.

I concluded that the explosions must be gunfire, since 8 a.m. is hardly a good time for fireworks. Straining my ears, I faintly picked up a distant chanting in the direction of Al Aqsa mosque and the Dome of the Rock. I strained my eyes as well, but it was far away, and I couldn't see anything out of the ordinary.

I walked back down. The gate to the Garden of Gethsemane was open now, and I slipped inside. I read the four accounts of Jesus' last night there and leaned my head between the metal bars for an unobstructed look at the olive trees and brown dirt, conceivably similar to His surroundings. I cried, thinking of the pain and yet the need for death, for surrender, in the life of Christ on that dark night, and in my own life.

Jesus, like the refugees, had left His beautiful home! *We were living in heaven,* the Syrians had told me. But Jesus actually had been living in heaven! He had come anyway, to a place of inconvenience, ridicule, hunger, suffering, and death, as the Lamb of God, to take away the sin of the world. Once more I thought of the words that had so touched me in one of the first refugee homes we had visited.

Jesus came for all people. He didn't come to certain people. He came for the Christians, the Muslims, the Druze, Jews, for everyone. The Jews didn't accept Him. They crucified Him. But whoever accepts Jesus and what Jesus did, he's the one who will be saved, because Jesus died to save everyone. As God prepared a lamb to die on behalf of Abraham's son, Jesus was the Lamb who died for all of us.

I was only saddened by the sign outside the garden. On the wall, someone had posted a beautiful plaque, quoting verses from Scripture, and describing Jesus' last night in the garden. Yet in a country where almost every sign is written in Hebrew, Arabic, and English, this sign was written only in French and English, and locals who understood primarily Hebrew or Arabic could not get the full benefit. Even Pilate, writing his sign just across the valley two thousand years before, did better than this, making sure his sign was written in three languages so that everyone would know the *criminal* was the King of the Jews.

I walked back across the Kidron Valley and began the long walk around the old walled city of Jerusalem. The gunfire had quit. I met a lady who said she also had heard gunfire on the Temple Mount. Later, I found that the clash had been a combination of firecrackers thrown at police and stun grenades by the police in return, with no casualties.

After my time on the Mount of Olives, I could only think of Christ and the immense sacrifice He had made. What would it do for each of the refugees we had met, if they understood that Jesus had left His country, for them? What would it do for the bushy-haired boy in the gray shirt who spoke bitterly about Jordan and the price for brides, to know that Jesus, who was despised and rejected of men, had died for him? What it would do for those clashing factions on the Temple Mount to know that Jesus was the perfect Lamb?

And I had been privileged to witness the many local workers in Lebanon and Jordan who were taking the opportunity to tell the refugees these truths.

CHAPTER 52

Not Quite a Refugee

I WAS STILL THINKING PHILOSOPHICAL thoughts as Keith, Jana, and I boarded a bus to the Jordanian border once again. We were all hoping this crossing would be a little less like a refugee experience.

"Don't let me forget my baklava," I told them as I tucked it into an overhead compartment.

The bus bumped along through acres of palm trees and greenhouses amid the desert dust, and I even got a nice glimpse of the Dead Sea for the first time.

But then, shortly before arriving at the border, we suddenly began to doubt if we would reach it at all, as our bus rolled to a stop due to an accident. The police had been letting the traffic through, but stopped with the car ahead of us. We were told it might take an hour for them to clear the road. We didn't have an hour—it was about 6 p.m., and the border was going to close at 7:00. If I didn't cross the border tonight, I might miss my flight to Chicago in the morning.

"There's nothing we can do," Jana said. "So I guess we may as well not stress."

It was great advice, but it also reminded me that the one thing I could do was pray. *God, you're going to have to arrange this,* I told Him, *or bring glory to yourself through whatever happens.*

It was 6:16 p.m., and I was in the process of texting my friends to ask them to pray for us as well, when Keith, who had been chatting with other passengers outside, came bounding in the bus door.

"This fellow will take us to the border," he said. "Let's go!"

Jana and I leaped up, grabbed our things, and hurried down the bus steps.

"Do you have the baklava?" she asked.

"Got it," I said.

Keith yanked our two suitcases from underneath the bus and the three of us, in view of the curious eyes of a whole line of cars, ran off the curb of the road and into the dusty ditch. Dust poofed up around our shoes and thorny green weeds grabbed at our ankles as we sped across the ditch toward a dusty gray Jeep Keith pointed out.

"I feel like a refugee," Jana hissed.

Across the Jordan River a super moon slid into the sky above the mountains of Jordan.

"He was just kind of sitting off to the side watching," Keith said of the man in the Jeep. "He told me he could take us, but he isn't sure if he has enough fuel in his tank."

We piled in, luggage everywhere, and our driver turned the truck away from a line of cars on a detour lane, and out across the uneven field. We clung to our luggage, bouncing helplessly through the dirt.

Does this man know what he's doing? I wondered. We had just jumped into the vehicle of a stranger.

Then he turned back to the main road, which was separated from us by a sizable ditch. Surely he wasn't going to try to go down through the ditch? Careful not to lose too much speed, he nosed the truck into the ditch, just missing a post, and up the other side onto the smoothly paved Israeli highway. We were on our way to the border once again!

Jana thought the man was Jewish because he was talking Hebrew. All I knew was that he was a clear answer to prayer. What man in a Jeep, especially one that is low on fuel, just sits beside the road watching traffic, available for taxi service?

"I do this for God," he said.

At one point as he barreled down a shortcut toward the border, he simply began to laugh, I guess at the whole situation. Was he an angel sent from God?

I was still afraid the border could be closed, but we pulled up and leaped out, and the security guard unbuckled the blue strap and let us in with the brisk question, "Do you have any weapons?"

Yes, ma'am, I do, I should have said. *It's called prayer, and it makes stun grenades and fireworks and rioting look like poor alternatives. It's the same thing that brought the walls of Jericho down for your forefathers many years ago,* I might have added, *and parted the waters of the wide Jericho River.*

This border crossing was easy compared to the previous one. From the border we hired a taxi to take us to Amman.

We were sailing along the highway when a police vehicle suddenly waved us over. Jana and I, now in full possession of the back seat, nibbling on snacks, looked at each other curiously. Perhaps this whole trip was a test of our solidarity with the refugees.

We had heard the story of the Syrian man with the seven bullets being flagged down by the police on the lonely drive from Daraa to Damascus. Perhaps it was on just such a night, at nearly the same time of night.

"We've gotten stopped before with taxi drivers," Jana said.

The taxi driver seemed a bit nervous, and there were about five armed soldiers or policemen standing around our car. Like they might have done at Syrian checkpoints, they asked for all of our passports, comparing photos with the people in the car.

I remembered how I had heard so much about the Jordanian Army welcoming the refugees at the Syrian border. Some of the young men beside our car were dressed in camouflage, and I wondered if any of them had been there, welcoming the children with juice, and hiding their guns behind them. *Really, they were so kind.* We had heard this sentiment more than once.

There would be no shootings tonight, no men thrown on the pavement or beaten before the headlights of the car. The officials admonished the taxi driver to slow down and gave him a warning. They seemed intrigued by the presence of the three Americans. Then, we were released to go on our way, up the mountain to Amman.

Back in Amman, I checked in at a hotel for my last night in the Middle East. It was hard to believe our time was over. I thanked Keith and Jana for their tireless support and guidance, but it seemed that words were insufficient. After depositing my bags, despite my exhaustion, I stepped out into the street and walked to a rooftop restaurant for dessert. I sat near the railing of the rooftop, looking down into the steady flow of traffic on the street and the young men dancing in an empty lot, the spirit of the holiday still pervading everyone. I wanted to hang on to this experience as long as I could, knowing I might never be back.

I went back to my hotel, and even though I was almost too tired to think, I set my alarm for early morning, just before sunrise. There was going to be an eclipse of the moon, and I wanted to see it.

In the wee hours, I stumbled sleepily up a flight of outdoor stairs to the hotel's rooftop. It was a bit eerie, but I had the roof to myself.

Sure enough, the full super moon we had seen rising over the Jordan River earlier in the evening was now a mere crescent, shadowed by the shape of planet Earth.

Then, like an orchestra, the morning calls to prayer began to sound from the minarets of Amman. First it was a distant chorus. Then the mosque right beside the hotel started its call.

It was haunting and sad. My mind recalled the words of a man in Lebanon who worked with Muslim refugees: *Every time when I pray I feel like the Muslim people are very important to God. I love these people. I hate their religion. I hate the Quran because I believe it is an evil book. But I love these people more than my life, really. I love to see them come to Jesus.*

I thought of how the mosque speakers in Syria had been used during the war: to announce that everyone should move to lower floors of their buildings because the area was being bombed. Despite all the hate, the mosque leaders wanted their people to be safe.

I lingered on the rooftop of the hotel, as I had lingered on the rooftop of the restaurant. I drank in the darkened moon and the pink linen of the eastern sky. If I never came back, I wanted to remember this deep love for Amman, for the Muslims, for the Syrian refugees.

But I also wanted to be able to go home. I had baklava in my suitcase to take to the people I loved. Like the refugees, I thought of home as a place of familiar faces and streets and wonderful memories.

Unlike the refugees, I would soon be back home.

Epilogue

Exhausted and suffering from jet lag, I felt a bit lost on the first days at home.

It was good to be back, and there was so much to be thankful for. I enjoyed the ease of hearing English and eating American food. My three friends picked me up at the airport late in the evening and stocked my refrigerator. My co-worker Sue agreed to work just a little longer so I could rest. My geraniums were beautiful when I arrived, because my neighbor had watered them. My neighborhood was just as I had left it.

But, after being frustrated every day that I could not understand Arabic, I was shocked to find myself wishing to hear it again! My surroundings in my own house were oddly familiar, yet they were too . . . familiar? I couldn't quite process my own longing.

Jana, still in Jordan, texted me encouragement throughout the morning as I tried to give thanks for my many blessings through the mild case of reverse culture shock I was feeling. Her texts gave me a feeling of sitting with her on her rooftop with all of Amman beneath us.

I wrapped myself in a scarf from Jordan and began to read my Arabic/English New Testament, because even though I couldn't read the Arabic, the script felt warm and friendly, like the people in the Middle East. I picked up the tile I had purchased in Jordan, the letter *nuun,* made by refugees to ask for prayer. *It's kind of like the cross,* someone had said, *a symbol of shame they are claiming as an honor. N for the Nazarene.*

I took the baklava from the Muslim Quarter of Jerusalem to the hospital. I went up to the cardiac floor where everyone was rushing around in their normal state of busyness. I met a cardiologist I knew who had once lived in Asia. He was with his nurse, a good friend of mine, and I offered them baklava.

"Thank you," the nurse said.

"Shukran," said the cardiologist.

Endnotes

1 U.S. Passports and International Travel. Bureau of Consular Affairs, U.S. Department of State. May 29, 2015, < http://travel.state.gov/content/passports/en/alertswarnings/lebanon-travel-warning.html>, accessed on June 3, 2015.

2 Karen Miller Pensiero, "Aylan Kurdi and the Photos That Change History," *The Wall Street Journal Online*, September 11, 2015, <http://www.wsj.com/articles/aylan-kurdi-and-the-photos-that-change-history-1442002594>, accessed on April 11, 2016.

3 "Israel Shrouded in Dense Sandstorm," *Times of Israel*, September 8, 2015, <http://www.timesofisrael.com/israel-shrouded-in-dense-sandstorm.>, accessed on April 11, 2016.

4 Terry Carter, Lara Dunston, and Amelia Thomas, Syria and Lebanon, Lonely Planet Publications, Oakland, CA, July 2008, p. 198.

5 Thomas L. Friedman, From Beirut to Jerusalem, Picador, New York, NY, 1995, p. 79.

6 Carter, Dunston, and Thomas, pp. 31–32.

7 *Syria Deeply*, <http://www.syriadeeply.org/timeline/>, accessed on April 23, 2016.

8 "Free Syrian Army," Wikipedia, <https://en.wikipedia.org/wiki/Free_Syrian_Army>, accessed on July 29, 2016.

9 Friedman, p. 98.

10 Ibid., p. 100.

11 Carter, Dunston, and Thomas, p. 352.

12 Ibid., p. 155.

13 Dylan Collins, interview with Haian Dukhan, "Tribal 'Blood Ties' and Syria's Civil War: Q&A," *Syria Deeply*, December 11, 2015, day 1,732 of the Syrian conflict, <http://www.syriadeeply.org/articles/2015/12/9039/tribal-blood-ties-syrias-civil-war-qa/>, accessed on April 23, 2016.

14 Friedman, pp. 87–88.

15 Dylan Collins, interview with Haian Dukhan, <http://www.syriadeeply.org/articles/2015/12/9039/tribal-blood-ties-syrias-civil-war-qa/>, accessed on April 23, 2016.

16 Carter, Dunston, and Thomas, p. 66.

17 Dylan Collins, interview with Haian Dukhan, <http://www.syriadeeply.org/articles/2015/12/9039/tribal-blood-ties-syrias-civil-war-qa/>, accessed on April 23, 2016.

18 Yazan al-Homsy, translated from Arabic by Naziha Baassiri, "510 Days of Siege and the Darkness Endured," *Syria Deeply,* November 6, 2013, day 967 of the Syrian conflict, <http://www.syriadeeply.org/articles/2013/11/2574/510-days-siege-darkness-endures/#!>, accessed on April 25, 2016.

19 Matthew Weaver, "Battle for Baba Amr - Timeline," *The Guardian,* March 1, 2012, <http://www.theguardian.com/world/2012/mar/01/battle-baba-amr-timeline-syria.>, accessed on April 25, 2016.

20 Yazan al-Homsy, translated from Arabic by Naziha Baassiri, "When the Grave Becomes a Luxury," *Syria Deeply,* November 6, 2013, day 967 of the Syrian conflict, <http://www.syriadeeply.org/articles/2013/11/2581/grave-luxury/>, accessed on April 23, 2016.

21 "Christianity in the Middle East," <https://en.wikipedia.org/wiki/Christianity_in_the_Middle_East#Persecution_of_Christians_in_Middle_East>, accessed on May 11, 2016.

22 Carter, Dunston, and Thomas, p. 160.

23 Friedman, p. 83.

24 Ibid., p. 95.

25 Ibid,. p. 96.

26 Carter, Dunston, and Thomas, p. 66.

27 Ibid., p. 172.

28 Ibid., pp. 42–44.

29 Mark Twain, *Innocents Abroad,* Chapter 44, The Literature Page, 2003–2012, p.335, <http://www.literaturepage.com/read/twain-innocents-abroad-335.html>, accessed on April 25, 2016.

30 Ibid.

31 G. Frederick Owen, "Archaelogical Supplement-Damascus," *The Thompson Chain-Reference Bible,* 5th Edition, B.B. Kirkbride Bible Company, Indianapolis, 1988, p. 1,739.

32 Carter, Dunston, and Thomas, p. 105.

33 Yazan al-Homsy, translated from Arabic by Naziha Baassiri, "510 Days of Siege and the Darkness Endured," *Syria Deeply,* November 6, 2013, day 967 of the Syrian conflict, <http://www.syriadeeply.org/articles/2013/11/2574/510-days-siege-darkness-endures/#!>, accessed on April 25, 2016.

34 Orwa Ajjoub and Mais Istanbelli, "Snapshots from Syrian Cities on the Fourth Anniversary of the Uprising," *Syria Deeply,* March 16, 2015, day 1,462 of the Syrian conflict, <http://www.syriadeeply.org/articles/2015/03/6960/snapshots-syrian-cities-fourth-anniversary-uprising/>, accessed on April 25, 2016.

35 Joe Sterling, "Daraa: The Spark That Lit the Syrian Flame," *CNN,* March 1, 2012, <http://www.cnn.com/2012/03/01/world/meast/syria-crisis-beginnings/index.html>, accessed on April 25, 2016.

36 Omar Abdallah and Tamer Osman, "Syrians Desperate for Healthcare as Assad Regime Barrel Bombs Hospitals," *Syria Deeply,* July 3, 2015, day 1,571 of the Syrian conflict, <http://www.syriadeeply.org/articles/2015/07/7593/syrians-desperate-healthcare-assad-regime-barrel-bombs-hospitals/>, accessed on April 23, 2016.

37 "Syria: Barrage of Barrel Bombs Destroys MSF Health Facility," Medecins sans Frontieres, June 18, 2015, <www.msf.org/article/syria-barrage-barrel-bombs-destroyes-msf-health-facility>, accessed on April 25, 2016.

About the Author

Katrina lives in a diverse neighborhood in Elkhart, Indiana, where she works as a nurse in heart surgery and is part of an outreach church. She began her writing career by telling stories to her brother Scott while they pulled weeds on the family property in Wisconsin. Her parents passed on to her and her five siblings a love for reading, writing, crossword puzzles, and playing Scrabble. Since traveling to the Middle East, the region and its people have become close to her heart.

In addition to maintaining a weekly blog at www.500-words.com, Katrina has written *On the Winning Side, Blue Christmas, Shatterproof, Inferno in the Lost Pines,* and the text for *Faces of Syria.* She enjoys hearing from her readers and can be contacted at katrina@500-words.com.

The Way to God and Peace

We live in a world contaminated by sin. Sin is anything that goes against God's holy standards. When we do not follow the guidelines that God our Creator gave us, we are guilty of sin. Sin separates us from God, the source of life.

Since the time when the first man and woman, Adam and Eve, sinned in the Garden of Eden, sin has been universal. The Bible says that we all have "sinned and come short of the glory of God" (Romans 3:23). It also says that the natural consequence for that sin is eternal death, or punishment in an eternal hell: "Then when lust hath conceived, it bringeth forth sin: and sin, when it is finished, bringeth forth death" (James 1:15).

But we do not have to suffer eternal death in hell. God provided forgiveness for our sins through the death of His only Son, Jesus Christ. Because Jesus was perfect and without sin, He could die in our place. "For God so loved the world that he gave his only begotten Son, that whosoever believeth in him should not perish, but have everlasting life" (John 3:16).

A sacrifice is something given to benefit someone else. It costs the giver greatly. Jesus was God's sacrifice. Jesus' death takes away the penalty of sin for everyone who accepts this sacrifice and truly repents of their sins. To repent of sins means to be truly sorry for and turn away from the things we have done that have violated God's standards (Acts 2:38; 3:19).

Jesus died, but He did not remain dead. After three days, God's Spirit miraculously raised Him to life again. God's Spirit does something similar in us. When we receive Jesus as our sacrifice and repent of our sins, our hearts are changed. We become spiritually alive! We develop new desires and attitudes (2 Corinthians 5:17). We begin to make choices that please God (1 John 3:9). If we do fail and commit sins, we can ask God for forgiveness. "If we confess our sins, he is faithful and just to forgive us our sins, and to cleanse us from all unrighteousness" (1 John 1:9).

Once our hearts have been changed, we want to continue growing spiritually. We will be happy to let Jesus be the Master of our lives and will want to become more like Him. To do this, we must meditate on God's Word and commune with God in prayer. We will testify to others of this change by being baptized and sharing the good news of God's victory over sin and death. Fellowship with a faithful group of believers will strengthen our walk with God (1 John 1:7).